SHATTE~~RED~~

Three deadly tornadoes and the towns that survived them

CHRISTIAN LIGHT PUBLICATIONS INC.
P.O. BOX 1212
Harrisonburg, Virginia 22803-1212
(540) 434-0768

© 2012 by TGS International, a wholly owned subsidiary of Christian Aid Ministries, Berlin, Ohio.

All rights reserved. No part of this book may be used, reproduced, or stored in any retrieval system, in any form or by any means, electronic or mechanical, without written permission from the publisher except for brief quotations embodied in critical articles and reviews.

ISBN 978-1-936208-87-6
Cover design: Velinda Miller Photography & Design
Text layout design: Felicia Kern
Front cover photo: © B. W. Shepherd/Ozarkjournalist
Printed in the USA
Printed September 2012
For more information about Christian Aid Ministries, see page 333.

Published by:
TGS International
P.O. Box 355
Berlin, Ohio 44610 USA
Phone: 330·893·4828
Fax: 330·893·2305
www.tgsinternational.com

TGS000541

SHATTERPROOF

Three deadly tornadoes and the towns that survived them

Katrina Hoover

Table of Contents

Dedication vii
Acknowledgments ix
Author's Preface xi
Introduction xiii
Tornado Footprints in the Past xv

Part I: Hackleburg, Alabama

Life Before the Tornado 23
The People 27
Wednesday, April 27, 2011 39
The Storm 49
EF5 Tornado Touchdown—3:05 P.M. 61
The Monster Is Gone 67
First Baptist Hackleburg 73
The Rubble 77
The Wasteland 91
Searching for Hope 99
A Spirit of Resilience 109
Volunteers 115
Shatterproof 121
Rebuilding Lives 127

Part II: Ringgold, Georgia

Before the Nightmare 143
The Storm Approaches 153
Danger in the Air 157
8:15 P.M. 163

Like a War Zone 169
Night With No Rest 179
The Aftermath 183
Down to the Bare Bones 189
Grace Enough 199

Part III: Joplin, Missouri

On the Grid 211
Life—As It Was 221
Pressure Builds 229
Code Gray 233
The Vacuum Cleaner 241
Snapshots 245
After 5:41 P.M. 251
Healthcare 257
Documenting the Disaster 261
Fire Departments and EMS 267
Freeman Hospital 273
A Search for Life 281
Helping the Needy 289
Emergency Workers 297
Joplin's Continuing Story 305
Preparing to Soar 313
   Planning a Refuge—Tips for Tornado Safety 319
   Conclusion 321
   Endnotes 323
   About the Author 331

Dedication

Dedicated only to our God,
Healer of all things shattered,
Author of all things shatterproof.

Acknowledgments

Many thanks to:

- » Sarah Miller, my excellent assistant on my first research trip to Joplin, Hackleburg, and Ringgold.
- » Bill Shepherd, freelance photographer, for sharing both his story and several photos.
- » John Lowe, disaster exercise coordinator, for connecting me to the Center for Preparedness Education conference on the Joplin tornado in Omaha, Nebraska.
- » Sherilyn (Troyer) Yoder, editor and friend, who worked out many of the kinks in my writing.
- » Velinda Miller, graphic designer and friend, for the beautiful cover.
- » The characters in this book, who graciously shared their very personal stories. You impacted my life, and I think you will impact the life of anyone who reads this book. I would love to meet up with you again and hear your continuing story!

Author's Preface

This book is largely based on firsthand accounts. In other words, I was sitting in the living rooms, storm cellars, or offices of the characters and taking notes while they talked. When I returned to my computer, I attempted, as accurately as possible, to weave their details and direct quotes into a readable story. For the most part, the stories end in the fall of 2011. Changes that took place after that time are not recorded in this book.

I don't doubt that there are so many more people who could have been interviewed. I realize that the experiences related by one may not be the experiences of all. I ask for the understanding of anyone whose story I was not able to include. As it is, there are so many characters in *Shatterproof,* that I have not even been able to mention all of them by name.

In several cases, I relied on secondhand accounts from newspapers or online sources. These are publicly available sources, and I have made every effort to document each source in the endnotes. I also attended a conference by the Center for Preparedness Education in Omaha, Nebraska, where I was privileged to meet a number of Joplin healthcare professionals. Many of my accounts about Joplin healthcare following the tornado are based on the information presented at this conference.

The scientific and historical parts of this book, mostly found in the gray sections, are based on my notes from three excellent books. Anyone interested in further tornado reading should consider finding these books.

In his book, *F5: Devastation, Survival, and the Most Violent Tornado*

Outbreak of the 20th Century, Mark Levine discusses the tornado outbreak of 1974, presenting scientific research and personal stories side by side. His account is professional, suspenseful, heartfelt, and well-written. *F5* is published by Miramax Books, New York (2007).

The Mighty Whirlwind, by David Wagler is a personal and homespun account of the Palm Sunday tornadoes of 1965. He focuses on northern Indiana, including Elkhart, Shipshewana, and Goshen. *The Mighty Whirlwind* is published by Pathway Publishers, Aylmer, Ontario, Canada (1966).

In the Shadow of the Tornado, by Richard Bedard, is unparalleled for its figurative language and warm tone, recounting the Woodward, Oklahoma, devastation of 1947. Bedard also includes scientific information about tornadoes and tornado forecasting. The book is published by Gilco Publishing, Norman, Oklahoma (1996).

For those interested in tornado chasing, *Tornado Hunter,* by Stefan Bechtel and Tim Samara, focuses on those who run toward tornadoes rather than away. *Tornado Hunter* is published by the National Geographic Society, Washington D.C. (2009).

—Katrina Hoover, September 2012

Introduction

It's September 15, 2011, and I'm sitting at a Starbucks in Dunlap, Indiana. I'm out on the coffee shop's patio, remembering the last time I sat on a Starbucks patio just outside the shatter zone of Joplin, listening to tornado stories. I'm reading *Tornado Hunter* by Stefan Bechtel, taking notes.

It's on the drive home, on a perfect fall day, that I start to feel a bit guilty. The sun is shining whitely against the swoop of the electric wires, and they've turned to white-hot gold, dazzling streaks against the September sky with a kind of radiance I don't expect to see again until I get to heaven.

The world is so perfect here in Elkhart County, the trees swaying in the breeze, the sun turning wires into gold. I'm glad that my world is still okay, and I'm glad that we don't have to wait for years and years until the trees grow back. Elkhart County had its day in 1965, but that was before my time. Now the only thing that annoys people is construction. There's a certain complacency and pride stamped right into the cement of the sidewalks. Starbucks, Target, and Walmart appear to be invincible icons of prosperity and capitalism. It's unthinkable that they could be destroyed in five minutes.

Hackleburg, Ringgold, and Joplin know this is not true. There is no promise of tomorrow, no guarantee any neighborhood will stay standing.

When a massive disaster strikes and a neighborhood disintegrates, what is left that does not shatter? When survivors told me their stories, often with tears, I searched their words for the answer. When I walked beside piles of debris and stripped trees, I searched the scenery for the answer. When I read news articles from a distance, I searched between the lines for the answer.

This book is a collection of the answers I found. I hope that if a disaster strikes my hometown, there would be as many shatterproof people, attitudes, and organizations as I found in the cities described in this book.

Tornado Footprints in the Past

March 18, 1925—The Tri-State Tornado: This monster was called the Tri-State Tornado because it hit the ground in Missouri and didn't come up for air until it had crossed Illinois and entered Indiana, 219 miles later. Although record-keeping was not thorough at the time, it is believed that the tornado may have traveled as fast as 73 miles per hour—an exceptional speed. This was a single tornado, not a tornado outbreak. It killed 695 people, more than twice as many as any other single tornado in U.S. records.[1]

April 9, 1947—Woodward, Oklahoma: Woodward was a tough cattle town that had survived the Great Depression and the days of dust storms. Indian legend said that the rolling hills around Woodward protected it from tornadoes. But then came a surprise tornado that Richard Bedard describes in his excellent book, *In the Shadow of the Tornado*. It blew a path across the prairie almost two miles wide on its way to Woodward. It scrubbed little towns off the face of the land, sending "washing machines tumbling out of the skies like footballs, half a mile from their laundry." Of one little town in the path, Bedard says, "Board by board, it flew apart." It came through after dark, hurling a delivery truck into a house where a woman was bending over to get her baby out of the crib. It caught people in restaurants and theaters, spinning 95 people to their deaths in Woodward and taking a total of 181 lives.[2] The cloud was "low and thick and black as ink," one man said as he hurried across town to his business to see why the power had gone out. "It looked like you could cut it with a knife."[3]

April 11, 1965—The Palm Sunday Tornadoes: "Palm Sunday will go down in history as the day the Midwest exploded," wrote Paul Schlemmer in the *Columbus Dispatch*.[4] An outbreak of thirty-seven tornadoes danced across the area, hitting northern Indiana with crippling force, on what was described in Indiana as "a nice day" until about 6:50 p.m. Communication and power fizzled as a tornado tossed aside several "indestructibles": a telephone building that crashed and burned south of Elkhart, and ten 165-foot steel utility poles carrying 138,000 volts. By the time many people became aware of the danger, they had about seven seconds to reach their basements. Although it struck Amish country, where radios and TV were not used to warn of the impending danger, no Amish were killed. In one barn the roof was ripped off, but the horses continued to munch their hay inside.[5] When the tornadoes finally retired, 260 people had been killed.[6]

April 3, 1974—The "Worst Outbreak in History": Mark Levine's book, *F5,* calls April 3, 1974, the worst outbreak in history. It included six F5 tornadoes, ten F4 tornadoes, and thirty-five F3 tornadoes (see "Mr. Tornado and the EF Scale" on page 34). An F4 tornado struck Limestone County, Alabama, wiping out a trailer court. Half an hour later, an F5 tornado descended, overlapping the same path of destruction. The local sheriff survived being dragged down the road by the force of a tornado—*twice.*

"That one was close," a local man said of the second tornado. "I'm almost getting used to it."[7]

The tornadoes were not confined to Alabama. In Louisville, Kentucky, 20,000 hardwood trees fell in the city's prized Cherokee Park. In Xenia, Ohio, three school buses crashed onto the school stage shortly after the school day ended. Thankfully, Daylight Savings Time had started early that year, or many children would probably have still been at school.

By the end of the outbreak, 335 people had been killed and 6,000 injured. Over 2,584 miles of tornado track had been cut into the country by 148 tornadoes. Property loss left 27,000 families with about $600 million in damage.[8]

PART ONE:
HACKLEBURG, ALABAMA

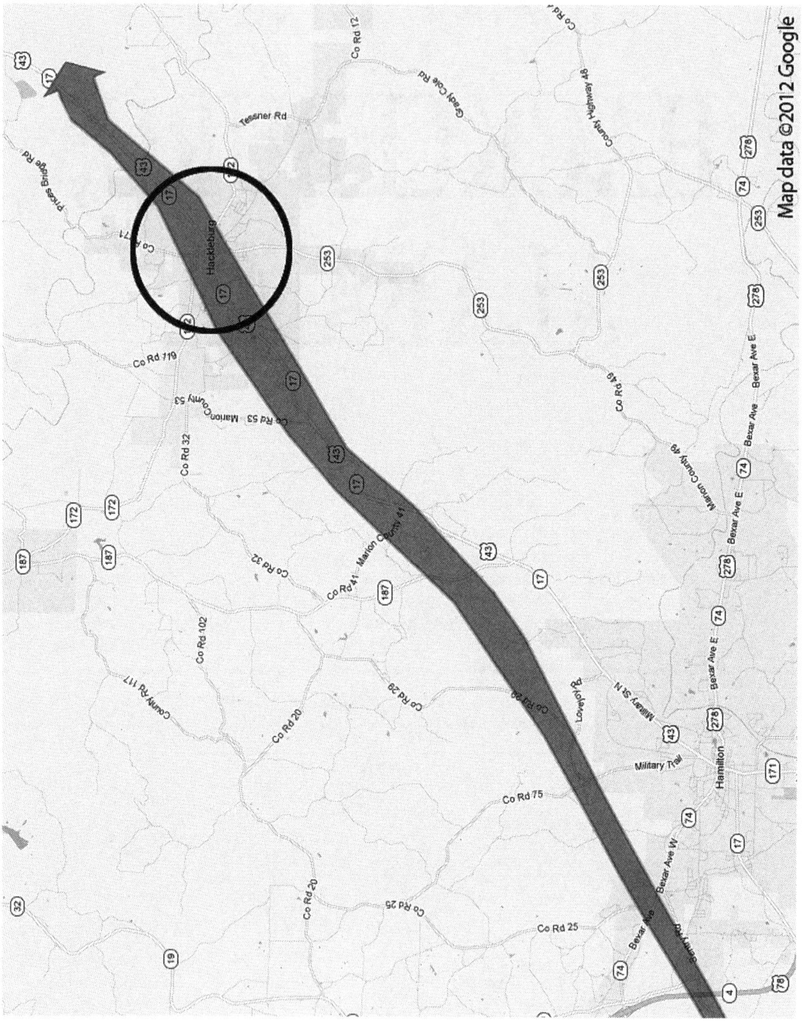
Map data ©2012 Google
Hackleburg
Hamilton
Tessner Rd
Co Rd 12
Co Rd 119
Co Rd 32
Co Rd 41
Co Rd 29
Co Rd 20
Co Rd 75
Co Rd 25
Co Rd 102
Military Trail
Bexar Ave E

Hackleburg, Alabama

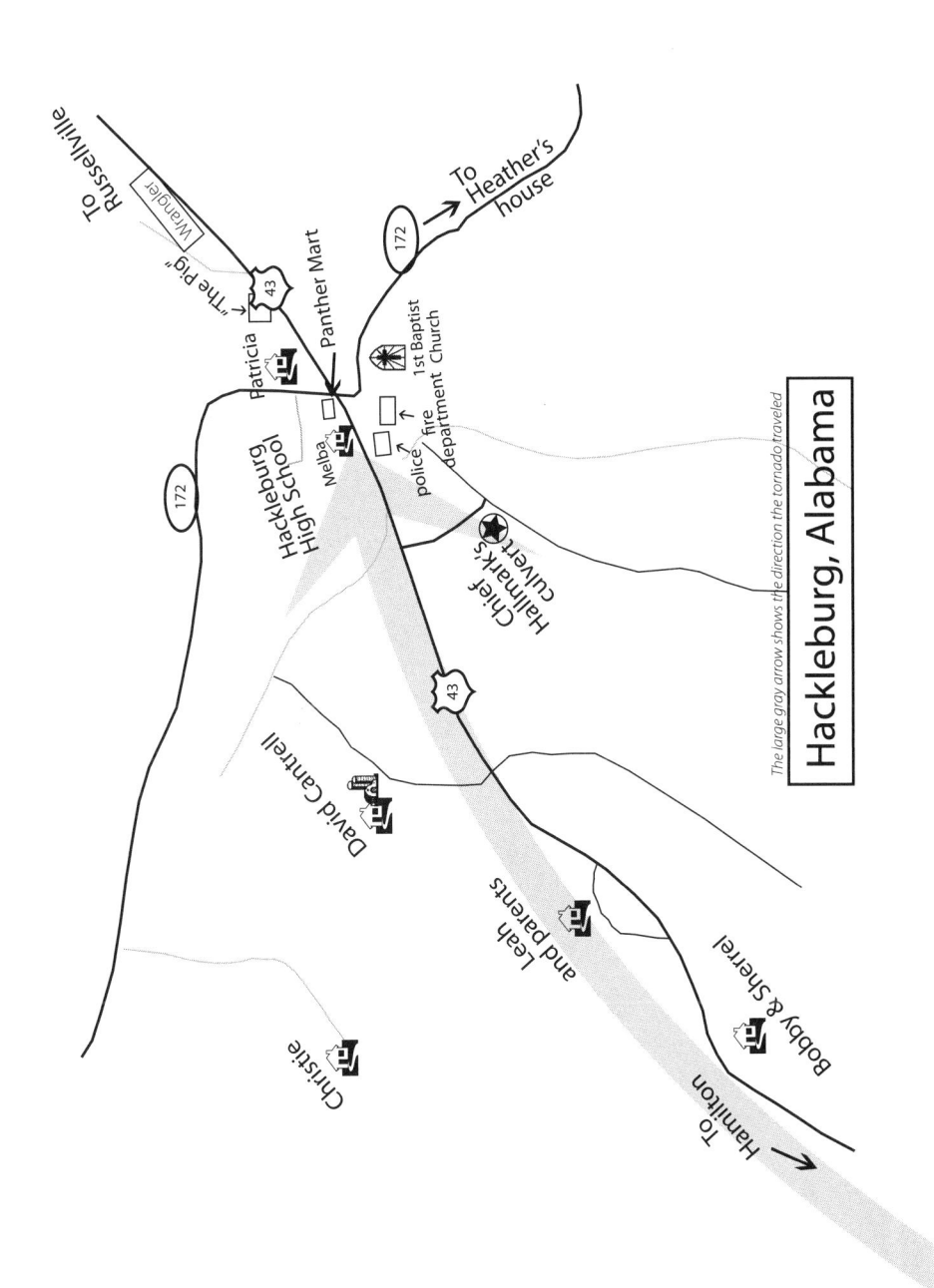

The large gray arrow shows the direction the tornado traveled

To Russellville

"The Pig" — Wrangler

Patricia

Panther Mart

172 — To Heather's house

1st Baptist Church

Melba

police, fire department

Hackleburg High School

172

Chief Hallmark's Culvert

43

David Cantrell

Christie

Leah and parents

Bobby & Sherrel

To Hamilton

21

Frequently encountered characters

Residents listed in roughly geographical order of the tornado's path:

- Bobby and Sherrell Barnwell, their daughter Bridgett and her new baby Mitchell
- Leah Phillips and son Nathan
- Christie Lindsey, Panther Mart employee
- Melba Gunnin, janitor at First Baptist Hackleburg
- Pastor Steve Lawrence and his wife Donna, First Baptist Hackleburg
- Wynn Knowles, high school senior and Panther Mart employee
- Patricia Raper, gardener, cook, and senior center manager
- Heather Cole, high school student from Franklin County
- Theresa Hutcheson, Panther Mart cashier

Emergency Personnel:

- Kenny Hallmark, police chief
- Steve Hood, fire chief
- David Cantrell, assistant EMA director, Hackleburg assistant fire chief
- Willie Holcomb, volunteer firefighter
- Rob Ayers, street department employee and volunteer firefighter

1
Life Before the Tornado

*The tornado has become the black hole of meteorology.
We really don't know how it works.*
—*National Geographic,* April 2004

On a map of Alabama, the top half of the state is a criss-cross of interstates. The interstates extend from the hub of Birmingham like six spokes on a wagon wheel. In the center of the space between the top and top-left spokes (I-65 and I-22), a national forest blots the map. Halfway between these trees and the Mississippi line, Hackleburg's 1,500 residents live in the shade of giant oaks, sprawling pecan orchards, and a massive Wrangler warehouse.

So few outsiders know about Hackleburg that it is usually described in relationship to larger places. It's the town "close to Hamilton" or "a hundred miles north of Birmingham." It's a town you pass through on your way to somewhere else. Travelers looking for Walmart, McDonald's, or a Best Western will have to continue north to Russellville, and by the end of the day they may have forgotten they drove through the little intersection at Hackleburg.

Those who pull up to Hackleburg's Panther Mart find the atmosphere warm and welcoming. In the morning, breakfast sandwiches or biscuits and gravy can be purchased there. Breakfast meats are layered between soft biscuits that fall apart with every bite. The Panther Mart swarms with locals buying a tasty breakfast along with their gas fill-up.

For those seeking more variety, Grace's Restaurant is just a few steps away. The cozy dining room has a flowered wallpaper border. The hanging stained-glass lamps are all different, personalizing each table. It's not a big building, but no one seems to mind sacrificing personal space for Grace's home-style foods. It's a social gathering place, especially in the morning, where men gather over coffee and linger over talk. Hackleburg doesn't have a newspaper; it has Grace's. A favorite meal choice is called a plate lunch. It's like a buffet, only the waitress spoons out the food. Grace's also has daily specials, such as chicken and dressing or good old southern pork chops. Banana pudding or peach cobblers await those who still have room.

Most of the tables at Grace's seat about four people, but there's one table that seats eight. Bankers from Hamilton and Florence meet their Hackleburg partners here. Agricultural groups take it some days. If there are road construction crews close by, they claim the table for eight.

First Baptist Church of Hackleburg is made up of several buildings. The older brick structure was built in 1942 after a tornado destroyed the original building. The sanctuary is a warm-colored room with maroon carpet and wooden benches upholstered in red. Stained glass lets in light through splashes of blue, yellow, and red. Even though it is no longer big enough to house the several hundred Sunday morning worshippers, it breathes peace and safety.

Pastor Steve and his wife live close by. They remember the long discussion in 2009. Should First Baptist build a new church or not? After many meetings, the building project was approved. The old church building stayed, but a new one was added only a few feet away.

The new building, a blend of technology and tradition, has ample capacity for attendees. There's an artistic foyer and little rooms for small group meetings and Vacation Bible School classes. There's a fellowship hall that can be used as a gym.

With two buildings, First Baptist now has the square feet to host small meetings and big gatherings all at once. The generous space has already been put to good use. If there is ever a need to house a large crowd of people, First Baptist Hackleburg is the ideal place.

The commercial section across the highway from First Baptist includes Dollar General, Dr. Morrow's family practice, and Piggly Wiggly. Not just a grocery store where you buy fresh meat and lettuce and milk, Piggly Wiggly is also known as "The Pig," a social destination. If you wish to see or be seen, this is the place to go. While their husbands drink coffee at Grace's, some elderly ladies make three or four trips to The Pig each day, just for the experience.

Farther out of town, the giant steel Wrangler warehouse on the hill employs dozens of people. There's a special turning lane on the highway to accommodate all the semis that pull in and out of the warehouse. The Wrangler industry provides many jobs, and its taxes help support the town.

\\\\\\\V////////

The smaller roads in Alabama look like a bowl of spaghetti thrown over the interstate wheel on the map. Following the single piece of spaghetti that is State Highway 43, one can see that the road goes up and down, this way and that, through northern Alabama. It heads north out of Tuscaloosa, cutting cross-country over the spokes of the wheel. It bends left to go through Hamilton, and then to the right for the fourteen-mile journey up to Hackleburg. On the way to Hackleburg, Highway 43 plunges passengers up and down hills and throws them around sweeping curves, bringing motion sickness to weak stomachs. The road is hemmed with acres and acres of trees.

Both Hackleburg and neighboring Hamilton are in Marion County. The county EMA (Emergency Management Agency) office is in Hamilton, the larger of the two towns. The EMA helps the county deal with disasters. Assistant director David Cantrell, a red-haired man in his early thirties, says, "EMA is an enabler. We're a resource outlet—a backup for the local departments. If you need a hundred fire trucks, we'll find you a hundred fire trucks."

It's a part-time job for David. Thankfully, disasters are not a daily occurrence. Besides, David has two other big roles. He is Hackleburg's assistant fire chief, and he is the associate pastor at First Baptist Hackleburg, working alongside Pastor Steve.

Emergency management, fire department, and church are three separate roles, but they all give David opportunities to serve others. He's a serious man who reads Oswald Chambers and C.S. Lewis. His words are careful and effective. Although David doesn't waste smiles, he inspires trust.

"When David says something, you just go with it," says one of the firefighters. "He's a highly intelligent man—99.9 percent of the time, he's right."

David isn't the only person in Hackleburg who wears a number of hats. Kenny Hallmark is both the police chief and the high school basketball coach. In addition, he's the father of three children. His multiple roles don't keep him from focusing, however. "I take my job seriously," says Chief Hallmark.

Both David and Chief Hallmark have been busy recently. Hackleburg has had odd weather so far this year, with several foot-deep snows and a few EF0 tornadoes. The snows have caused enough school closures that the district has run out of built-in bad-weather days. If they take off one more day, they'll have to have school on Saturday.

2
The People

I dreamed this tornado came.
—Hackleburg resident Sammy Lindsey

Nathan dashes up to the porch ahead of his mother. After a day at work at the call center in nearby Hamilton, listening to people complaining about their Internet connections, Leah Phillips still has a smile for the energy of the son she loves so much. Nathan's third birthday is coming up on June 26, and Leah realizes that today his birthday is exactly two months away. What kind of cake will he want this year? Last year he was almost too small to care. She pictures wrapping gifts in bright colors and singing "Happy Birthday" with MeMe and PaPa, her parents.

Leah ran some errands after work before picking up her son, who had spent the day with MawMaw, his other grandma. Mother and son are arriving home now around 8 p.m.

"Nathan, remember, MeMe is still tired from her surgery," Leah cautions, knowing that Nathan will burst into the house and expect giant hugs and kisses from both of his grandparents. Nathan often stays with MeMe while

Leah works, but Leah's mom had a heart catheterization recently. With a new stent in place, she feels fine but is still taking it easy.

Leah greets her parents.

"How was your day, Mom?" she asks. "You need to get more minutes on your phone so I can talk to you during the day." Her mother is putting eggs in a pot to hard boil, but Leah can see that she's tired. Leah draws Nathan's bath water while the hugs and kisses make their rounds.

After the bath and some mommy time in the rocking chair, Nathan is ready for bed.

"Let's say your prayers," Leah coaches. "Dear Jesus . . ."

"Dear Jesus."

"Help—"

"Help me to be strong."

"Help me to be—"

"Help me to be a good boy."

"Help MeMe to get better."

"Help MeMe to get better."

Leah smiles to herself, knowing what will happen next.

"In—"

"In Jesus' name, Amen!" Nathan cries triumphantly.

MeMe has taught him that part. Whenever they sit down for supper, hands are folded under the table and a prayer of thanks is sent to heaven. It always ends with "In Jesus' name, Amen," and Nathan has learned that part best of all.

Leah tucks in her son and gives him one final kiss before slipping back to the living room.

"Mom, the eggs!" Leah cries. "Never mind, I'll get them," she adds hurriedly, seeing that her mother has fallen asleep in her chair. The eggs her mother was attempting to cook are popping and cracking. Leah lifts the lid. The water is completely gone and the bottom of the pan is scorching.

Hard-boiled, all right, Leah smiles to herself as she turns off the flame.

It doesn't matter. The eggs come from her parents' own chickens, so there will be more tomorrow. Leah empties the eggs into the kitchen sink to cool and leans against the counter. It's dusky outside, but Leah can still see the raised garden box right outside the window. Radishes and onions wave at her from the box and remind Leah why she has learned to love this homestead she and Nathan share with her parents. Leah's mother enjoys growing herbs, and she also cans vegetables and meat in glass Mason jars. This raised box below the kitchen window makes up a very small part of her garden space. The real garden is farther back behind the house and will soon be leafed full of greens: collard greens, turnip greens, and squash. Leah's dad builds what his wife needs for her projects, from retaining walls to chicken houses.

Leah's mother is not just a gardener. She has a penchant for collecting. As far as Leah knows, her mother has $10,000 worth of registered animal furs. In addition, she has a tremendous assortment of trinkets. Who knows when someone might need just such a thing? And, her mother reasons, how much space does it take up anyway to store tiny collectibles?

Leah turns from the window with the cozy sense of being wrapped invisibly in the arms of a dark, friendly forest, sheltered in a sturdy, thirty-year-old house with the people she loves the most. Despite her mother's odd habits, her parents' home is the private harbor where she and Nathan drop anchor. In a swelling and stormy world, she is so glad that her little son always knows there is a safe place to vanish. Even in broad daylight, only the tip of the house roof can be seen above the trees from the end of the driveway.

At 4 a.m. the next morning, a thunderstorm cuts the electricity in the house, so things are shadowy when Leah leaves for work. Normally Nathan stays at home with MeMe on Wednesdays, but because of her mother's surgery, Leah will drop him off at MawMaw's house again. MawMaw lives in Hamilton, closer to Leah's workplace.

"Goodbye, Mom, see you tonight," Leah says, giving her mother a kiss. "Bye, Dad!"

On the way to work, Leah sees she's running low on gas. There's no time to fuel up before work, so she makes a mental note to get gas in the evening. She leaves Nathan with MawMaw and drives to the call center.

\\\\\\\\\V/////////

Bobby and Sherrell Barnwell live south of Hackleburg on a hillside dotted with wonderful trees and Bobby's hunting shacks. Their house is crowned with brand new shingles. Bobby and Sherrell's daughter, Bridgett, lives in a house close by. Because the two houses have separate driveways, the Barnwells have beaten out a path from Bridgett's house to their own. Whenever Bridgett has a question or needs to borrow something, she runs down the path through the dancing shadows of trees to her parents' house.

The last few months, Bridgett has been more careful on the path and less steady on her feet. Then just a few weeks ago, on April 11, she gave birth to a son, Mitchell. When Bridgett was released from the hospital, she refused to leave her new son, who needed to stay a few more days. Finally, the nurses gave her a cot outside the intensive care unit and let her stay.

Now Bridgett and Mitchell are home. Excitement is high at the Barnwells' with the arrival of the new grandson. They visit him often and love to babysit. They're also delighted because Bridgett loves her baby so much and wants to take good care of him.

Bobby and Sherrell have lived on their lot for more than thirty years. After the 1974 tornadoes that ravaged Alabama, they added a storm shelter to the side of the hill. For a while they used it frequently, but as the memory of the horror stories faded, their use of the shelter lessened. Furthermore, they learned that by the time a storm got bad, it was almost as dangerous to run across the yard to the storm shelter as it was to ride it out inside the house.

The Barnwells have weathered more than storms. Six years ago, Bobby was talking on the phone to another daughter when she had a heart attack. By the time help arrived, she had passed away. She was forty-two years old.

At the cash register of the Panther Mart, Christie tries to ignore her tired feet. She'll be up all night, spending the night with her Aunt Freddie, so rest is a long way off. Aunt Freddie, who is confined to a hospital bed and has almost no movement on her left side, lives with her husband Junior and their daughter Vicki. Uncle Junior and Vicki care for Freddie, but Christie often stays with her aunt overnight to give them a break.

After spending the night with her aunt, Christie will return home to sleep until it's time to return to work at the Panther Mart for the evening shift. Tonight as Christie heads out the door to sit with Aunt Freddie, her husband Sammy tells her about his dream.

"I dreamed this tornado came," he says. Not surprising, because Hackleburg weather has been unsettled all week. "We couldn't get Aunt Freddie to safety." This is not shocking either. Aunt Freddie, with her catheter, oxygen, and feeding tube, would never be able to move quickly to a storm cellar.

Christie pauses with her hand on the door and smiles at her husband.

"I'll be okay," she says.

In fact, she feels that Aunt Freddie's house is the safest place to be.

"God takes care of those who can't take care of themselves," she adds.

There's a thunderstorm at 4 a.m., but no tornado. Aunt Freddie wakes up, and Christie props her up in bed. Cousin Vicki's puppy, Casper, a tiny little spot of fur, curls at the foot of Aunt Freddie's bed like always. Together, Christie and Aunt Freddie watch the lightning and the little tree frogs clinging to the window. Aunt Freddie is alert and cheery. When the blackness of night bleaches to watery gray, Christie gives Aunt Freddie a hug and a kiss, promising to be back in the evening after her shift at the Panther Mart.

Melba lives on Nix Road not far from the Panther Mart. A fig tree dominates her front yard. She's a glass collector, a hobby shared by her next-door neighbor. Her neighbor comes over to take a look at the contents of Melba's china cupboard, and Melba visits the neighbor to admire her glass collection as well. It's a friendly competition. In fact, the whole neighborhood is friendly. Hackleburg is a busy and populated place compared to the Tennessee farm where Melba grew up, but she likes it.

Melba washes the few dishes from her small supper. She's always liked vegetables, and she can transform okra into something delectable. She has diabetes, although it's not crippling. Still, she watches her diet and tries to wear good shoes to keep her feet safe from injury, since it's harder for a diabetic's bruises to heal.

It's good she lives so close to First Baptist Church because she is the church's cleaning lady. There will be prayer meeting tomorrow night, so Melba plans to go to church in the morning and do some cleaning. She straightens up her own house a little tonight, but now that it's just her, there are no dishes or clothes to pick up after others, no magazines or newspapers to put in the rack.

Like her diabetes, the death of Melba's husband two years ago is an ever-present cloud in the back of her mind. How strange that you could live with someone for so long, almost never thinking about someday being apart. All her life she has tried to see sunshine behind every cloud. But she wonders if it's even realistic to expect sunshine to emerge from the cloud of her husband's death.

\\\\\\\\\\\\\\V////////////

Wynn Knowles is about to graduate as class salutatorian from Hackleburg High School. He already has his graduation invitations, and he's getting ready to send them out.

Wynn lives close to the school as well as Hackleburg Community Church, a pleasant, modern-looking building with a green roof. Wynn's father is the pastor. His father's assistant, the youth pastor, does so much with their family that he can almost pass for a family member as well.

\\\\\\\\\\\V/////////

A talented flower gardener, Patricia Raper moves through her yard, in which one could imagine to be lost on the cover of a landscaping magazine. Four shades of pink peonies stretch the length of Patricia's garden, which takes up as much space as her house. Purple verbena thrives in a bed in the front lawn. Four rows of irises stretch from a wooded area to the storm cellar behind the house. Dug into the side of a hill, the storm cellar has a flower bed with fifty-two shades of irises for its roof.

At the front of the brick house reside seven Knock-out rosebushes. The rosebuds are dragging on the ground. Because of all the snow and ice this past winter, Patricia never trimmed the bushes. Bending over, Patricia rearranges a new row of pots, six more Knock-outs. These roses are yellow, and they will stand in front of the pink ones. They'll match the yellow lilies on the other side of the doorstep.

Patricia stands up, resting gloved hands on her hips, nodding with grudging satisfaction that she has placed the pots at the proper distance from the older row. She will plant them in the ground soon.

Patricia, who could rightly claim retirement herself, is manager of the senior citizen center in the neighboring town of Phil Campbell. Besides that job and her landscaping hobby, she takes care of domestic duties for herself and a fourteen-year-old niece who has always lived with her.

Patricia was born in Hackleburg, up on the hill past the giant Wrangler factory. Her childhood home was surrounded by giant trees. When the Corps of Engineers wanted an article written about the historic trees, they came and found Patricia. She knows just how much coolness they provided to the house where she grew up. She remembers sailing through the air on a wooden swing hanging from their branches. Patricia and the trees have grown up together.

Just north of Marion County, Heather Cole, age seventeen, lives in Franklin County with her mother and older brother Bradley. In her bedroom, Heather has a huge bulletin board pinned full of pictures. Many of them are pictures of her with her father.

Heather still misses her father, who passed away in 2010 after a gallbladder surgery that should not have killed him.

"It's okay," she says, but she clings to several tangible reminders of his presence. In her car, Heather keeps an informal memorial, including a bottle of her father's cologne and a picture of the two of them together. Her most treasured possession is his black jacket, with his name embroidered on the front.

Mr. Tornado and the EF Scale

The name "Mr. Tornado" goes to a researcher who grew up, not in tornado country, but in Japan. This man is said to have advanced "the human understanding of tornadoes more than any other single individual."[9]

Mr. Fujita had a brilliant eye for drawing maps and a keen mind for visualizing how things worked. A few days after Hiroshima was bombed in World War II, Fujita was hiding in a bomb shelter three miles from the target for the second atomic bomb. Because of the cloud cover, the pilot changed the target, flying the B-29 on to Nagasaki.[10]

Fujita closely studied the wreckage caused by the atomic bombs, noting that the damage formed a starburst pattern. Based on the burn marks on cemetery flower pots, he was able to prove that the bombs had exploded high in the air, not after they reached the ground.

In 1953, Horace Byers, head of the Thunderstorm Project in the United States, invited Fujita to come to Chicago after seeing copies of his research. On the plane ride over, Fujita put the expensive ticket to good use by sketching the clouds. He arrived in Chicago after a three-day train ride from California, sustained by Coca-Cola and fig bars.

His timing was excellent, because the States had just been ravaged once again by three deadly tornadoes in Waco, Texas; Flint, Michigan; and Worcester, Massachusetts. In particular, the downtown Waco tornado was disturbing, shattering the myth that tornadoes prefer lonely towns on the prairie and tend to avoid cities. In fact, there was some suspicion that the atomic bombs being dropped in the Nevada desert as a Cold War practice had caused the tornadoes by disrupting the atmosphere. The Atomic Energy Commission attempted to put fears to rest by insisting that this could not be the case because the atom bomb explosion "is a tiny force compared with the energy unleashed by a natural storm."[11]

In 1955, 82 people were killed by a tornado in Udall, Kansas, at 10:35 p.m., half an hour after TV announced that the threat of danger was past. In 1957, Fargo, North Dakota, was struck by tornadoes that destroyed 1,300 homes and killed 13 people. This tornado was so slow that many people were able to take photos of it, and there was even one video.

After the Fargo tornado, Mr. Fujita became famous. He found all the photos he could from that storm and shrank them all to the same scale, determining which angle they had been shot from. He walked the damage paths over and over. Because of his gift for visualizing things and noticing details, he was called the "Sherlock Holmes of storms." *Weatherwise* magazine called him "the best meteorological detective who ever lived."[12]

After Fargo, Mr. Fujita had the freedom to do as he pleased

because his work brought large grants to the University of Chicago. His skills were so great no one cared about his poor English, and some people even suspected that he exaggerated his accent to get attention.[13] Despite the name "Mr. Tornado," he didn't actually set eyes on one himself until he was sixty-one years old. However, he saw plenty of evidence, going to northern Indiana after Palm Sunday in 1965 and Alabama in 1974.

Mr. Fujita explained that in Japan there were four things to be feared: earthquake, lightning, fire, and father. In the United States he made a new list: tornadoes, lightning, fire, and crime.[14]

Perhaps Fujita is most famous for the Fujita scale. This scale rates the strength of tornadoes based on the damage they cause. Although the scale was updated on February 1, 2007, and called the "Enhanced Fujita Scale," changing the letters to *EF* instead of *F*, the basic work is Fujita's.[15]

- EF0—More than half of all reported tornadoes are EF0. These gentle tornadoes damage gutters and siding and might peel off roofing (winds 65–85 miles per hour).

- EF1—About 30 percent of tornadoes are EF1. They cause moderate damage by stripping roofs, destroying mobile homes, and breaking glass and outside doors (winds 86–110 miles per hour).

- EF2—10 percent of tornadoes are EF2. They tear off roofs, lift cars, snap trees, and hurl light objects (winds 111–135 miles per hour).

- EF3—An EF3 causes severe damage but only

applies to about 3 percent of tornadoes. These tornadoes damage large buildings, push trains over, strip bark off trees, and throw cars around. Buildings with weak structures may be picked up and tossed (winds 136–165 miles per hour).

· EF4—Less than 1 percent of tornadoes cause EF4 damage, which is considered devastating. This damage is the same as an EF3, only worse, with well-built houses being completely leveled (winds 166–200 miles per hour).

· EF5—Less than 0.1 percent of all tornadoes do this kind of damage, which is considered to be incredible. Cars fly for one hundred yards. Strong houses are picked up whole. Steel structures are badly damaged, and skyscrapers receive significant damage (winds more than 200 miles per hour).[16]

Although wind speeds are assigned to each category, the scale measures damage, not wind speed. For this reason, there could be no level higher than EF5, because the definition for EF5 is, essentially, the most incredible damage imaginable from a tornado, which is judged to be caused by internal speeds of more than 200 miles per hour. Whether the wind speed is 200 miles per hour or 700 miles per hour, the tornado would still be an EF5.

Although EF3, EF4, and EF5 tornadoes account for less than 5 percent of all tornadoes, they cause 88 percent of tornado deaths.[17]

After re-making tornado science, Fujita died in 1998.

3
Wednesday, April 27, 2011

I've got trees coming out of this wall cloud.
—Marion County deputy

David Cantrell is one of the first to awaken in Hackleburg on April 27, 2011. He drives to Hamilton at 2 a.m., arriving at the EMA office ahead of the morning's first storm. The head director is there. David and the director check satellite radar. They listen to James Span, a Birmingham meteorologist.

"It will either be the worst day in history, or nothing," Span says. It is impossible for him to predict if the system will break open, but if it does...

The EMA office has known for a few days that volatile weather is brewing. Dr. Greg Forbes, a meteorologist with the Weather Channel, has developed an index to measure tornado conditions. This index, called the TOR:CON, indicates the likelihood of a tornado within fifty miles of a given area. Today there is a TOR:CON rating of 9 out of 10 for this region, which means there is a 90 percent chance of having a tornado within fifty miles of Hamilton. A TOR:CON rating this high has never been forecast here before.

The National Weather Service's prediction is no brighter. "We've never seen anything like this before," they announce.

\\\\\\\\\\V/////////

The early morning thunderstorm that Christie and Aunt Freddie watched is not deadly, but it cripples. When it disappears to the east, it has damaged electric lines, cell phone towers, and fiber-optic cables. Long-distance telephone service, Internet service, and weather radios are all compromised, on the least convenient day of the year. Because the weather radios are not working, the only outlet for weather forecasting is television, and that is available only for those who still have electricity.

As night turns to dawn, a question arises. *Should we have school today?* Ryan Hollingsworth, Marion County's school superintendent, stops in at the EMA office around 6 a.m.

It's a hard decision. Because of the snow days, another day off will force the school to operate on a Saturday, which no one wants to do. Furthermore, the morning storm has passed, and though the forecast is still worrisome, a glance at the radar over Mississippi shows no immediate threat.

Mr. Hollingsworth strides down the hall of the EMA office. He chats with the director, looking at the radar before heading back down the hall. He drops into David's office.

"What do you think, David?"

"I don't know." David leans back in his chair and eyes the superintendent. "I don't know why—I just have a really bad feeling." For a man who can usually prove his statements, this is unusual.

The superintendent nods and walks out. It's not long before Marion County residents hear that school has been called off for the day.

"I'm surprised," says the EMA director. "When he left my office, he was leaning toward just calling a delay and starting school at ten."

About 10:00 the sun comes out, and it's easy to think the threatening weather is past for the day. David and the director answer phone calls. People want to know what to expect.

Although the weather radios are out, David uses a new texting system they have just put in place. Using his iPhone, David is able to hit one button and send weather messages to hundreds of people. This is a huge blessing because of the Internet and weather radio outages in Marion County.

Still, with the damaged communication systems, there will be no way to warn everyone when a real tornado comes out of the clouds. And even for those who do receive a warning, by the time they get it, the tornado will have already traveled some distance.

\\\\\\\\\\V//////////

At 1:00, David steps out to look at the sky again. The sun is out, but it feels like a smile from a mean teacher. David can see three layers of clouds in the atmosphere, each blowing a different direction.

"What does that mean?" someone beside him asks.

"It means it's bad."

Ten men gather in the EMA office in Hamilton. In the center of the meeting room is a big screen showing the weather radar images. The images reset and update every three minutes. To the left of the radar screen, the television broadcasts on a 35-inch flat screen. David is sitting behind the others, most of whom are watching the weather on the TV. Meteorologist James Span reports on a live tornado about fifty miles east of Hamilton, heading straight for the camera tower filming it. Although the tornado is chilling, David keeps his eyes on the radar over Mississippi. The Mississippi state line is a mere twenty miles west of Hackleburg. Whatever begins in Mississippi will probably come to Alabama.

One of the Marion County deputies is a meteorological guru. He loves following the weather. He's standing behind David, leaning on the doorway, also watching the radar colors. Greens and yellows mean moderate intensity, and oranges and reds are more severe. There is no red in Marion County right now. It's not even raining.

David and the deputy, however, are watching the radar over Mississippi. When it refreshes, they notice that a red spot in Mississippi has exploded over the last three minutes.

A man watching the TV screen leans over and punches David on the arm. "What are you looking at?" he asks.

"The radar. If it does in the next three minutes what it did in the last three, we'll have a storm."

David and the deputy wait another three minutes. The screen refreshes and they stiffen—the storm area has doubled.

"Did you just see that?" the deputy asks. He's not just talking about the huge, red storm, but about something else that he's never seen before. In the center of the red mass is a black hole. It's as if the middle of the cloud is so dense it won't send a recognizable signal.

Both men get up and leave.

The deputy drives to the interstate. David drives to the local airport to monitor the weather from there. The National Weather Service stays in touch with them via two-way radio. The EMA men keep in touch with each other as well.

Seeing a dangerous cloud, the deputy hollers into the radio, "That cloud's rotating."

"Yes, sir, it is," David replies.

A small tornado drops out of the rotating cloud. David thinks it's probably an EF0. It knocks over some trees. David continues watching it.

As others from the EMA office leave to keep an eye on the weather from their vehicles, someone radios, "What do you see?"

"It was a huge system, but it didn't do much," comes the response.

A minute later, another deputy radios from north of Hamilton. "There's a huge wall cloud up here," he says.

David decides to follow the cloud and heads north on Highway 43 toward his hometown of Hackleburg.

Police Chief Hallmark and all the Hackleburg emergency workers have also been watching the weather forecasts closely the last few days. At 4 a.m. on April 27, Chief Hallmark sets off the tornado warning sirens at the police station and takes his family to the adjoining jail, a safe place in the event of tornadoes.

That first storm of the morning passes, knocking out power but causing little damage. Chief Hallmark and his staff discuss what each person's task will be in the event of severe weather. However, the sun comes out and the day begins to look nice. Chief Hallmark's family leaves the jail and goes home.

At 3:00 in the afternoon, the chief brings his family back to the jail and the sirens sound again. One of the sirens has been struck by lightning and is waiting to be fixed. Several other emergency workers enter the jail cell for refuge.

Chief Hallmark, however, gets into his police cruiser and heads out of town, south on Highway 43. He keeps in touch with David and the others to the south. They've seen a small tornado slip out of the sky. They are also describing a huge wall cloud north of Hamilton, heading for Hackleburg. As David follows this cloud up Highway 43, Chief Hallmark says, "I'll go down 43 and see it from the top."

"You should start seeing it soon," David crackles over the radio. Chief Hallmark's car dips into the hills and hollows south of town, and he can't see anything.

"I don't see anything yet," the chief says.

That's when another deputy north of Hamilton radios an announcement. This deputy is a reserved man, who usually doesn't say much over the radio.

"I've got trees coming out of this wall cloud," the quiet deputy reports suddenly.

David grabs his radio. "That's not a wall cloud; that's a tornado—just get out of the way!"

Chief Hallmark reaches the top of the hill. He sees it.

Chief Hallmark is the first to really set eyes on the giant, because he is seeing it from the front. The quiet deputy, standing behind the tornado to the south, can see only black sky. But Chief Hallmark can see the tornado clearly, a mass of black dipping out of equally black clouds, but outlined behind by lighter sky.

Immediately he makes a U-turn.

"I have a visual on a large tornado heading up Highway 43," he reports. He turns on his lights and siren and steps on the gas.

On the other side of the cloud, David hears the chief radio, "I'm going 80-something, and it's gaining on me. I'm not sure that I'm going to be able to outrun it."

Most tornadoes travel 30–40 miles per hour. This one is traveling 65 miles per hour.[18] The chief is going faster, but he is confined to the road. And, he stops to warn people, like the driver who's parked beside the road taking pictures.

As the chief nears Hackleburg, he passes a house trailer. The boy who lives there is a friend of his son.

The young man is in his trailer with his mother and a friend. They aren't paying attention to the weather until the boy hears Chief Hallmark's siren. He goes to the window and sees the officer racing past, lights flashing in the eerie duskiness. Behind the car, he sees the tornado coming straight for his house. He rushes his mother and friend to the bathtub, saving their lives.

The chief hurries on, but now he has a car in front of him that's poking along at 60 miles per hour. Glancing in the rearview mirror, the chief sees houses exploding. He slows at a side road, wrenches his car to the right, and slams to a halt. He leaps out and dives into a culvert. All around him, trees are snapping.

\\\\\\\\\\\\\V//////////

Willie Holcomb, a volunteer firefighter, has been at his job in Hackleburg for several hours. Since he started work, the temperature changed from cool to steamy. Willie is sweltering in his shirt. The air feels oppressive and suffocating. Under this spell, the rows of houses look too plastic, as if they could melt.

In the afternoon Willie hears the sirens. He quickly heads to the fire station and parks beside four other vehicles. Willie glances at the clock on his dashboard before hurrying inside. It's after 3:00. Other firefighters are hanging around the station. Willie talks to a couple of them and together they decide to head over to the jail.

Everyone knows that the jail is the storm cellar of choice. Located at the back of the police station, the jail is small but made of block walls. The cells were made before World War II. Rows of heavy, hard-backed volumes of Alabama law line the one side of the little jail. There are two cells, each with a toilet. One cell is used for storage. Hackleburg does not produce enough dangerous people to warrant keeping two cells prepared.

The remaining jail cell is now crowded with emergency workers. The door swings shut. It's a door of heavy metal slats criss-crossing on each other, suggesting a game of checkers to bored inmates. The openings between the slats also allow the occupants to see pieces of debris circling ominously through the air.

\\\\\\\\\\\\\V/////////

Firefighter Rob Ayers is another man with more than one responsibility. He works for the street department as well as the fire department. On the afternoon of April 27, 2011, he and a co-worker are cutting up a tree that has fallen on a county road a few miles from Hackleburg. When they realize the danger, they leap into their truck and barrel down the road. They can see a black pillar behind them.

"Step on the gas!" Rob tells his friend. "If we slow down, we're dead." They're driving 90 miles per hour, honking their horn, shouting at people to take cover, pointing behind them to the pillar of black.

They dash into town and Rob leaps out of the truck at his home. He remembers the old advice, "Don't look back, because if you do, you'll lose three seconds," and hurtles inside to get his family into the basement. The truck rushes on to a storm shelter.

\\\\\\\\\\\\\\V//////////

Meanwhile, David heads up Highway 43, five minutes behind the tornado. He arrives at a house that has a car on its roof. The house looks nearly ready to collapse. He sees a woman in the window. She leans out and yells to David that she and her small children hid in the bathtub. They're okay, but they need a place to go.

David gets out of his vehicle. It's pouring rain.

"Let's wait a minute before getting the children out of the bathtub," he says.

His radio beeps. It's the National Weather Service. "You said you had damage on Highway 43, right?"

"Yes."

"You need to get under something because there's another one coming right through."

In the pouring rain, David lifts his face to the already terrified mother.

"Get the children and get back in the bathtub," he says.

His own words drain him. *I've got to tell her to get back into the bathtub of a house that's collapsing?*

He returns to his truck, but then he sees a nearby SUV turned upside down. He knows that vehicles are tornado death traps, so he looks for a ditch, but the closest one is laced with whipping barbed wire. When the weather service announces that the tornado is not far away, David bails out of his truck into a nearby swimming pool he's just spotted.

"I'll be in the swimming pool if you need me," he radios.

He sits in the pool, which has only a foot of water in it. It's quite comfortable in the pool, a moment of relaxation in a day that won't be getting any easier.

After about three to four minutes, David emerges. The second tornado has eased to the west, on a track parallel to the first one. David makes sure that the mother and children are headed for the ambulance that has pulled up.

Highway 43 is blocked and David can't continue to Hackleburg that way. But if his home town is in trouble, he's going to get there however he can.

4
The Storm

The last thing I saw was three pieces of tin and a couple of tree limbs coming over the post office.
—Hackleburg resident

Leah is taking lunch break at 3 p.m. at the busy call center in Hamilton.

"Did you see the news?" a co-worker asks as microwave doors slam. "A tornado hit Cullman." Cullman is about seventy-five miles away.

"Do you think we're going off the phones?" someone asks. The call center is a place that's supposed to be available at all hours for people who are experiencing technical difficulties with their computers or Internet service. Going off the phones is a major deal.

A big aluminum building houses the call center, one of those structures that appears in days and can be destroyed much faster. There is no good hiding place, no storm shelter, no tornado protocol except gathering in the middle of the building, as far from potential danger as possible.

Leah, watching the news, chews thoughtfully, then sets down her sandwich and reaches for her phone. She texts MawMaw and asks where Nathan is and if everything is okay.

MawMaw replies that they are fine and Nathan is playing down in the basement.

Leah knows she will not relax anyway—not until Nathan is in her arms. She can't call her mom in Hackleburg, because MeMe doesn't have any more minutes on her phone. But she doesn't worry about her parents. They live in a thirty-year-old house surrounded by older trees, all of which have weathered many storms.

\\\\\\\\\\\\\V//////////

On this gray Wednesday, Bridgett walks down the path through the trees with her two-week-old baby. She needs to run to The Pig to get a few things for her evening meal, and she wants to leave Mitchell with Grandma and Grandpa Barnwell.

After Bridgett leaves, Grandma Sherrell takes Mitchell out of his carrier. It's such a pleasure to hold him. She's worried about the storms, although the tornado forecast she heard did not mention Hackleburg. Still, she takes Mitchell into the hallway with a pillow, just in case. Grandpa Bobby is having an afternoon snack at the kitchen table.

Bridgett arrives at The Pig and does her shopping. When she hears the tornado rumors, she hurries through The Pig, grabs the groceries she needs, checks out, and hurries back down Highway 43 to her house and her baby. She's pulling into her driveway when she sees the tornado, and it's really close. She jumps out of her vehicle and kneels down, placing her hands over her head.

Shoppers still at the Piggly Wiggly leave their carts. Three elderly ladies crouch in a cooler. Workers point people to small, enclosed places in the huge, quickly-built building—a tornado death trap.

\\\\\\\\\\\\\V//////////

After leaving Aunt Freddie's house, Christie falls into her bed at home to enjoy a deep, daytime sleep until four o'clock when she'll have to get ready for work. But at three, Christie's husband wakes her.

"Christie, there's a tornado warning. We need to go to the storm cellar."

Christie lifts herself on one arm, looking at him sleepily. Slowly she sits up. Is a weather warning worth losing the last hour of sleep? She rubs her eyes, yawns, and slides into a pair of slip-on shoes. She follows him to the storm cellar.

\\\\\\\\\\\V/////////

Theresa Hutcheson, the cashier on duty at the Panther Mart, gets a text from a friend, warning her of a bad storm. Cell phone service has been unreliable all day, but texts still work.

Theresa looks out the window. She's heard the forecast on the radio, but there is no wind, rain, or hail right now. Everything is still.

She is texting back when she sees her husband's Ford Expedition whip into the parking lot and pull to a rocking halt outside the door. She hurries to the door and sees her teenage son leap out of the passenger seat.

"Mom, it's coming behind the store! Get out, get out! Get in the truck!"

Dazed, Theresa rushes back into the Panther Mart and grabs her purse. She hurries out, then turns back and carefully locks the door. It never occurs to her to tell her husband and son to come inside.

In the Expedition, they turn left, driving to a storm shelter. But trees are blocking their path and they have to turn back.

When the tornado reaches them, the Expedition is close to a small white building. Theresa pulls her feet onto the seat and puts her face on her knees. Her husband is still at the wheel. Their son dives to the floor.

\\\\\\\\\\\V/////////

Up on the hill, the Wrangler factory has decided to call off the second shift due to the threatening weather. Only about a dozen people are left when the tornado arrives. They rush to the office of the massive warehouse. Like Theresa, the Panther Mart cashier, one of the ladies turns back for a purse. A steel beam meant to hold a warehouse in its arms snaps like a loose LEGO. It hits her in the head as her co-workers dive under desks.

> ## Procrastination
>
> **1965:** In northern Indiana, a woman stopped to put a pie into the refrigerator on her way to the cellar. Others attempted to close exterior doors that were swinging wide. The uselessness of this effort was obvious after the storm, because the doors had disappeared anyway.[19]
>
> **1974:** People were unconcerned about the tornado warnings because the weather looked so nice. Tending to be skeptical of exaggeration, they were quick to assume that the announcers were being overdramatic.[20]

Near the post office stands a man watching the storm. He has watched storms for many years while standing outside, and he expects to do the same this time, but then the world flies to pieces.

He hears a sound like five choppers landing near him. "A sound that you'll never forget but that you'll never want to hear again," he relates later. When he sees three pieces of tin and a couple of tree limbs flying over the post office, he takes shelter quickly.

Melba moves through First Baptist Hackleburg with a vacuum cleaner and a dust mop.

There have been weather warnings all week. As she finishes up her cleaning, several people come through the church doors.

"It's getting scary out there, Melba," one says. "Have you heard if we're cancelling church tonight?"

Melba has not heard.

It isn't long, though, before area churches with Wednesday night prayer services begin to cancel, and soon First Baptist Hackleburg cancels too.

At home, Melba looks out the window as hail begins to pour down from a sky that seems to have no beginning and no end. *It's larger-than-normal hail for Alabama,* she thinks. With the instinct of a glass collector, she grabs her camera and slips outside. "We'll need evidence if we want to remember the hail storm of 2011," she chuckles to herself. If only her husband were here to make his little comments about the hailstones! After all their years together, she can still hear his voice, clear as a bell in her memory.

Melba snaps pictures before stooping to the ground and picking up the finest specimen, like plucking her favorite dish from the china cabinet. She slips back inside and places it into the freezer, smiling at her own childish delight in the large piece of ice that has so recently been bouncing up and down in the clouds. Melba continues to listen carefully to the announcements. She hears the Hackleburg siren. "There is a tornado on the ground," the voice says, warning Hackleburg residents to take cover because it is coming their way.

Melba and her husband had always concluded that their hallway would be a safe place in a tornado, but now that she's the only inhabitant of the house, Melba rushes into her bathroom and opens the linen closet. The top of the closet is lined with shelves of clean-smelling washcloths and towels. Her vacuum cleaner is in the bottom of the closet. Melba yanks it out and gets into the space herself before pulling the folding closet doors shut.

As a child, Melba lived in Tennessee, not far from the tracks, where the old coal trains lumbered past. Coal trains that got up a lot of steam had a certain *shhh-shhh-shhh* sound as they came closer and closer. Crouched in the linen closet in place of the vacuum cleaner, Melba hears that sound now.

Down at First Baptist Hackleburg, Steve and Donna Lawrence and about a dozen others take shelter in the hallway outside the old sanctuary.

\\\\\\\\\\\\\V/////////

On Tuesday night Wynn played basketball with friends at a neighborhood park close to the high school. They talked about the weather forecast the last few days and how things were predicted to get bad. But as they jostled each other, reaching for the rebound beneath the basket, they never imagined that the weather could take their neighborhood park. They've been through the tornado cycle. Wynn has lived here for four years and has heard many tornado forecasts. Like obituaries, tornado forecasts are routine in northern Alabama. The possibility of tornadoes affecting the life of a teenager doesn't seem very likely.

Wynn is sound asleep when Mr. Hollingsworth cancels school Wednesday morning. When his mother calls to his room with the announcement, Wynn can't believe the wonderful turn of events. He rolls over, enjoying the unexpected vacation.

Around 10:00, Wynn gets up and eats breakfast. After this leisurely start, he works on addressing graduation invitations. His graduation will be a big deal for his relatives, because he's the class salutatorian.

The news gets interesting around 3 p.m. Meteorologist James Span keeps announcing what's happening around Alabama. Looking at the news, Wynn watches the tornado heading into downtown Cullman, the same tornado that David Cantrell and the deputy are ignoring down at the EMA office. *I can't imagine something like that going through our town,* Wynn thinks. *Cullman isn't that far away.*

James Span goes on to announce that there's a major storm cell heading into northwest Alabama. Wynn is still thinking *oh, well*—until he hears the announcer say something else.

"If you live in Marion County, seek shelter now," the voice says. The radar is showing a major hook echo, which is an unmistakable tornado signature.

Marion County? This is getting personal, Wynn realizes.

At 3:25, the power goes out. Wynn and his family see the storm coming, an ominous black wall cloud set against a clear background. Lightning blasts through the huge blackness of the cloud, shaking the world with its power, zipping energy through its tens of thousands of feet. FLASH. Darkness. FLASH.

It's the most terrible thing I've ever seen, Wynn realizes with horror.

The whole family is watching it now, and the youth pastor arrives to check up on them.

"We need to find a safe place," Wynn's dad says. He insists that his wife and three children get into the closet immediately. He and the youth pastor stay on the watch just a little longer.

The four in the closet hate to miss out on the action.

"What does it look like?" Wynn hollers out of the closet.

"Tell us!" pleads his little brother.

"That's definitely a tornado right there!" they hear their dad say.

"Oh, wow, that's huge!"

The two men dash toward the closet. Wynn's father is a big man. At six foot three, the youth pastor is even bigger. And the closet is small. But all six of them pile in. Wynn sees the look on his dad's face as he dives into the closet, and it terrifies him. He's never seen such an expression of terror there. His father pulls the closet door shut, and Wynn sees his knuckles shining white in the near-darkness.

His father begins to pray loudly, speaking peace to the storm, quoting the Gospel of Matthew, and praying for other church members by name.

At the senior center she manages, Patricia is restless. Weather warnings keep blaring over the radio and television, and the air tosses like a feverish child. She thinks about her house and wants to get home.

By the time she does get off work, the sun is shining.

"Well, I guess they missed their prediction again," Patricia chuckles as she drops a load of laundry into her washing machine. She hums to herself as she measures the detergent and turns the dials to the right place. It's 2:30; plenty of working hours are left in the day.

She hears a car door slam outside. She walks to the door, past a hall tree carved by her great-uncle.

"Are you home, Grandma?" says a voice as her front door swings open.

It's her grandson, and the air is low in his tire. He knows she has an air compressor. Together they tinker with the compressor, and he fills the tire to the proper pressure.

Back in her kitchen, Patricia loads dishes into her new dishwasher. She's had it only a month, and it's such a pleasure to slide the dirty breakfast dishes onto the racks and have them appear an hour later, magically clean. She hits the button, starting the cycle.

It's strange how few dishes she has now compared with the days of the family cookouts. Patricia's house once hosted fish fries that filled the block with appealing smells and made un-invited neighbors jealous.

Patricia's husband invited guests, and Patricia cooked. Cousins, siblings, and in-laws packed in, knowing that Patricia would be at her gas stove, dropping fish, hush puppies, and French fries into the boiling oil of the Dutch ovens.

Patricia's hush puppies, laced with jalapeño peppers, bit back at the mouths of the guests. For those with cautious tongues, Patricia fried up safer hush puppies, flavored with onions but no peppers. Unlike many inferior of their kind, Patricia's hush puppies turned themselves in the boiling oil, frying evenly.

For dessert, Patricia would chop apples, mingling the white flesh with dough and sending them into the boiling vats as well. After they emerged from the sizzling oil, they tumbled into a blizzard of confectioner's sugar and then into the hands of eager relatives who were more than willing to risk damage to their arteries.

Since her husband's death in February 2008, Patricia no longer puts on the large fish fries that she did when she and her husband owned catfish ponds. But Patricia hasn't parted with the huge cast iron pots and Dutch ovens she used at those events. They are lined in a neat row in her pantry. Patricia smiles just to think of them as she moves around her kitchen, wiping down counters, while water swirls through her dishwasher and churns in the washing machine drum.

As she shakes out her dish cloth, Patricia hears the sound of the large feed trucks that sometimes rumble by. Strangely, there is no familiar sound of brakes slowing for the intersection. Instead, the sound increases and seems to get closer. Patricia steps into the living room curiously and notices the door.

Her door is shut, but it is gaping two inches at the bottom, pried open by unimaginable pressure. Patricia runs to her bedroom closet, pulling the door shut after her. She's almost more afraid of closed-in spaces than of severe weather, but still, a tornado can't be ignored. She has a storm shelter too, but there's no time to reach it.

Her closet has two doors, one on each side, so she holds onto both of them as the tornado bears down.

\\\\\\\\\\\V/////////

As the tornado lumbers on northeast of Hackleburg, it creates more drama. In the eastern part of Franklin County near the town of Phil Campbell, school is not canceled but is called off early due to the threatening weather. After dismissal, Heather Cole heads home. Her grandmother calls her.

"Heather, go to my house. There's a bad storm," she says.

Heather drives to her grandmother's house and calls her brother, asking him to come there too. The weather doesn't look bad, but she doesn't want to be alone.

After Bradley arrives, he and Heather take it easy. Bradley sits on the porch, and Heather relaxes on the couch. Then their other grandma calls. She's the one who often gets concerned about nothing.

"The tornado is in Phil Campbell," her grandma says. "Get in the hall and stay there!"

Heather isn't sure what to think, because she knows that grandmothers worry easily. However, the power is out now. Maybe her grandma is right.

Then her first grandmother calls back. "Heather, you need to go into the bathroom right now!"

Heather hurries outside for Bradley. He doesn't seem concerned at first, and she doesn't want to wait around for him to get concerned. Exasperated, she tells him she'll be in the bathroom, and rushes inside.

She runs back into the bathroom and climbs into the tub like everyone always says you should. Finally Bradley comes in with a blanket and pillow, which he hands to her.

"What am I supposed to do with this, go to sleep?" she teases to ease the tension.

"Put it over your head," he says.

He kneels down on the floor beside her because the bathtub isn't big enough for both.

Heather hears pounding noises—something hitting the walls. The toilet is shaking.

"Bradley, what is that?" Heather cries.

"It's the tornado," he says. He looks down and sees open space where there used to be a floor, and they both begin to scream.

Studying Tornadoes

By the time of the monster tornadoes of 2011, weather science had developed far beyond what it was during other historic tornadoes. However, the bottom line in all tornado research is basically the same. There's a lot about tornadoes that is unknown. "The tornado has become the black hole of meteorology," the researchers admit. "We really don't know how it works."[21]

Many attempts have been made to describe tornadoes. The word *tornado,* believed to come from the Latin word *tornare,* means "to turn." When tornadoes hit the ground, the whole world seems to turn upside down.[22] Or the word *tornado* might have been a mauling of the Spanish word for thunderstorm, *tronada.*

Everyone agrees that statistics and photos are useful, but they do not truly explain the tornado. The questions are much bigger than the answers. Why do tornadoes take one house and leave its neighbor? Why the unearthly greenish colors in the sky, and the indescribable shriek? How do animals know the tornado is coming? And how do those 200-miles-per-hour winds, the fastest on earth, appear in an instant in someone's kitchen or living room?

"Tornadoes resist analysis," said a *National Geographic* writer in 2004.[23] Richard Bedard calls them a "maddening atmospheric puzzle."[24] Why are they so difficult to study?

Tornadoes are rare. They are forgotten from season to season. People think of weather as a neutral background to their plans. A family cookout could be ruined by the weather, but no one really expects their *family* to be ruined by the weather. People do not think the tornado will come for them, and they are usually right. Even in areas where tornadoes are common, the chance that a house will be struck is not very high.[25]

Tornadoes are not predictable. They turn up suddenly and disappear quickly, whether the scientists have predicted them or not. Even if researchers are in the right place at the right time, there isn't much time to send warnings.

Tornadoes are dangerous. They are "earth's most extreme form of extreme weather."[26] Tornado writers find there are not enough words to describe them, and they use verbs that are normally reserved for criminal violence: whipped, flexed, exploded, jerked, tattooed, sliced.

Tornadoes are mindless. A traffic reporter in a helicopter who escorted a 1974 tornado out of Louisville, Kentucky, realized this. "A tornado is mindless. That's the scariest thing about it. When someone is shooting anti-aircraft guns at you—there's a reason for that. But a tornado . . ."[27] By trying to think like a human opponent, enemies anticipate the other's next move. With tornadoes, that doesn't help at all. Tornadoes don't think, so you can't out-think them.

Still, occasionally the weather "seems to disclose her most closely held secrets, however briefly."[28] It is in these times that scientists gain valuable information that can save lives later.

5
EF5 Tornado Touchdown— 3:05 P.M.

God thundereth marvellously with his voice; great things doeth he, which we cannot comprehend.
—Job 37:5

Behold, [the enemy] shall come up as clouds, and his chariots shall be as a whirlwind.
—Jeremiah 4:13

The voice of thy thunder was in the heaven: the lightnings lightened the world: the earth trembled and shook.
—Psalm 77:18

The storm system that blasted through Alabama in the early morning hours of April 27 produced scattered tornadoes, with four tornadoes reported before 6:30 a.m. These spinning storms were the more common EF2s and EF3s. The National Weather Service's record is silent for several hours. Then suddenly the entry appears, "HACKLEBURG TORNADO (MARION COUNTY), 3:05 p.m."

The damage path begins southwest of Hamilton, just five miles from the Mississippi line. The National Weather Service color codes this path on their map in shades similar to radar. EF1 is neon green, EF2 is yellow, EF3 is tan, EF4 is red, and the ominous EF5 is a suffocating purple shade. At its source, the tornado is neon green—a mild EF1. The National Weather Service reports tree damage here: hardwood trees with trunks snapped, few trees uprooted. This is the small tornado finger David Cantrell and the deputy witnessed dropping out of the sky.

The tornado dances lightly over Highway 78, and a few miles later, the NWS reports more uprooted trees. The symbol is still neon green, an EF1. Directly north of Hamilton, a yellow triangle suddenly pops up, and here the rating is EF2, with the following note: two homes with roof sections gone, but walls still standing.

Here the monster widens to nearly three fourths of a mile. It rolls its fat body closer to Highway 43, as if it wants to stay organized and follow the road. It smashes past the house where the woman and two children hide in their bathtub, past the swimming pool where David takes shelter. Then, about halfway between Hamilton and Hackleburg, there's a red triangle: EF4 damage. "Degree of damage to houses" is marked as "all walls collapsed" with the comment "uninhabitable."

The storm seems to relax in the next few miles, with a tan EF3 and a few more green EF1s. There's a restaurant with exterior walls collapsed and interior walls standing, and more snapped and uprooted trees. There's an eighteen-wheeler overturned and blown off the highway, but that's just EF1 damage.

Moving up the map with still four miles to Hackleburg, there's a purple triangle with this description: "Hundreds of trees snapped, one well-constructed residence destroyed with slab swept clean: EF5. Estimated wind speed, 201 miles per hour." The rare killer is on the prowl, and it's headed straight for the little town of 1,500 people.

Again the tornado catches its breath, as if saving extra energy for later. There's a yellow EF2, with the collapse of load-bearing walls at an auto center. Then there's a tan EF3, with "hundreds of trees snapped or uprooted and a few debarked." Then a red EF4: "All walls collapsed in one- or two-family residences. Homes uninhabitable. A few cars blown at least a hundred yards. Estimated wind speed, 170 miles per hour."

The tornado flies right over the heads of Bobby and Sherrell Barnwell and little Mitchell under the pillow. It strikes their home, where Sherrell is taking shelter in the hallway with her two-week-old grandson. Bobby hears glass shattering and the crunching of the stove and refrigerator being picked up and hurled back down. He looks up and sees a winter wonderland of papers from his desk whirling above him.

The tornado lunges up the path to Bridgett, kneeling beside her vehicle with her hands over her head, hoping her baby is okay.

\\\\\\\\\\\\\\V//////////

Now just two miles from Hackleburg, the tornado's roaring mouth is three fourths of a mile wide, and the triangles on the NWS map are all purple. The tornado roars across Hayfield Road, where Leah's mother, MeMe, is recovering from heart surgery in the strong brick house with the herb garden outside the kitchen window. The map shows five purple EF5s in a row saying, "slab swept clean, slab swept clean, slab swept clean, numerous houses destroyed, numerous cars thrown or flipped." [29]

The tornado rings Chief Hallmark's car with fallen trees, roaring over his hiding place in a culvert. It narrowly misses Christie and her husband in their storm cellar. She's wide awake now. Her husband steps out of the storm cellar, and they can both hear the roar.

It howls over Aunt Freddie with her oxygen tank and left-sided weakness.

\\\\\\\\\\\\\\V//////////

The three-quarter mile swath of purple on the map swallows Hackleburg. It charges over Melba, hiding in the linen closet in place of her vacuum cleaner. It chews through the empty Hackleburg High School and fills the tornado drill hallways with heavy blocks that would have killed the students had they been at school that day. It blows apart Grace's Restaurant and smashes the stained glass lamps that personalize each table. It rushes over Cedar Tree Cemetery, taking out the cedar trees and knocking over the gravestone of Bobby Barnwell's daughter, the one who died of a heart attack while talking to her father on the phone.

It sweeps over Willie and his friends in the jail cell. Knowing the town well, Willie immediately thinks, *second shift is going on at the factory*. He sees things flying through the air but doesn't hear anything. Later he wonders if he really couldn't hear or if he was just in shock.

The tornado roars past First Baptist Hackleburg, where Melba cleans. It leaves this church standing with hardly a mark, both the old sanctuary where Pastor Steve and a dozen people are taking cover, and the new church.

It whines over Hackleburg Community Church, ripping through its green roof, making the tin look like torn gift wrap. It hits the parsonage where Wynn and his family, along with the tall youth pastor, are hiding in the closet. They hear the wind rising, and everything is shaking as if there's both a tornado and an earthquake. There's a roar like a jet engine.

"Some people say a tornado sounds like a train," Wynn remarks later. "That would be a wimpy tornado."

About halfway through the forty-five seconds of horror, the smell of freshly-torn earth meets the noses of the closet-dwellers. With a chill, they realize the house must be torn open.

\\\\\\\\\\V/////////

The tornado pounces on Patricia as she hides in her closet with two doors. It snatches her new yellow rose bushes and hurls her cast iron pots and Dutch ovens away from the neat pantry shelves. It discards her car and her niece's piano like factory products that didn't make the cut, sprinkling piano pieces behind. It stops the washing machine in mid-wash and throws the drum outside. It grabs the carved hall tree and yanks open the refrigerator door, as if it hasn't already gobbled enough, as if it's looking for leftover fried fish or maybe an apple fritter dipped in sugar. It whirls off with her keys and papers from work.

From her closet, Patricia can see into her fourteen-year-old niece's room. Her niece is not at home today. Patricia sees tin, chipboard, shingles, insulation, and tree limbs zipping through the window, striking the wall above the girl's bed and then bouncing down onto the bed, where the slight form of the young girl curled the night before. *What if this were 3 a.m.?* Patricia can't help but wonder, but mostly she can't think because she's clinging to the two closet doors. One of them is open and one is shut, and she can't seem to control them.

The tornado catches up with Theresa, the Panther Mart cashier, and her husband and son in their Expedition. The Expedition stops beside a small white building, and her husband puts the vehicle in reverse. His foot pushes the gas pedal to the floor, gunning the engine, but the vehicle won't move an inch. The back end of the Expedition rises into the air. Theresa, her head in her hands, can do nothing but pray. She hears something that sounds like bricks hitting the windows. Then a metal roof sweeps out of nowhere and crashes against the Expedition, knocking its back end out of the sky and back to earth.

\\\\\\\\\\V//////////

The tornado cuts close to Rob Ayer's house, where Rob and his family have just landed in the basement after Rob rushed home with his co-worker, driving ninety miles an hour.

The tornado blasts into The Pig, where three elderly ladies crouch in a meat freezer. It bites open the Dollar General, dumping the yellow sign beneath lumber and tin and scattering shopping carts with yellow handles.

It crashes against the Wrangler plant, where an employee runs back for her purse. It tosses steel beams like a child sorting pieces of LEGO bricks. It moves on to the house where Patricia grew up. It hits the giant trees she swung on as a child, the trees that have stood through a hundred years of storms, knocking them flat.

The tornado leaves Hackleburg, but heads on to Franklin County where Heather Cole is in the bathtub with the pillow her brother gave her. She holds it over her head while her brother kneels beside her and the shivering toilet.

"Are you okay?" Heather screams.

"Yes," she hears Bradley say.

Everything is whirling and shaking.

"Are you okay?" she screams again.

"Yes."

She feels something that can't be described.

"Are you okay?" she yells the third time.

Again, she hears him say, "Yes."

Then they are on the ground in a ditch, a hundred yards from where the house had been. The bathtub, broken in half, is lying fifty feet away.

"Are you okay?" Heather asks again.

"No," Bradley replies.

Has the world come to an end? Heather wonders. *Yes, I'm sure this is the end of the world.*

That day, Alabama experienced more than sixty tornadoes statewide, but the destruction in Hackleburg was especially severe. The tornado that entered Marion County at 3:05 p.m. disappeared at 3:28 p.m. In those 23 minutes, it had traveled 25.14 miles, giving it an average speed of approximately 65 miles per hour.[30] Even as it traveled this fast, the rotating winds inside the tornado swirled much faster, up to at least 200 miles per hour. According to the National Weather Service, 120 structures were destroyed in the town of Hackleburg.

The National Weather Service doesn't comment on the emotional aftermath experienced by the people hiding in those bathtubs, linen closets, storm cellars, and airborne cars. No one's made a system to rate what's happening inside the minds of the elderly ladies in the meat freezer. Science has enhanced the Fujita scale, but it hasn't even suggested a scale to assess the mental upheaval of the people crawling out of the rubble.

6
The Monster Is Gone

Then, in perhaps the rudest turn of all, that monster was gone, unanswerable for everything it had done.
—Richard Bedard, *In the Shadow of the Tornado*

When the action finally stops, Chief Hallmark crawls out of the ditch, his uniform painted with mud, grass clinging to his radio and badges. His car is trapped by huge trunks and limbs that won't be moved by one man. He radios into Hackleburg for help, reporting that he needs help getting out. He knows it's his responsibility to take care of the town of Hackleburg.

"How are things at the station?" he asks over the radio.

"We don't have a police station anymore," the voice replies.

"You better not tell me that, I just put my family there. Have you seen them?"

"I can't find them anywhere."

\\\\\\\\\V//////////

As David Cantrell hurries back to Hamilton to find a way back to

Hackleburg, the radio traffic turns him cold. He hears Police Chief Hallmark radioing for help because his car is trapped by trees.

"Hackleburg is gone," someone says.

They must be exaggerating, he concludes.

He hears that Fire Chief Steve Hood is getting off work in Hamilton and heading for Hackleburg.

"Don't go up Highway 43; you can't get through," David tells the fire chief. "Tell anyone driving to Hackleburg to take a different route."

After taking back roads, David finally pulls into Hackleburg and parks by the small Wrangler sewing plant across town from the Wrangler warehouse. He gets out of his truck and stares. His truck door hangs open.

There's a voice cutting through the fog. Someone has walked up behind him.

"What do we need to do?" the person asks.

As an EMA director, assistant fire chief, and assistant pastor, David gets asked this question all the time. Usually, he gives good answers. If he doesn't know what to do, he finds out.

Now he says, "Pray, because I don't know."

He looks toward the fire station. The overhead doors have blown in on the trucks. Someone is tearing the doors off with a backhoe so they can get the fire trucks out. He decides to go there.

Late afternoon blurs into evening as David fans out through town with other rescue workers. He reaches an apartment complex. The top floor of the apartment has completely exploded, and the bottom floor is not in good shape.

In one of the apartments that are still standing, David finds an elderly lady who did not go to the storm shelter. She sat out the storm in her bathroom and is still there, sitting on the toilet.

"My roof's leaking," she tells David.

"No, ma'am, you don't have a roof," David corrects her. He convinces her that she must get to safety. There's another storm coming.

With the help of three other men, David slowly helps the lady out. She's a large woman, unable to move easily on her own, and they carry her over the debris on a straight-backed chair. They get about halfway across the yard to the storm shelter when hail begins to pelt them. They stop, set the chair down, and shelter the woman from the hail.

"I think I'd have been better off just to stay on the toilet, boys," she observes.

After riding out the hail, they continue to the shelter. David looks in through the door and all he can see is eyes. Designed to hold eighteen people, it is now packed with about thirty. In the direct path of the tornado, the shelter shows a dent where a power pole scraped across its roof. It's no wonder everyone is bug-eyed.

At midnight, rescuers stop combing the countryside for survivors. Now they respond only to calls and texts for help. But in the darkness, with broken gas lines and no power, finding anyone or anything is difficult.

A mobile command center arrives and is planted in the Panther Mart parking lot. David and the others work there all night preparing for morning. They put up a white board with a listing of search areas on one side. They collect maps. By 6 a.m., volunteers pour in, with about six hundred registering the first morning. They divide them into groups of four or five, with at least one medical member in each crew. They give maps and radios to the groups.

"This is where you need to go," they tell each group, pointing out one of the regions on the white board. They try to include a local person in each group to lead the way. When teams report back with their finds, David and his helpers erase that team's search area from the white board.

At four that afternoon, David drives to his farm. He's amazed that the buildings are still standing.

"There's no way anything is still there," people had told him, but he hadn't known for sure. Everything on the other side of the road is gone, but his home and barn are still standing. He changes clothes and rushes back to the action.

That night at 1 a.m., he goes home to rest. It's been forty-eight hours since he headed toward Hamilton to the EMA office to check the radar.

\\\\\\\\\\\\\\\V/////////

When Chief Hallmark finally makes it back to town, he finds that his family switched shelters in the final moments before the storm. In a dangerous move, Hallmark's wife, their three children, and a cousin had raced across town to a friend's storm shelter. As they ran, they got hail in their shoes. When they entered the storm shelter, it took two of them to pull the door shut. The door's hinges had broken. The air vents at the top of the shelter had become choked, and grass had come through.

The chief's shoulders shake with emotion when he finally finds his family. He had thought they were gone.

His family thought the same of him. "I thought Daddy was dead," his seven-year-old daughter Alex said.[31]

\\\\\\\\\\\\\\\V/////////

When things stop falling out of the sky, Willie crawls out of the jail cell. The tornado has gulped up the roof and block wall on the front and west side of the police station. In what had been the office, drywall, brick, glass, computer pieces, maps, and radios spew over the floor like tornado vomit. The sign that says "Police Department" now points to a pile of rubble.

Next door, the roof is also gone from the fire department office. The glass door with the white "Hackleburg Fire Rescue" insignia hasn't flown apart, but rather lies folded in on itself like a newspaper. At the fire house, not only have the front doors blown in on the trucks, but the back doors are completely gone. Together, the firefighters work to free the trucks.

Driving out in one of the trucks, Willie gets just far enough to find himself blocked. Then the call comes to take cover again; another tornado is coming. Everyone piles back into the jail cell as the rain and hail soak the ruined buildings and make everything slippery.

Finally, Willie emerges into a world that will never be the same. There are so many needs, so many people asking for help, that it's impossible to get to them all. Oddly, cell phones and radios work best for the first fifteen minutes after the tornado. After forty minutes, communication is a nightmare. But despite the trouble with communication, calls do come in—all of them frantic.

The roads are blocked by trees and debris. The power is gone. Willie works into the night, clearing roads, helping people in need, and doing whatever is found to do.

When Rob realizes that the tornado has passed his home, he steps out of the basement. The street department truck comes and picks him up. They head to the collapsed apartment building. Then they move on to the Wrangler warehouse. Word is out that one person is missing there.

Rob starts toward the building.

"What are you doing?" one of his buddies asks.

"Going in," he says.

"I don't think you should."

Rob can't stop himself.

He enters the warehouse office and squeezes himself out to the plant, into a forest of twisted metal and scattered files. He calls as he steps among the debris, but there is no answer. At the other end of the ruin, Rob kicks his way out of the building.

"Did you find her?"

"There was no response."

More help is on the way, including heavy rescue trucks. Rob knows that the job will take more hands and more equipment, so they move on.

In the aftermath of the tornado, Rob wears both the hats of firefighter and street worker. The street department is responsible to get the roads opened. The fallen trees they were cleaning up before the storm now seem so insignificant. They're not even sure if the backhoe they were using to clean up the trees is still where they left it. They head back to check.

On the way, they find a wounded man whose wife did not survive the tornado. He's having trouble breathing.

"We've got to get him help," Rob and the men decide. They have a backboard, but nothing to tie the man onto the board to keep him from slipping off. They're in a woods, and it's going to be a bumpy ride out as the rescuers climb over and under trees. Cars have been thrown into the woods, so they pry them open. They hope to tear out a seatbelt to use as a strap, but the seatbelts have locked fast. Finally, they find an extension cord. They strap the man to the board with the cord and take him to safety.

7
First Baptist Hackleburg

Brother Steve, I got blowed across the yard.
—boy in church parking lot

Down at First Baptist Hackleburg, the tornado has passed with hardly a scratch to the buildings. Pastor Steve emerges from the old sanctuary. He heard the noise, and he's sure there's been some damage, but he has no idea what is in store for the spacious church.

Pastor Steve and two other men get into a truck and take off, but they get only about half a block before they can go no further. Dazed by what they see, they get out and walk, doing whatever they can to help whomever they meet.

At The Pig, a lot of the shelves are still standing. Fat heads of lettuce and mounds of bananas are standing in the gloom as if they still want to be for sale.

Pastor Steve finds an elderly woman he knows. There's fifteen feet of debris between them. Although she's not hurt, she needs help getting out. He crawls over to her, carefully balancing on fallen tin, navigating past broken glass and nails. He wonders how to get her out.

It begins to hail.

"Ma'am, you're going to have to let me pick you up," he says firmly.

"Oh, Brother Steve, you can't do that!" she argues, distressed about being a burden.

But this is no time to argue with the pastor. He hauls her up anyway, slowly and carefully.

The owner of The Pig collects the contents of the scattered cash registers and stuffs the money into bags. He hands a bag to Steve.

"Can you keep this for me?" he asks. There are thousands of dollars inside. Steve doesn't want to be responsible for the cash, but this is only one of the many undesirable but necessary things that must be done.

\\\\\\\\\\V/////////

As word gets out that First Baptist Hackleburg is still standing, people pour in that direction. Pastor Steve heads back, feeling a need to be with his church. He finds it swarming already. No one comes to him and says, "Steve, you're in charge," but as the pastor, Steve knows that the responsibility of making good decisions falls on him, ready or not.

Within the first hour, the place is packed with nearly four hundred people. Nurses arrive, both church members and others who have heard about the meeting place. They set up a triage center, a place to quickly determine who needs what kind of help.

Bathroom use is a problem. Not only are there too few bathrooms, but the power is off and the water isn't working. The toilets won't flush.

Steve finds five-gallon buckets. He looks at the people standing around, wishing for something to do. He approaches a couple of young men.

"Can you find us some water?" he asks. "Look for swimming pools, anywhere you can find some decent water that we can pour into the toilets."

He sends the men to find more buckets if they can, and to keep the water coming. He tells others that if anyone has contact with the outside world, they should let people know that one of the main needs at the shelter right now is portable toilets.

It's been a gray day, but now true darkness is about to fall as the sun, already veiled, prepares to exit entirely. With the help of others, Steve stockpiles flashlights, candles, and matches in a race with the coming darkness. Everyone silently promises that if they *ever* again have a chance to buy extra batteries, flashlights, candles, and matches, they will stock up.

Word reaches a Porta-John company in Hamilton about the Hackleburg shelter that is hauling five-gallon buckets of swimming pool water to flush its toilets. The owner somehow finds a way to deliver the valuable little cubicles yet that night.

People are carrying in the wounded, and Pastor Steve directs them to the old sanctuary, the warm red room with the padded benches and the stained glass letting in colored light. Steve pushes the benches to the side of the room.

It's hard for ambulances to get around, but the biggest problem is that there just aren't enough ambulances. The first few callers get help, but then the ambulances are all used. Dispatchers are forced to admit to callers that all ambulances have already been called. "Please hold on until we can get someone to you," they say.

"There are no ambulances available right now," the police say to an injured elderly couple. Volunteers help the lady sit in a metal lawn chair and lift her onto the back of a pickup. Later they move her to another truck, wrapped in blankets. Her husband rides to the hospital on the back of a truck, resting on a table padded with blankets.

Wounded people walk to the church with scratches and bruises; sometimes blood is running. Steve is out in the parking lot when he turns around to see a ten-year-old face, washed in blood.

"Brother Steve, I got blowed across the yard," the boy says.

On the other side of the church entrance, a lady arrives in a car that doesn't look drivable. She's elderly, and as she steps out of the vehicle, Steve sees a small dog clutched tightly in her good arm. Her other arm is broken and bleeding, with the bone exposed.

An ambulance has arrived. The elderly lady with the complex fracture wants nothing to do with them if they won't let her dog go along. Finally, Pastor Steve promises to take care of the dog, and she agrees to go to the hospital. He puts the dog back in her car for safekeeping.

Steve asks his wife what they can use to cover people to help them stay warm. Donna hurries over to her own linen cupboard, returning with armloads of sheets.

Night falls and the warm sanctuary is dark, glistening only with the electric glow of flashlights and dancing candles. The murmur of voices and the eagerness of occasional reunions create a rumble of noise, but it's not chaotic.

The church bus also hauls injured people. Many people just have small cuts or bruises. Others have head injuries. There are diabetics who are crashing and need something to eat. The Panther Mart opens its doors. Crackers and peanut butter are pulled off the shelves and handed out. No one thinks about how much the food costs, and no one cares.

\\\\\\\\\\\\V///////////

Pastor Steve becomes the man who knows too much. He hears about the death of a woman, but is told not to tell anyone until the whole family is located. Unfortunately, her husband arrives at the church, looking for her.

"Have you seen my wife?"

Steve answers him vaguely.

The church becomes the meeting place, the place to go if you're looking for someone. In a corner of the parking lot, two small children sit with their mom and grandpa, but where is their father? They don't know, and their father doesn't know where they are.

"Has anyone seen my wife and children?" Steve hears the father's desperate voice across the parking lot. From a distance, the man sees his family and he begins to run, leaping in and out of the flashlight beams. Tears roll down his face, and he jumps around like a first-grade boy let out for recess.

8
The Rubble

Although [tornadoes] are capable of lifting a tractor trailer truck off the ground, they are, after all, merely a momentary disturbance of wind, dust, and water vapor.
—Stefan Bechtel and Tim Samaras, *Tornado Hunter*

At the call center in Hamilton, Leah waits with the other employees in the center of the building, since a tornado warning has been issued in the area. She clutches her phone and worries about Nathan. The news creeps in around 3:45.

"Hackleburg's been hit by a tornado!"

"Hackleburg's been hit by two tornadoes!"

Off-duty employees text their co-workers at the call center. "Tornado hit Hackleburg right north of the city limits sign."

She knows there are two city limits signs, and one of them is very close to her parents' house. Leah asks, "Which one?" But no one seems to know what she means by that.

Her mother, MeMe, has no minutes on her phone, so there's no way to reach her.

An employee calls to the others in a strained voice. "The Wrangler plant's gone! The Piggly Wiggly's gone!"

The call center employees stare at him in stunned silence at news so impossible. The Wrangler plant is gone? The massive three-story white structure with the proud word WRANGLER at the top? The giant small-town skyscraper on the hill under the ancient trees? The blue jeans distribution plant with dozens of semi-trailers backed up to its cement bays? The company that employs dozens of Hackleburg residents and supports the town with tax money? How can something so massive, so familiar, and so important, be gone without asking permission?

And The Pig? What happens when a grocery store collapses? Are potato chips and baking soda scattered throughout the streets? Where will Hackleburg residents buy bottled water or bread or milk? What if houses are destroyed and people need to buy food just to stay alive? Where are the grocery carts and the cash registers, the fresh flowers and the produce?

But above all the questions that race to everyone's brains is the question no one wants to ask: "Is everyone okay?"

Leah leaves Hamilton with a friend and drives north. They make it as far as a barbecue restaurant, and then they can't get through. People grab chainsaws and attack the blockades of trees, but Leah knows it will take hours. She also sees that her gas tank is practically empty.

"We have to go back to Hamilton," she tells her friend. "I'll go to MawMaw's where Nathan is, and then we'll get gas and try again."

After squeezing her son tightly, Leah borrows MawMaw's lawn mower gas. But it's not enough to last long. The gas pumps aren't working in Hamilton due to loss of power, so Leah and her friend drive to Mississippi for gas. By the time they do that and get back on the road to Hackleburg, it's 8 p.m. People are still trying to break through, cutting trees. Leah still hasn't heard from her parents.

Leah's friend gets a call. She's driving, but she answers her cell phone. She steps on the brakes.

Instantly Leah knows something is wrong.

"What?" she begs her friend.

"They're gone, Leah," her friend finally says. "I'm so sorry."

"How do you know?" Leah screams. Her friend touches her arm. There's nothing to say.

After a lengthy pause, the friend speaks again, her voice like soft cotton to a wound. "They said they were taken to the funeral home in Hackleburg. Let's go home. It's too dark, and we can't go farther, and you need some rest." She turns the car around.

But rest is not something that Leah will get easily tonight.

\\\\\\\\\V/////////

When his office papers stop swirling above him, Bobby Barnwell picks himself up. He realizes he's okay, but the roof and walls of his house have disappeared. It's wet. He needs to find Sherrell and his grandson Mitchell.

Sherrell is still in the hallway, and she's kept the pillow over the baby's head the whole time. Mitchell's been quiet, but now he begins to cry.

At least someone will find us if he cries, Sherrell thinks. She's staring at the pine branch, twice as big as a baseball bat, impaled in a nearby door. Bobby finds them here in the hallway. It's raining and hailing, so he holds an old door over Sherrell and the baby as they head toward the storm house, the only safe place left.

Bobby and Sherrell look up toward their daughter Bridgett's house. Has she arrived home from The Pig? Is she okay? She will be worrying about her baby. They need to tell her that Mitchell is okay after riding out an EF5 tornado under a pillow in his grandmother's arms.

"Bridgett!" Bobby bellows up the path toward where his daughter's house used to be a few minutes before. "Bridgett!"

There's no answer.

His words bounce back over the jumble of broken trees. Every limb and trunk is prostrate. Because of all the downed trees, reaching the storm house is challenging. To get there, Bobby and Sherrell have to pass the storm house and then walk back. Bobby steps across the limbs first, finding footholds. Then Sherrell hands him the baby, and she walks across. Handing Mitchell back and forth through the trees like a baton, they make it to the storm cellar.

"Bridgett!" Bobby hollers again. "Bridgett!" He looks toward the path, but it's covered with trees.

Later in the day the Barnwells' son and grandson arrive. That's when they find out that Bridgett did make it home from The Pig, but did not survive the storm.

\\\\\\\\\V/////////

Christie and Sammy leave their storm cellar, get in their vehicle, and drive as far as they can. There they stop in stunned silence, looking out over a view that stretches too far. In the distance, they can see Aunt Freddie's house. It is a pile of boards.

They get out and walk because driving is impossible. There's a man crawling out from under a roof, holding a pair of shoes. They pass another house with nothing left but a porch.

They arrive at the pile that was once Aunt Freddie's house, the house Christie left that morning.

Christie collapses to the ground.

"Aunt Freddie!" she screams. "Aunt Freddie!"

The normally calm, controlled cashier cannot stop screaming as she calls her aunt's name.

"We have to get help," says her husband, but Christie can't stop screaming.

Sammy leaves her and steps into the rubble, searching. Never before has he searched so hard for something he does not want to find.

The first discovery is Christie's cousin under a rain-soaked blanket. Gone.

Then he finds Uncle Junior, and he's still alive.

"Christie! Come here! I've found your uncle!"

Christie stumbles blindly toward his voice, her stress level mounting until it feels as though her head is about to explode.

"I have to call an ambulance," she hears her husband say.

It's raining again, and then there's hail, and everything is so wrong it's hard to know what to do or how to plan. It's hard to think past the moment, so they just do what they see needs to be done right now.

"Here," says Sammy, ripping off his raincoat. "Hold this over him. Maybe if I go to the top of this hill, my phone will have service."

Christie stands above her uncle, shielding him from the downpour, her own reddish hair plastered flat in the rain and hail, like the house blown flat by the tornado. Everything is dripping.

When her husband returns, he keeps searching. Aunt Freddie. Where is she? Finding Uncle Junior alive has given everyone hope. An ambulance breaks through for Uncle Junior, and more rescuers arrive, and still they haven't found Aunt Freddie.

Then they uncover Casper, the little puppy, who is no longer living.

Christie knows Aunt Freddie is nearby.

Christie's husband hands the puppy to her, and his eyes meet hers. He also knows they are about to find Aunt Freddie. He steps closer to her.

"Christie, take the puppy and go put it by your cousin," he says. "You don't want to be here."

Christie turns away, but she can't turn off her senses. They dig, and she hears the crunch of walls being lifted, the clack of bricks spilling, and the tinkle of broken glass sliding. She knows the dust would be rising if everything were not dripping wet.

She lifts the soaked blanket and slips the puppy into the arms of its mistress. She glances back through the rain to where the rescuers dig through the broken world.

Then the digging stops, the rescuers stand silently, and Christie's husband kneels down somewhere in the middle. Christie knows the search is over.

Crouched in the linen closet, holding the folding doors shut, Melba realizes that the debris is no longer flying. Instead, there's a great silence.

I guess I need to try to get out, she thinks. It's hard to think straight, but it's clear that there is only one thing to do right now, and that's to find an exit.

She works at the folding doors, and the one is jammed fast by a board or a piece of furniture or something. The other one wiggles, and she jerks at it. Something catches at the top, and for a second she thinks, *I'd better not push too hard or I'll break the door.* Then she realizes that everything is broken already. She shoves harder and towels tumble down from above. She squeezes through the gap.

The next thing in her way is a rafter. She looks doubtfully at the thin canvas shoes she's wearing. Her doctor has told her plenty of times that her diabetes makes foot injuries much more dangerous. He's warned her to wear rubber shoes and make sure she doesn't stub her toes or step on glass.

Glass. For the first time, Melba thinks of her glass collection. After a second, she decides that her glass collection is the least of her worries.

Just as Melba squeezes into the daylight, the hail starts again. Since the roof of her house has blown off, the hail pelts her. She ducks back into the closet. When it lets up, she pulls herself back through the opening.

My old secretary desk, right where it should be! It's soaked, and there are a few melting pieces of hail clinging to it, but it's there. She smiles at the familiar shape, but suddenly it seems so wrong. How did the world become a place where normal things are surprising?

She sits on the desk and looks out on the world. She looks to the right and sees that her neighbor's house has literally exploded. She looks to the left, and that house has collapsed too. She looks at her fig tree in disbelief. There's not a leaf on it, not a branch, nothing but a trunk and a few stubs stripped of bark. She looks down the street that had been a cozy neighborhood lined with towering shade trees just moments before, and she doesn't recognize anything. She feels like she's waking up and finding herself planted in another world—one she's never even visited before.

Over everything, Melba feels the awful silence. There's a stillness throbbing in her ears, and suddenly it's almost as deafening as that shrieking train.

Am I the only one still living? she wonders.

She hears voices. Two neighbors run toward her from behind, shouting, "Melba, are you all right? Melba! Melba!" She hears desperation in their voices.

Like Daniel calling from the lion's den, she answers, "I'm okay! I just can't get out. There's furniture blocking my way and lots of broken glass!"

"She's okay!" Melba hears the men say to each other, and then she hears them scrambling up what used to be the side of her house. Their faces appear. They're fighting tears of relief as they step through the rubble and help Melba to safety.

"You don't know how glad we are to see you," one says. "I didn't even want to come up here. I *knew* you were in the house, and I *knew* you were dead."

A neighbor's car is on top of his house, and he walks around in shock. He's the father of the two little boys that Melba has seen biking in the streets, and they've been tossed into another neighbor's garden. When the father comes to his senses, he frantically begins to search for the boys.

Before he gets far, he hears them calling.

"Papa, Papa!"

Again, when the world falls apart, it's the normal things that surprise and thrill. The short word *Papa* never sounded so surprising or so good.

When the noise and movement stop, Wynn's dad emerges from the closet. There's a crack in the ceiling of his house.

"The church is gone!" his family hears. The reality is that Hackleburg Community Church is not completely gone, but with the roof caved in, it's mostly destroyed.

Insulation and shingles are still falling from the sky. After about thirty seconds, Wynn's patience runs dry, and he and his little brother follow their dad. They find him looking to his right, then to his left. To the left, their neighbor's trailer is gone.

The neighbor's nephew walks toward them through the destruction.

"Preacher, there's another one coming," he says.

It's raining now, and the house is about to crumple. Wynn's car is gone, wrapped in a piece of a neighbor's house like a bad gift-wrapping job. The youth pastor's Honda Element is still drivable, although the windows are gone, all the tires are going flat, and insulation is wrapped around the rearview mirror. All six of them pile into the Element and head to Wynn's grandparents' place, outside the tornado's path.

"Has the tornado hit yet?" Grandpa asks, not knowing of the first one.

Without stopping for conversation, they load up their grandparents and take them along to the nearest storm shelter, where they wait out the next wave of the storm.

Huddled in the storm shelter, after the first horror, the questions sprout. "My friend lives that way . . . is he okay? What about school? Where will we stay?"

\\\\\\\\V//////////

I've got to get me some shoes is Patricia's first thought when the tin quits blasting against her niece's bedroom wall. She runs to her bedroom to find her shoes and realizes that her car is with her in the house. She realizes she should not go barefoot in this world. It's a world where glass carpets the ground, tin clings to pillows, and cars drive into kitchens.

She finds her shoes. She sees the refrigerator door hanging open, a ketchup bottle on the floor. She sees the fish aquarium not far from her car. The fish are swimming around as if they don't mind sharing the house with a car. It starts to rain again, great big monster tears of remorse. Hail pelts the ground. She stands on her doorstep, looking out on the foreign world.

Out in the yard, she notices the washing machine drum, which she had just filled with clothes. She spots a piece of her niece's upright piano, and then another piece on the other side of the yard. Her new line of yellow Knock-out roses, waiting to be planted, is gone. She looks around the yard and sees a flash of yellow. With her shoes now on, she steps carefully over and finds one of the rose bushes half crushed by a piece of furniture. It's badly damaged, but it will grow out.

Patricia sees her grubbing hoe sticking out of the rubble that had been her small garage. She pulls it out and walks back to her front doorstep, which is littered with glass and debris.

"Don't want nobody coming up and getting hurt," she says to herself as she sets to work brushing off the soggy mess with her hoe. As she does this, she remembers her niece's graduation invitations and pictures. What if they are gone? She's going to need them, and there won't be time to order new ones!

She glances in the direction of the high school. She can almost *see* the high school. The landscape that obstructed her view this morning has been peeled away. Maybe the high school has been peeled away too.

\\\\\\\\\\\\V//////////

Theresa and her husband and son crash back to earth in their Expedition. They realize that the storm is gone and they are not dead.

"Thank you, Lord!" she breathes. She's been praying without words, dangling up there between earth and sky.

Her husband backs away from the small white building.

"Look at The Pig!" says their son. The giant grocery store is shattered. Nearby, the bright yellow of the Dollar General sign can be seen from the middle of the collapsed structure.

They drive as close as they can to the grocery store. There's a man walking toward his car, blood dripping from open wounds.

"Are there others hurt?" Theresa asks.

The man shakes his head in a daze, looking at her as if he's never seen a human before.

"I don't know." He pauses. "Well, all I can tell you is I won't be here trying to hold the fort down." He turns to go and looks like he could collapse. As her husband and son rush toward the nearby Piggly Wiggly, Theresa helps the man settle into his car.

The craziness continues as the two men plunge through the rubble of the smashed store, yanking open cooler doors and helping people over the debris. Theresa helps them sit and tries to calm them. When they've helped seventeen people crawl out, including the three elderly ladies, Theresa and her husband decide they should check on their younger son, who is staying out of town with friends.

They pile back into the Expedition and fight through debris to the house where their son is staying, around trees and past rescue vehicles and pickups with people on the back.

They pull up to the driveway. The house is gone.

Just as they begin to panic, people emerge from the hillside storm cellar. Theresa and her husband burst into smiles. Their son is okay.[32]

\\\\\\\\\\\\V//////////

Heather looks for her phone, but it's gone. Bradley is lying a few feet away, and she sees his phone. She can't move her legs, but she reaches as far as she can and grabs the phone. She calls her sister.

"Hello?"

"Help me, help me!" Heather screams. She can't think of anything else to say.

"Calm down, Heather, what's wrong?"

"Help me," she sobs.

Her grandpa is calling now. She answers.

"Heather, where are you?"

"Outside."

"Why, did the weather get bad?"

"Yes, it *did* get bad. Your house is gone."

"Are you okay?"

"I'm hurt and I'm stuck, but I'm all right," Heather sobs. "But Bradley's not. He's bleeding."

"Bradley!" she calls to him. He doesn't answer. He's slipping in and out of consciousness.

"Call 9-1-1," says her grandpa.

Heather dials 9-1-1.

"We'll have some trucks on the way," the lady replies.

It's hailing hard now.

"What's that?" Heather asks.

"Hail," Bradley replies, coming to.

She calls 9-1-1 again and again, but they are swamped with calls. The lady answering the phone admits that some of their trucks are stuck.

Finally Heather's cousin arrives. She is a nurse and had already driven by the site once without seeing Heather and Bradley.

"It won't help to call 9-1-1," Heather tells her cousin and the helpers she's brought with her. "I'm fine. Go get Bradley."

Using the neighbor's door as a stretcher, the rescuers lift Bradley and carry him to the bed of their pickup. They try to hold a shirt over him to block Heather's view, but the plan fails.

"His insides were outside," Heather recalls later.

The rescuers help Heather to the cab of the truck. Her grandma arrives along with another cousin. The cousin takes one look at Heather and begins to panic. Heather does not realize that her face is black and blue.

"No, you can't—you can't scare me like that," Heather begs.

The truck drives to where an ambulance is waiting, and Bradley is moved to the back of the ambulance.

"You need to go in the ambulance too," someone says.

"Can my grandma go along?" Heather asks.

"No."

"Then I can't go," Heather sobs.

"You have to," says Grandma, but Heather refuses. She stays in the truck, and they drive to the hospital.

When the truck pulls into the Russellville hospital, past the yellow "Emergency" letters posted on the tan bricks, Heather's mother is already there. Overworked nurses crowd patients into the halls, holding up sheets to give them privacy as they undress them.

"Is it okay if we cut off your clothes?" the nurses ask Heather.

"It's fine," she says. But when the scissors head toward her sweatshirt, she remembers how much she paid for it. She asks them not to cut it and takes it off herself.

Bradley is taken to another hospital. He stops breathing on the way but is revived. Doctors order his ambulance on to Birmingham.

Nurses fear that Heather may be paralyzed, but then her feet move. They relax and tell her that she can go home because she has no broken bones. Heather, however, begins screaming with pain. The next morning, doctors discover that she has a collapsed lung that is filling with fluid. They take her to surgery and place a chest tube inside her.

Debris Paths and Oddities

Unlike hurricane damage, tornado damage paths are random. Hurricanes spread their damage for hundreds of miles, and the closer you get to the center, the worse the damage becomes. Tornadoes, on the other hand, destroy only what they touch. Travelers unaware of the tornado may come upon the path suddenly.[33]

April 11, 1965, Goshen, Indiana: Reuben and Pauline Kulp were visiting friends in an upstairs apartment in Goshen only blocks from the Goshen College gym, which would become a temporary morgue for tornado victims. When the Kulps and their friends heard sirens, they suspected there had been an accident. Even the next morning, when Reuben left for work, he still didn't know what had happened only miles away until he came upon the rubble.

May 4, 2007, Greensburg, Kansas: A tornado destroyed the whole town but missed its ten-story grain elevator, which remained "like a gravestone."[34]

April 27, 2011, Hackleburg, Alabama: The water tower still stood above the ruins of the town, having escaped a Hackleburg tornado for the second time.

9

The Wasteland

*Picture where you are from, and then imagine it all in pieces.
It was almost like walking out on a moonscape.*
—Rob Ayers, volunteer firefighter

Weird stories start floating in. The truck driver who was caught in the tornado and spun around twice while he locked his brakes and gripped the steering wheel. The 92-year-old lady with a board through her shoulder. The people stripped of their clothes, whether dead or alive. The man with rug burns whose basement carpet was pulled out from under him. The baby found in someone's back yard, reunited with its mother three days later. A man too tired to take shelter who had flopped on a mattress for a nap. His body was found in a ravine, still on the mattress, and his head three miles away.

Rescue workers who find body parts are particularly impacted. The *Times Daily* records comments from the volunteer fire chief of Phil Campbell. "We saw things that were unimaginable," he says. "You didn't know, when you picked up a piece of debris, what you would find under it."[35]

Chief Hallmark's seven-year-old daughter Alex is in the wrong place at the wrong time and hears adults talking about the human head that was found behind the Hallmark home. She begins to have nightmares.

People older than Alex are having nightmares. One firefighter dreams he sees faces and hears voices calling his name, saying, "We're still out here."

He recalls search and rescue the night of the tornado, trying to reach someone's house. As he had walked through the woods, another rescuer called to him.

"I've got bodies down here!"

"Alive or dead?"

"Dead," the man called through the darkness.

"Let's move on so we can help the people who are still alive," the firefighter suggested.

"If I leave, I won't be able to find them again," the unseen man said. He stayed.

For a while the Hackleburg death toll seems to hover around thirty. Soon someone discovers they are counting people twice. When the pieces are put together, there are only eighteen complete bodies.

\\\\\\\\\\\V//////////

Sleep in Hackleburg is nearly as scarce as cell phone service the night after the tornado. As morning breaks on April 28, 2011, the people see what the darkness of night could hide but not erase. Lifting exhausted eyelids, the people stand and stare as the light bulb of the world exposes a vast swath of rubble and waste. How could it be that yesterday morning this same sunlight had washed over houses with porches and flowers, cars buzzing down clean roads, and tall, stately trees?

In the frenzy of greater loss, no one has really thought much yet about the trees. Where giant branches arched over the town protectively just yesterday, there are only toothpick arms. No one is thinking of how many years it will take to shade Hackleburg once again. It will be much easier to rebuild a

Piggly Wiggly or a Wrangler factory than to create a tree-lined street.

The next several days run together. Chief Hallmark takes charge, knowing there are "seventy-two hours for life." This means that after seventy-two hours, the chance of finding a trapped person alive is much less likely.

"It was the most hectic week I've ever had in my life," he later says. "For seventy-four hours, I never stopped. No sleep, no shower."

"It's been a good learning experience," the Chief says. "But there's no way to plan for sixty-three tornadoes in one state. The hospitals were flooded."

However, even this hectic week is not as bad as the feeling of helplessness Hallmark experienced standing by his trapped car, hearing that his family was nowhere to be found. Hallmark has been through a lot in his career: he's been shot, and he's had a partner who was shot. But nothing compared to that initial feeling of helplessness after the tornado.

"I can't put it into words," Chief Hallmark says. "Until you are able to see it and experience it . . . things you took pride in, gone . . . people broken. . . . Until you see how powerful a tornado is, how quickly everything can be destroyed . . ." He trails off. "Yet that's not even a speck on how powerful God is."

Frustration grows as spectators from out of town arrive. Local firefighters and rescue personnel admire those who truly come to help. A fire department from Pass Christian, Mississippi, stretches its own

Adrenaline

1965: A woman reported that her husband freed her by lifting a piece of roof. Later, it took three men to lift the same piece.

1974: A civil defense officer reported that he kept going on coffee and No-Doz pills. He was so caught up in the moment through that first long night that he forgot that he would normally be sleeping at that time of day.[36]

department thin to come and help the Hackleburg Fire Department. But these people who are just driving through to look, while firefighters cut through tree trunks and shovel up debris, anger the genuine workers.

"You get to see the best and the worst. Let us get our dead out before you start filming," Rob fumes.

In moments when there's time to talk, Hackleburg firefighters discuss the timing of the storm. What would have happened if the storm had come at 3 a.m. instead of 3 p.m.?

"This whole town would be dead," says Willie. "And if anything like this happens again, Hackleburg will be a ghost town."

Added to the emotional trauma of the tornado is the confusion of running a town that has lost every important part of its infrastructure. Communication? Gone. Transportation? Gone. Electricity, grocery store, high school? All of them are gone. The Panther Mart opens its doors and cleans off its shelves, handing out bread and drinks and snacks, but these things are soon gone as well.

"There was more mass confusion here than in Hurricane Katrina," a state trooper who also helped with the hurricane tells the fire department.

"It was chaos," says Rob Ayers, "but the best I've ever seen humans working together. It wasn't just firemen, but young people and senior citizens. There was a man with a suit and tie working beside a couple of little children, a complete spectrum of people with no thought of self."

Highway 43 is closed, and not just by debris and trees. It becomes the helicopter landing pad, the heavy equipment lot, and the lunch room. Law enforcement and the National Guard patrol the ruined area to prevent looting. Military checkpoints are established going into the town. There are no street lights, no street signs, no house numbers, and no stoplights. Even the locals feel lost.

"Picture where you are from, and then imagine it all in pieces," Rob says. "It was almost like walking out on a moonscape." It does bring images to mind of men crunching through the barren, useless surface of the moon.

People move from day to day without adequate sleep. Firefighter Willie Holcomb is one of these. He showers at the mobile unit parked at the Panther Mart. For the first two weeks, all the sleep he gets comes from napping in his truck.

For a while the small town of Hackleburg is stranded without help. When the supplies do start finding their way in, Hackleburg residents are blessed with the overwhelming response of surrounding communities. Trucks full of supplies, food, and water line up along the road.

By the end of the second day, the FBI arrives to handle the missing persons list and keep track of who's who. It is a difficult job. The morgue is a morgue of parts, as rescuers bring in a torso here and an arm there.

By day three an army tent appears, and complete registration is available for volunteers. Each helper receives an arm band to allow them entrance to the disaster zone and to separate them from the people hanging out of their car windows with cameras.

By day five an eighty-man team from the Alabama task force arrives with cadaver dogs and two Chinook helicopters. With specialized equipment and backpacks of supplies, the teams fan out over the debris fields left by the tornado. At the end of the day, each team produces a GPS map, showing the area they have covered.

\\\\\\\\\V/////////

The weekend was scheduled to be Hackleburg's spring festival, Neighbor Day. This year's Neighbor Day doesn't include craft booths and antique car shows, but it's the best Neighbor Day Hackleburg has ever had. The National Guard estimates that 20,000 volunteers appeared in town on Saturday.

First Baptist Church continues to be the center of disaster relief. After the first few days, the wounded have been taken care of. Next, the church becomes a distribution center for food and clothes. The Red Cross sets up in their parking lot.

A man named "Pops" sets up a grill and makes burgers.

"The best cheeseburgers I've ever eaten," street worker Rob says. "This man went way above and beyond."

Part of the parking lot becomes a veterinarian's office, treating horses impaled by lumber and dogs lacerated by debris. Surgeries are performed in a makeshift operating room.

First Baptist also becomes the pharmacy. Volunteers bring shopping carts full of medications from the ruined drug store. They're escorted by police to protect drugs that could be used illegally.

Pastor Steve doesn't see much looting. However, he recalls one unfortunate incident. A gentleman donated fifteen brand new generators to elderly people. "Use them, I don't want them back," he said.

Later, however, another man visits the generator recipients and tells them the generators must be returned. This second man is found to be a thief, cheating the elderly people out of their gifts.

\\\\\\\\\\\\\\\V/////////

When Willie has a chance to check on his pickup behind the fire station, he finds that it has survived better than the other vehicles parked beside him. The first vehicle in the row could now pass for a convertible. The second has lost its windows. Another is missing the back glass. Willie's truck has received only a few dents on the passenger's side and damage to the mirrors.

News comes to the department that a veteran paramedic from another station has been killed by the tornado. Many people know her as an excellent co-worker. "And it didn't matter if we didn't know her," says Willie. "In the fire and rescue field, even if you've never met someone, it's as if you already know them. Everyone is family."

When the time comes for the paramedic's funeral, the fire chief asks Willie to lead the procession with the rescue truck.

Leading the procession, Willie's not thinking about the number of vehicles behind him until he looks in his rearview mirror at the top of a long hill. He can see at least a mile, and the funeral procession stretches as far as he can see.

At the cemetery, Willie takes the time to grieve for the first time since the tornado hit.

"We got down to where they buried her," he says slowly. "It really . . . it really hit me."

10
Searching for Hope

This is what it feels like to be totally helpless.
—Wynn Knowles

Leah's friend begs her to take sleeping pills as the evening turns to night. Nathan is sound asleep and doesn't know what happened. In his mind MeMe and PaPa are at home in their recliners inside the brick house with the herb garden outside the kitchen window.

In fact, if it hadn't been for MeMe's surgery, Nathan would have stayed with her today. This thought twists Leah's heart like a dish cloth being wrung, but unlike the cloth, no teardrops fall from Leah's eyes. She cannot cry.

Why? her heart wails. *God, did I fail you? Why did you take them both from me?*

Leah finally agrees to the pills after midnight and drops into a weary sleep.

At 6:00 a.m., the morning after the tornado, Leah drags herself awake to the beeping of her alarm clock. Her faithful friend climbs into the vehicle with her again. Driving on back roads, over power lines and around trees, they inch toward the house. The sun is up, but it doesn't keep them from getting confused.

"Charlotte, that's my road," Leah says suddenly to her friend who is driving again.

"No it's not."

"That's my road," Leah repeats.

It is her road.

They crawl over tree trunks, stepping carefully around splintered limbs. They get to the bottom of the hill that leads up to Leah's parents' house.

"You stay right here," Leah's friend says firmly. "I'll go up and just . . . make sure everything's okay, and then I'll call you up."

"Okay," says Leah, and she's shaking. She wants to go right away, but at the same time, she never wants to go. It seems impossible that the sun has risen on a world so changed.

She watches her friend climbing the hill until she can't see her anymore. It's not long before Leah begins to breathe fast, and finally she yells up to her friend.

"What is it? What do you see? Can I come up?" Her voice sounds like a stranger's.

"Okay, come up. It's okay," says her friend.

Leah stares at the ground ahead of her as she climbs, at the twigs she's stepping over, at that page that must have been ripped from a book that sat in her mother's library only yesterday, less than twenty-four hours ago. She sees clothes and pieces of the doghouse. She catches a glimpse of color, and she's afraid it's her mother's sweater, so she looks away and keeps climbing. The hill seems more like a mountain. The debris in her path takes on a personality of its own. The air feels like ink that will never wash away.

Her friend is there at the top of the hill. Her arm steadies Leah as she raises her head and looks at the scenery. There's so much brown and gray, lumber and splintered limbs and mud and the roots of uprooted trees. Her parents' car is there, about where it always was, but the house and the garage are not. Their safe is in the middle of the yard. Bricks lie here and there.

Pieces of metal roofing wrap around the property like crumpled ribbon.

Leah sees a white box, and then she sees that it's their microwave, the one that was right there beside her on the counter just two nights ago when she ran to rescue the hard-boiled eggs. The microwave is bent and the door is gone. "Gone where?" is the question Leah wants to ask about more than just the microwave door.

"No one could have survived that," she whispers.

"No," her friend agrees softly.

The heavy silence is broken by the sound of birds and insects. What did the birds and insects do during the storm? Or are these new birds and insects that weren't here when the storm came through?

Leah looks out to the lake not far from the house. From the floating pieces, she can see that a lot of the house must be in the lake. The lumber pools together, washing in a mass toward the shore. There are people down there too.

Furniture is everywhere, and it's hard to tell which pieces of wood are splintered furniture, which are splintered lumber from the house, and which are splintered limbs from the trees. Leah sees a T-shirt she recognizes and another book from that room her mother had filled with books.

She sees more articles of clothing. She and Nathan have nothing but the clothes on their backs, so she fills her arms with hand-me-downs she wishes she wouldn't need.

They hear footsteps and voices. The people who walk up are some of the ones who were down by the lake, rescuers from another town. They look like they worked late into the night and got back up before they were rested.

"Are you okay?" one of the rescuers asks.

"Yes," Leah says. *What else is there to say?*

"Is everyone accounted for?" he asks next.

"I guess so," Leah says. "I was told last night that both of my parents are gone."

"You . . . uh, you didn't find him then?"

Leah stares. "What do you mean? Who?"

"Well, we were here last night, and we found the body of the woman, and a chopper lifted her out. But no one has found the man yet."

"They told me that they were both taken to the funeral home," Leah says.

The man looks down, and the people with him look away.

Before they can think of what to say, there's noise from the lake. A trained dog is barking.

"Don't go down there," Leah's friend says.

The rescue team sends a diver into the lake, but Leah stays away. Soon they tell her that a man's body has been found. They ask if there's any way to identify for sure if it is her father.

"He has a scar on his chest from open heart surgery," Leah says.

The rescue team does not take action until Leah leaves. She talks with the police and the coroner, and it's confirmed that they have found her father's body.

When the legalities are over, Leah and her friend walk to town. It's two miles, but walking is better than any other form of transportation in this transformed world.

Like the whole town, the ground in front of the funeral home is soaked with rain, but here there are drops of blood too. Leah tries to ignore them as she asks for a funeral home employee. She wants to know for sure that her mother is here.

"Well, I think we can help you. We have five unidentified women and three unidentified men right now," says the worker. The funeral home has also had a long night.

There's another woman there too, also hoping to identify her mother.

Leah begins to describe her mother, but the man shakes his head.

"You'll have to come in. I'm sorry."

"I can't," says Leah. She suddenly feels faint, and the air feels stuffy and hot.

"I'll go," offers her friend.

Leah's mind spins as her friend leaves. *Did they know it was coming?* Leah wonders. *Were they together? If they weren't found together, does that mean they were apart? Did they try to hide? Did they know what was happening, or was it painless?* Leah had been told that her mother was found with her dog. She wonders if her mom had been in the kitchen.

Her friend returns.

"I'm sorry, Leah, I just don't know," she says. "I couldn't tell."

The man stands respectfully close by, quiet for a moment. Leah stands beside the other woman who thinks her mother is there too, and they ache together.

Suddenly Leah remembers. "My mother just had heart surgery on Monday," she tells the man.

This is enough information, and Leah is told she does not have to go in.

"I'm glad you were able to find her," the other lady tells Leah.

"I'm sorry you haven't found your mother yet," Leah whispers. "Maybe she's really not in there."

The small funeral home is filled beyond capacity, so they are using a refrigerated truck to extend the space of their morgue. There's no easy way yet to get in and out of town, and transportation is reserved for the injured. The bodies of Leah's parents lie in the refrigerated truck for six days. Every day she goes back to the funeral home.

"Have they been moved yet?"

"No, I'm sorry, not yet."

Although her parents' latest will has disappeared like most of their things, Leah is so glad that she has talked with them and knows what they would want to have done.

On Friday, two days after the storm, more of Leah's family arrives. They spend a day and a half together at the house site, searching for important documents. They search for the key to their parents' safe deposit box without success. Finally they cut off the door, smiling when they find some of their mother's valuables and registration papers for her furs.

On Monday Leah's family leaves and she is alone on the hillside now, continuing to sift through the rubble, searching. She is homeless and on leave from work. Nathan's birthday will be coming soon, and she wonders if she will even have money to buy him a cake. She is sad that her family left so soon.

Bobby and Sherrell Barnwell go to stay with a relative the night of the tornado. Every step is slow; it takes four hours to cut their way out of their own 200-yard lane.

Settled in at the relative's home, Bobby sleeps on a recliner, and Sherrell sleeps on a couch with Mitchell close by in a bassinette that survived the tornado.

The Barnwells are not set up to care for a baby. However, friends and family generously donate diapers and bottles, an infant seat, and a stuffed giraffe.

Bobby returns to the house site, trying to clean up. U.S. Steel helps with the big things in Hackleburg, and then the Corps of Engineers helps with smaller debris. But even after they leave, there are still piles of things to sort through.

A group of Mennonites arrive at Bobby's house, one older man and a group of younger men.

"I had the best time with them," Bobby says. "They never complained. They tore down my chimney and moved the bricks."

Melba stays at a friend's house. They boil drinking water until the water is pronounced safe again. Although her house has no roof and no walls, she is able to retrieve some furniture and pictures.

"I'm fortunate in so many ways," she says.

For a while Melba is lost in the sense that her relatives can't find her.

Then one of Melba's cousins from Tennessee calls a tornado hotline.

"I can't find out if my cousin is okay," she says frantically. "I can't find out anything about her. Her name is Melba."

The person taking the call knows Melba personally.

"I saw her today," she says.

Another friend calls the hospital, looking for Melba.

"Melba's fine," says a nurse who also knows her. "I hugged her today."

\\\\\\\\\\\\\\\\\V//////////

The next few days Wynn digs through the remnants of his house and helps salvage Hackleburg Community Church. The church's beautiful green roof is twisted and collapsed, with the metal caved into the sanctuary. Church people turn out to help at the Knowles' home, although the Knowles are not the only church members hurting. In fact, five church members have lost their lives.

Wynn remembers a volunteer walking up to him on Saturday. "Hey, are you hungry?" she asked. "Do you need a biscuit?"

"Sure," Wynn said.

This is what it feels like to be totally helpless, he realized. *I am completely vulnerable. My mom isn't cooking, and our house is gone.*

Besides the vulnerability and helplessness, there is the pain of not knowing. Communication is still so sketchy that, until they return to school, students will not be able to know for sure if all their classmates are still alive.

\\\\\\\\\\\\\\\\\V//////////

Patricia and her son sift through their things.

"As long as it's lying there scattered, you just keep sifting through it," says her son. "Once you bulldoze it, it's finished."

Besides all the debris, her son buries five hundred pounds of newly butchered meat that spoiled in his freezer when the power went out.

How does it feel?

"You can't focus for a few days; you can't get anything done," he says. "If you'd at least have a vehicle, you'd have a place to start."

He still can't get that smell out of his mind, the smell right after the tornado. It was an earthy smell of torn-up trees and earth. But it was more than that. The oil sucked from lawnmowers and the sewage sucked from sewers and the insulation sucked from walls tossed into the air together created a smell that was both unforgettable and indescribable.

Patricia lost her car and had to use her sister's car for more than two months.

"People don't have any idea what it is until they wear these shoes," she says. "You forget that you don't have things," she laughs. "I say, 'I'll go get my . . . ,' and then I remember I don't have it anymore."

Patricia is not sure that the tornado is to blame for the loss of her cast iron pots, though. Reports of looters looking for iron circulated. The pots would have been worth quite a bit.

Patricia appreciates the help from volunteers, although she remarks that they stay to help clean up for only about forty minutes at a time. Then they move on and another group comes after a while.

\\\\\\\\\\\\\\V//////////

Heather's mother, faced with the worry of two children in separate hospitals, divides her time between Birmingham and Russellville. Friends and family visit Heather.

"Is there anything in particular you want us to look for in the rubble?" they ask her. Although Heather was at her grandparent's house at the time of the tornado, her home has also been destroyed.

"Yes, see if you can find my daddy's black jacket," she says. "Is my car okay?

I want the picture of me and my daddy, and the cologne bottle in my car."

Not long after, they return with the picture, the cologne, and best of all, the black jacket. However, Heather's bulletin board full of pictures has vanished without a trace.

After several days in the hospital in Russellville, Heather begins to lose blood. She is moved to the ICU where she can be given more blood and be watched closely.

"Can my grandma stay with me?" Heather asks.

"Yes," they assure her.

"To see where the bleeding is coming from, we will have to do exploratory surgery," they tell her grandma. They also discover that Heather has a broken tailbone.

"Don't cut her yet," says her grandma. "Her mama's coming."

When Heather's mother arrives, the decision is made to move Heather to Birmingham.

In Birmingham, Heather is right across the street from the hospital where they've taken her brother Bradley. At the new hospital, she is told to lie still without any unnecessary movement: breaks have been discovered in her spine and pelvis, which went unnoticed in Russellville. Heather goes to surgery and pins are placed in her spine and pelvis.

Heather's uncle visits her in the hospital.

"I hear you're bleeding," he says. He prays over her.

After the prayers, nurses give Heather another pint of blood. It's the last one they need to give her, because the bleeding stops.

Bradley is also getting better, but they have not seen each other and Heather misses him terribly. In her last glimpse of him, he was being carried away on a neighbor's door with horrible injuries that could not be covered with a shirt.

One day a friend supplies Heather and Bradley each with a computer. Across the busy street and the walls of concrete and steel that separate them, Heather and Bradley chat with each other.

"It was the best moment ever," Heather says.

On Mother's Day, Heather and Bradley are both released from the hospital. Heather needs to use a walker yet, and Bradley will spend a number of weeks in a hospital bed at home. But both are recovering well and will be back to normal in a matter of time.

Heather is glad to be in her own bed, but soon she moves out to the living room to sleep on a cot closer to Bradley.

"I have lots of nightmares," she says, "not of that day, but of other tornadoes coming." There are family members in the tornado dreams too. But thankfully, she always wakes up before the nightmare tornado hits.

11

A Spirit of Resilience

We need the Wrangler plant to come back.
—Fire Chief Steve Hood

As a pastor, Steve Lawrence at times has to stifle his own pain and go on. As he moves from need to need among the tornado victims, however, he notices the lack of anger in the people coming to him. Fear? Of course. Confusion? Massive. But over it all rises a spirit of resilience. No one says, "Oh no, what are we going to do?" Instead, people face reality and begin to do what needs to be done.

"There was just so much to do," Pastor Steve says. "For a while, all we could do was the next thing."

Hackleburg schools are demolished. The scene is chilling to Ryan Hollingsworth, David Cantrell, and the EMA director as they think of their uncertainty about cancelling school that day. What if they had decided that cancelling just wasn't worth it?

"I know where those children would have been," says David. "National response plan says to put the children in the hallway. In this case, that was the most fatal area. Once you go past a certain point, reinforced concrete is no longer good to you." In one part of the school, the hallways are filled with cement, three concrete blocks deep. The elementary school is even worse than the high school.

The school year is not over, so the school administration begins looking for places to finish it out. They come to First Baptist Church, and Pastor Steve and his congregation agree to help. The red sanctuary with the stained glass windows is converted into two elementary classrooms. They use the new sanctuary for general assemblies, and the new gym for games and physical education.

"We thought the students would come in all traumatized," says Steve. "But they all came smiling."

One thing that helps is a visit from meteorologist James Span from Birmingham. He talks to the students about how a tornado works and explains the odds of such a destructive tornado ever happening again in Hackleburg.

Police Chief Hallmark points out that tornadoes touching down in larger cities like Birmingham and Tuscaloosa get lots of attention from the media and news cameras. But in those cities, a short walk moves you to a safe world with unharmed buildings and "normal life."[37]

In Hackleburg, though, businesses might not come back. Most critical is the Wrangler factory, a huge part of the Hackleburg economy. "If the Wrangler factory does not come back, Hackleburg will never be what it was," Hackleburg Fire Chief Steve Hood says through the open window of his F-150 pickup, parked along the street by the ruined police department. "It will make the difference between the police department being a four-man department or a two-man department. We need the Wrangler plant to come back."[38]

The warm July sun burns down on broken ceiling tiles, a two-liter pop bottle, a computer mouse, and a white teddy bear. Out front, the panel of glass that says "Hackleburg Fire Rescue" lies in several large pieces on top of each other, cracked but not falling apart.

\\\\\\\\\\V//////////

The morning after the tornado, Dr. Morrow's staff comes in to sift through the rubble of what used to be their office. In the days that follow, they work with the same dedication. The community doctor has set up shop in a camper and two army tents. The tents are stifling hot during the day.

The owner of a nearby Coca-Cola bottling plant is one of the many volunteers who has come to Hackleburg. This man brings two semitrailers with him. He turns one trailer into a mobile shower. The other he turns into a temporary bunk house for people who need a place to stay.

As these two needs grow less urgent, the man approaches Dr. Morrow's staff. He looks at the army tent and the camper.

"Is there anything I can do for your office?" he asks.

A nurse looks at her surroundings. "We really need a better shelter for our patients," she says.

The man studies the tents and camper silently. Finally he says, "I can do this."

He takes a semitrailer and partitions half of it into six plywood exam rooms the size of large shower units. He makes a smaller room to house a toilet. The makeshift bathroom has a dangling pull string to operate the single light bulb. In between the bathroom and the exam rooms is the emergency room: an exam table with a privacy curtain, an electrocardiography (ECG) machine and other emergency supplies. On the other side of the bathroom is a small office area with a counter, a red sharps box for discarding needles, and a phone. Only one person at a time can squeeze into the office. Bins of medication stretch down the narrow hallway along the exam rooms. Blood pressure cuffs curl nearby.

In Hackleburg and Phil Campbell, forty of Dr. Morrow's patients have died because of the tornado. He's treating many others who have lung problems from the dust. One patient lost a dental cap. Others are depressed and anxious, some of whom he refers to mental health professionals. They talk about their sense of loss and their disconnect from reality since their environment no longer looks like it once did.

\\\\\\\\\\\V//////////

All summer long, Christine Borntrager travels from her home in Florida to northern Alabama to attend long-term recovery meetings. She is a representative of Christian Aid Ministries' Disaster Response Services program. The front of their brochure says, "Disaster Response Services reaches out to victims of natural disasters in the USA by coordinating volunteers to help with cleanup, repairs, and rebuilding."

For those without the financial means to hire a contractor, Disaster Response Services offers free labor. Homeowners pay for materials, but DRS assists with house plans and estimates.

Many homeowners qualify for home replacement money from FEMA.

FEMA, the Federal Emergency Management Agency, "coordinates the federal government's role in preparing for, preventing, mitigating the effects of, responding to, and recovering from, all domestic disasters, whether natural or man-made."[39] FEMA officially started in 1979, although it grew out of a number of other government programs. FEMA took the place of all these separate programs for earthquakes, hurricanes, and nuclear threat. After September 11, 2001, FEMA became involved with homeland security. In 2003, it became part of the newly formed Department of Homeland Security. In the aftermath of Hurricane Katrina, recorded as the costliest disaster ever in the United States, President Bush signed into law an act to balance FEMA's weaknesses.

FEMA will not come into an area unless the President of the United States declares the region to be a disaster zone. When FEMA does arrive, however, everyone there can apply for a FEMA number, whether they have insurance or not. By 2011 the maximum grant FEMA will give to homeowners after a disaster is $30,200. Those who get the money cannot use it as they please, however. Some is marked for home replacement. Up to $5,000 of it can be used for replacement of personal property like furniture and vehicles. FEMA will also pay the funeral expenses of victims. Those receiving FEMA money must keep all their receipts to prove what they used the money for, because they can be audited up to seven years later.

If people do not receive the help they need from FEMA at first, they can appeal. FEMA expects appeals.

FEMA has a vast resource base and produces helpful materials. For example, its Debris Removal Guideline sheets show a sketch of a house and a curb, with a ten-foot zone beside the curb for debris pickup. It explains how the debris should be piled: electronics in one area, hazardous waste (oil, paint, or cleaning supplies) on another pile, and tree branches and leaves on another.

According to Christine, even with free labor, the cheapest houses still cost $25,000 to rebuild. Because many people don't get that much home replacement money from FEMA, the long-term recovery committee in the community teams up with charities to see who can help. The Salvation Army, St. Vincent de Paul, and the Red Cross each send a representative to these meetings. When a need comes up, the reps say how much they can give to the cause.

Lowe's works with Disaster Response Services. They will call Christine when there are sales. In addition, they give DRS an automatic 10 percent discount off every purchase.

12
Volunteers

When there's a cloud in the sky, I'm a nervous wreck.
—Leah Philips

Leah has worked alone on the hillside cleaning up for two weeks when she meets a volunteer from Christian Aid Ministries named Allen. Allen and his group help her clean up the property. In the midst of negotiating with FEMA to get help, experiencing problems with her family, and struggling to provide for her son, Allen's help is like medicine.

Leah feels pressure to move to the "projects," government housing for those with low incomes. But because the projects do not have a good reputation, she does not want her son to grow up there. But where will they live?

Driving home one night to MawMaw's house, where her son is still staying, Leah turns down an unfamiliar street. She never goes that way, and she can't say why she changes course tonight. On the strange street she sees a property with a "For Rent" sign. She gets out and asks the owner the important questions. Then she says, "I'll take it."

"Well, it's not quite ready," the owner hedges.

"Do you want to rent out this place or not?" she asks.

He does, and she gets it.

During her time alone on the hillside of her parents' property, Leah has time to think.

"I have no patience usually," she says. "I like to control things. But now I just have to sit and wait. Everything is completely out of my hands. When you don't have anything on your plate, you have to try to find stuff to do. I don't know what's going to happen tomorrow—sometimes I don't know what's going to happen the next minute."

Leah notices that her attitude toward money has changed. "Money's not mine to have; it's mine to share," she says. She believes that it is her duty to donate her time and money to help others in need, even if she doesn't have much herself. "You're going to get it back tenfold," she states.

Her feelings about post-traumatic stress disorder, or PTSD, have changed as well.

"I used to hear about PTSD, and think, *Oh, whatever, it's just an excuse*," she says. "It's not."

Since the tornado, she has used up vast chunks of Internet on her phone, checking the weather.

"When there's a cloud in the sky, I'm a nervous wreck," Leah comments. Memories of the tornado are different from memories of hurricanes she's experienced. "In Florida, we had hurricane parties," she reminisces. "We knew they were coming. It was just part of life."

At times Leah has allowed herself to relax, to go away with friends. She's found that while she can laugh and have fun, something is always lurking in her mind.

"I'm laughing and talking, and then I think, *My mom's dead*," she says.

She recalls a night that she went away with friends. On the way home they stopped close to the property of her mother's house. Suddenly the fun of the night dissolved into a blackness of depression.

She isn't quite ready to go back to work, because she fears that this tendency toward mood swings may lead her to vent on her customers.

When she goes back, she will take calls from people with Internet problems.

"I'm afraid I would say, 'Oh, you're having a bad day because your Internet doesn't work. Do you want to hear about some real problems?' " she says.

\\\\\\\\\\\V/////////

For a while Bobby and Sherrell aren't sure if they want to rebuild on the site of their old home. Their home had been in a clearing in the middle of a forested hillside. Now the hillside holds a handful of trees torn up like weeds and thrown back down. The hillside shows the tornado damage more than flat land does. Here the slanted earth displays the power of monster tornadoes. Standing at the foot of the Barnwells' lane, it's hard to look at the hillside without getting dizzy from sadness.

And, Bridgett is gone. It will be hard to live there without hearing her laughter down the path.

"But it will never be the same regardless of where we are," Sherrell says.

In the end, Bobby and Sherrell move back onto their property in a FEMA trailer. They don't mind the trailer, although it's very basic. It's a simple, block-shaped trailer with cream paneling and a large handicapped bathroom.

Bobby isn't happy that he's being charged $400 rent each month for the trailer, but he's looking forward to having a house built by Christian Aid Ministries' Disaster Response Services. Christine has taken the case and will be sending volunteers.

Emotional Rubble

1947: A teen-aged girl kept having nightmares in which someone screamed chillingly. Soon she realized she herself was the one screaming.

A younger child woke up with no memory of anything in her life before the tornado. Her earliest memory was of being on an airplane, hearing moans and screams around her as she and other patients were transported to another hospital.

A pilot who had just gotten his pilot's license had taken his wife on a flight not long before the tornado hit Woodward. After the tornado, he never wanted to fly again.[40]

1965: A man who lost a leg said, "My body will make it—I hope my mind will."[41]

1974: A girl in Alabama continually had the same nightmare after the tornado. She was always in a car when debris started flying through the air, but she would wake up before the tornado actually hit.[42]

Post-traumatic stress disorder, often called PTSD, strikes people after highly traumatic events that involve deaths or injuries, either actual or threatened. Typically, individuals who develop PTSD responded to these events with intense fear and horror.[43] People with this condition tend to relive the experience they went through and have an exaggerated response to noises or sights that remind them of the traumatic event. In addition, they often become numb to other emotions for a time and feel disinterested in life and relationships.

What kinds of disasters cause PTSD? Often people think of war. However, experts list natural disasters such as floods, tornadoes, earthquakes, and tsunamis right after military combat.

What actually happens to a person with PTSD?

> When someone is in danger, feeling afraid is natural. This fear triggers many split-second changes in the body to prepare to defend against the danger or to avoid it. This "fight-or-flight" response is a normal reaction meant to protect a person from harm. Normally this reaction

dissipates when the danger is past, but people who have PTSD continue to feel anxious or frightened when they're no longer in danger. [44]

When a person has an attack and begins to relive the horror he experienced, the best thing to do is to orient him to reality. If he hears a roaring noise and begins to panic, he may need someone to calmly remind him that they are in a car wash and he is hearing a dryer blowing, not a tornado. If the person is not given this support, he may struggle with these flashbacks for life.

People with PTSD may also have trouble sleeping and may appear to always be looking, always aware of their surroundings.[45]

Even those who do not have full-blown PTSD may experience a milder form called "acute stress disorder." Similar to PTSD, acute stress disorder will cause a person to experience fear, anxiety, and trauma flashbacks. However, the symptoms usually last for less than four weeks.[46]

SHATTERPROOF//HACKLEBURG, ALABAMA

13
Shatterproof

After the tornado, folks who pretty much hated each other were shaking hands.
—Willie Holcomb, volunteer firefighter

One month after the tornado, Hackleburg seniors graduate in the football field just as they had hoped to do. However, having their gym and school destroyed was not part of their dream. Before graduation they stare at the hallway where they might have been had school not been cancelled on April 27. It's full of blocks, insulation, bricks, and several inches of water.

"My youngest son would have been there," says the fire chief.

The graduation is both happy and sad. Graduates sit on folding chairs in the newly cleaned field. Patricia describes the five generators that Channel 6 brought from Birmingham for the graduation. "They each were the size of a car," she says.

"But the graduation was sad," she continues. "You would look around and see the field house, the concession stand, and the high school, all destroyed."

The class valedictorian lost her home.

In her speech she says, "It didn't sound like a train or a loud swarm of bees. It just sounded like destruction."

Wynn Knowles is the salutatorian. He commends the crowd for persevering through the aftermath of a worst-case natural disaster. "You've stood on high ground, and that is what is going to get us through," Wynn says. His voice echoes over the football field.[47]

The governor of Alabama, Robert Bentley, attends the ceremony. His presence honors and encourages the hurting students.

"It's definitely drawn the community closer together," says Pastor Steve. From the earliest records of First Baptist Hackleburg until now, attendance records were broken on four consecutive Sundays after the April 2011 tornado.

"There's been some discouragement with the whole housing process," Steve says. "So much of our town is gone." With all the sorrow, people realize how much they need a community—and faith in Someone more powerful than they are.

Donna, Steve's wife, reports that one of the newspapers released a headline saying, "God Stomps on Hackleburg." This did not go over well with the people of the small town.

"God did not stomp on Hackleburg," she says.

Donna recalls the Vacation Bible School held not long after the tornado. She remembers the blessings that came from interacting with the children during that time.

The children seemed a little nervous every day, and when it got rainy or dark, terror descended. But she saw more than terror. "One minute, they were taking each others' stuff," Donna says, recalling fights over crayons or glue. "But the next minute a little boy would go around hugging people, saying, 'Jesus is going to take care of you.'"

"God's blessed us in a billion ways that you've never seen," says Chief Hallmark. Although his daughter Alex lost an uncle in the storm, she has conquered her nightmares about the tornado.

"I prayed a lot, and my mom has been hugging me," the little girl says.[48]

\\\\\\\\\V/////////

On October 3, 2011, there's a Hackleburg town board meeting, open to the public. New plans for the town will be unveiled by a committee that's been working for twenty-one Tuesday nights.

The board meeting is held in the town hall. On three walls, large FEMA print-outs of Alabama and Hackleburg are tacked up, showing the tracks of the April 27, 2011 tornadoes. There's also an aerial photo print-out of the village of Hackleburg, with the brown track of devastation carved across its middle.

The board members sit around a heavy wooden table. A bottle of water, a discarded pair of glasses, and stacks of files litter the edges of the table.

Wynn's father presents the plans for Hackleburg. "I've never given birth," he says, "but I've been with my wife on three occasions, and I know that the tension is relieved when you hear the baby cry." He expresses the hope that some of that joy will start to appear in Hackleburg.

Besides a new sewer system and a public water system, the committee pictures a town park and gathering space. Wynn's father points to an artist's sketch. Behind the park, there's an old railroad bed that can be converted to a bike and walking path. Closer to downtown, a historic bank building that was only partially destroyed by the tornado can be restored and used as a history center.

There are a few concerns after he sits down, but they are toned down by a balding man who speaks with effort while staring at the stack of papers in front of him. A FEMA man with experience in six states, he encourages the plans. A pleasant atmosphere is the way to attract revenue, he assures the board.

Christine Borntrager is now living north of Hackleburg, arranging for the building of fifteen houses by Amish and Mennonite volunteers from across the United States. Working with local case workers and long-term recovery committees, she hears the stories of people ravaged by the tornado. She is arranging houses for Leah Phillips, Bobby and Sherrell Barnwell, and Heather Cole's family.

Disaster Response Services uses a building north of Hackleburg as well as a bevy of RVs that have been pulled in for the winter. Christine's office resides in the middle of a large empty floor with a compact organization of filing cabinets, a computer and printer, clipboards, and a three-hole punch.

Until the volunteers arrive, Christine is alone on the base with Ginger, a dog she got while on an assignment after Hurricane Katrina. And she's busy. She can't even eat breakfast without getting phone calls.

She's worked in this capacity for ten years, and she knows what she's doing. She knows how to draw up lists of materials for the houses and how to evaluate foundations.

"You're the last one I can take," she tells one couple who had an afternoon appointment with her. Earlier that morning, someone without an appointment had called in. She had to tell them she was sorry, but she couldn't help them.

Some cases are painful. One woman with several young children did get a grant from FEMA, but it was stolen by her estranged husband. After a meeting where Christine presented the woman's case, a man came up to her.

"I want you to do whatever it will take to help that woman," he said to Christine.

"Are you saying you are going to help her with funding?" Christine asked.

"Find out what we can do, and I will stand behind you," he said.

It won't be a perfect situation, but Christine has ideas and plenty of connections to help the woman. Something will work.

Sticky Tornado Finances

1965: Some home-repair workers tried to rip off homeowners desperate for aid. The South Bend Better Business Bureau released a warning about this to protect as many people as possible.[49]

1974: The owner of a destroyed mansion was sure that his insurance company had given him much less than he should have gotten for his house, taking advantage of his confusion at the moment.[50]

2007, Nappanee, Indiana: After an EF3, Governor Mitch Daniels wrote a letter to President Bush asking for aid. Fifty-one homes had been destroyed, one hundred thirty-seven homes badly damaged, and more than two hundred homes suffered minor damage. One hundred seven businesses had been damaged or destroyed. Even with figuring in potential government assistance, Nappanee estimated that recovery would cost an extra $600,000 beyond government aid.[51] When the reply came from Washington, the answer was no, because the area was "self-sustaining enough that it did not need federal assistance." They decided to join the red-tape war and appeal the decision.[52]

By October, Dr. Morrow's new permanent office is rapidly rising, but patients are still seen in the semitrailer. The registration and waiting room area is in a smaller trailer, connected to the semitrailer by a network of wooden ramps and steps and rails. In the waiting room, patients crowd together. There's a mother with a baby who is about eight months old. He begins to wail. A nurse brings him a squishy football just the right size for him to grab. He rolls on his back and begins to chew.

"Just nothing like a baby to bring the silliness out in all of us, is there?" says an older woman. The little man has everyone's attention.

"Won't it be nice when the office is done?" one of the waiting patients asks. But it's a pleasant comment, not a complaint.

"It's coming along really well," someone else says.

The grouchy atmosphere that might be expected in a temporary, too-small, too-busy workplace is simply not present. The nurses laugh and take time for people.

Over in the semitrailer, even Dr. Morrow is smiling and relaxed. Above a short-sleeved orange button-down with a stethoscope dangling, the doctor's friendly eyes and welcoming smile give him a youthful appearance despite his graying hair.

Aside from seeing patients in a semitrailer and rebuilding an office, Dr. Morrow is making plans to start a corporation devoted to assisting doctors' offices after catastrophes. After what he's been through and the help he's received, he's eager to be a resource for others in need.

It's as if he's addicted to helping people.

Recovery

1947: After losing a leg in the tornado, a young amputee propped his leg stump on the family card table. He pinched the scarred skin to make it look like a face, entertaining his younger siblings. The same boy learned to ride bike, hunt, and fish.[53]

1974: A girl had an inch-long wooden peg embedded in her leg that went unnoticed by doctors. After a year, it worked its way out of her leg. She kept it as a souvenir.[54]

14
Rebuilding Lives

*We shall draw from the heart of suffering itself
the means of inspiration and survival.*
—Winston Churchill

As Nathan's birthday nears, Leah's discouragement grows because she has no spending money. She knows that he is only turning three and will never remember if his birthday gets skipped. But turning three should be a celebration, and celebrations need the cake, presents, fun foods, and balloons that she cannot afford.

The night before his birthday, Leah prays beside the tub as she helps her son take a bath.

The next afternoon, the day of Nathan's birthday, the phone rings.

"Hello," says the voice, "I'm calling from the Salvation Army. I hear you're looking for us."

"Uh . . . no, I haven't been," says Leah.

"Well, either way, why don't you come up here?"

"Where's 'here'?" she asks.

The caller explains.

When Leah gets there, she finds that someone has sent her a few items. They are small enough to fit in an envelope, but big enough to buy a nice birthday party and a whole lot more. Piggly Wiggly card, $150. Cash, $50. Visa gift card, $100.

Another time when she answers the phone, Leah gets a question.

"Could we have your address?"

"Who are you?" Leah asks warily.

The caller explains that he wants to remain anonymous, but that he had gotten Leah's number from the United Way. Leah agrees to give him her address.

Shortly afterward, she finds a check in her mailbox for $1,000.

Leah sits at the Panther Mart, tears in her eyes, recalling these moments of grace. "All those years of my mom making me sit in church," she reflects. Her upbringing is making more sense to her as she discovers more of who God is.

On the red-checked tablecloths of the Panther Mart, she fingers a piece of plastic. "My mom's driver's license," she says. "I found it just this morning where the house used to be."

Since Grace's Restaurant is gone, the Panther Mart is doing what it can to meet the locals' hunger for breakfasts and conversations. It's the new social destination, the place that creates childhood memories, sparks relationships, and collects local news. New tables have been moved in to host people lingering over breakfast coffee and looking for excuses to stay longer. Others come in the evening and grab a quick supper of burgers and wings.

The Panther Mart swarms with so many people that it's difficult to meet the demands. On mornings when the sun shines in through the floor-to-ceiling windows, there might be ten customers waiting in line at the cash register. Many of them are here for breakfast sandwiches, and the Panther Mart has eight stainless steel trays of foil-wrapped sandwiches in its warmer. It's so busy that two employees stand behind the counter, one ringing up sales on the cash register and taking orders, the other snatching sandwiches and filling white sacks. These ladies are efficient, polite, and fast.

A table full of older men poke at empty baskets and talk about President Carter, keeping close tabs on who comes in and out the glass door. They are the unpaid guards at the door, the unofficial committee who misses nothing. Strangers are welcomed heartily with Southern greetings and Southern smiles, but they are analyzed closely.

Out in the gas station parking lot, the parking spaces get full, so people park on the side of the lot. There are construction vehicles, trucks with flatbed trailers, and the police chief's new Tahoe.

After food is no longer served in the evening, the Panther Mart dies like a kite when the wind goes down. The transformation is stunning as the dusky parking lot empties and the gas pumps stand alone. The bright yellow of the Shell station symbol stands like a beacon against the gathering sky, close to the black silhouette of the faithful Hackleburg water tower that's stood through two tornadoes. Panther Mart employees come outside with brooms and clean up the premises. A few people trickle in for a late night snack or something for the next morning.

\\\\\\\\\\\\\V//////////

Bobby and Sherrell are settled into their FEMA trailer on the ruined hillside. Inside the trailer, across from the colorful infant seat, the walker, and the baby toys, is a small memorial. It's a picture of Bridgett, whose eyes are bright and eager. She looks like a woman in love with life.

In front of her picture is another frame, this one holding a black-and-white photo of Mitchell's eager young face.

"We've been so blessed with people helping us," Bobby says. "And we lost Bridgett, but we're blessed with this baby. I don't know what we'd do without him."

Bobby reports that Mitchell is quite a charmer. When they go to church, the grandparents don't get to hold him at all, because he gets passed around. All they can see is his head bobbing as he moves down the row from person to person. Mitchell doesn't mind. He's a sociable young man.

Bobby would love to see Bridgett dash down the hill just one more time. Yet his outlook is upbeat. "We have to put our faith in the good Lord," Bobby affirms. "You can't go around with your chin on the ground."

\\\\\\\\\\\V/////////

"I don't like to leave home now—too much reality. As long as I stay home it is still just a bad dream," Christie relates.

She finds an envelope in the mail one day. Inside is a picture of her and Aunt Freddie standing together at a family gathering, both smiling. The photo is scratched and scarred, but there's no question that it's Christie and Aunt Freddie.

It's from Tennessee.

The small photo had wafted into the atmosphere, flown thousands of feet high across the border of the two states, and landed in the path of someone kind enough to pick it up and post it on the Internet to be seen by people who were looking for belongings. Someone recognized the people and sent it to Christie.

\\\\\\\\\\\V/////////

Patricia picks strawberries with her niece. How Patricia's garden has survived as well as it did is a tribute to her tireless care of all things, the same spirit which made her sweep off her front step minutes after the tornado.

Patricia has lost many things: the dishwasher that was brand new two months before the tornado, her favorite thirty-two-piece collection of Vision Ware, her Dutch ovens and cast iron pots, and a loft full of Christmas items.

Diligently working at the site of her home, picking strawberries one day and removing old bricks the next, Patricia is a likely target for reporters wanting to hear tornado stories. Patricia welcomes them, rain or shine. The *Birmingham News* features her picture and quotes her in a news article.

\\\\\\\\\\\\\\\\V//////////

Sometime after she and Bradley are released from the hospital on Mother's Day, Heather Cole gets a phone call from a man who lives seventy miles away.

"I found your driver's permit in my garden," he says. "I was wondering if you'd like it back."

"Thank you," she replies. "I'm glad it was my picture you found and not me."

By October, Heather is back in school and it's impossible to tell that she has been seriously injured. She has one more surgery to take out the hardware. In the spring she will be back to playing softball.

\\\\\\\\\\\\\\\\V//////////

Melba, the church cleaning lady, has lost her glass collection. The linen closet she hid in is gone now too, carried away with the rest of the debris. Her fig tree is blasted off, but she does not want its remains to be bulldozed. When a school group stops by, looking for ways to help one day, she asks them to protect her tree stump. Perhaps she is thinking about the whirlwind and fig tree in Habakkuk.

> . . . they came out as a whirlwind to scatter me . . . But . . . although the fig tree shall not blossom, neither shall fruit be in the vines; the labour of the olive shall fail, and the fields shall yield no meat; the flock shall be cut off from the fold, and there shall be no herd in the stalls: Yet I will rejoice in the LORD, I will joy in the God of my salvation. The LORD God is my strength, and he will make my feet like hinds' feet, and he will make me to walk upon mine high places (Habakkuk 3:14, 17–19).

Taking the scattered bricks on her property, the students create a brick ring around the tree. With the rejected bricks from broken houses, they protect the life that remains in the veins of the fig tree.

A few weeks later, construction workers begin on Melba's new house. She stops by, watching preparations for the foundation. She feels like hugging the workers as they place the string to mark where the foundation will be laid.

"Didn't know a string could look so pretty," Melba says.

Not only that, but fig shoots are bursting up out of the brick ring. A pumpkin plant and an okra plant sprout there as well, the pumpkin vines spilling over the sides of the loosely built brick wall. Melba remembers that she had thrown a fall pumpkin there, and apparently leftover okra.

The unexpected greenery symbolizes Melba's gratitude. Just as the forgotten pumpkin washes green into a world of brown and gray, Melba's relentless gratitude washes beauty into a world ravaged by the nameless whirlwind that disappeared. Just as the fig shoots burst above the wreckage of bricks from broken houses, Melba's spirit proves that in her corner of Hackleburg the tornado did not get the last laugh.

"I have so much to be thankful for," she says. "The community is concerned about you. People come up to you and say, 'I'm so glad to see you; I'm so glad you're all right.'" In what has to be a testament to her own life and unconscious influence, Melba says that people she doesn't even know have come up to her and hugged her.

Melba's not sure why she survived the tornado when others didn't, but she is glad that she chose to hide in the linen closet. "I just think the Lord wasn't ready for me yet," she says. "I thank the Lord and I hope I can fulfill what He wants me to do. Even at seventy-one years old, I can grow."

The tornado is not the hardest thing she's experienced in her life. It doesn't compare to having lost her husband just two years ago after watching him suffer with several years of sickness.

But that just reminds her of one more blessing that she can see in the timing of her two biggest nightmares. Where many people would be bitter against God for taking not only their spouse, but also their house, Melba is giving thanks that her husband did not have to suffer through both his sickness and the tornado. What if he had been sick in bed during the time of the tornado? But "there are no 'ifs' in God's kingdom."[55]

"I just thank the Lord," she says, her face calm and joyful. "Two of us couldn't have fit in that closet."

The response of gratitude exemplified by Melba and other Hackleburg residents still shines above the ruins of the town. Brighter than the yellow Panther Mart sign, more unwavering than the lofty water tower, this positive spirit in the face of destruction is something a tornado cannot shatter.

Tornado Formation: Where and Why?

Simply stated, tornadoes form when air masses meet between cold mountains or plains and warm water. Around the world, you will find them in these places:

- In Asia, between the Himalayas and the Bay of Bengal and between the Gobi Desert and the Yellow Sea.
- In Europe, between the Alps and the Black Sea.
- In Africa, between the Kalahari Desert and the Indian Ocean.
- In Australia, between the Great Outback and the waters of Southeastern Asia.
- In South America, between the Andes Mountains and the warm Amazon Basin.

But all these continents together receive only one fourth of Earth's tornadoes.[56]

Where do the other three fourths of the Earth's tornadoes happen? In the United States, between the Rocky Mountains and the Gulf of Mexico. The land that claims the right to "life, liberty, and the pursuit of happiness" receives a thousand tornadoes per year on average. Ninety percent of the earth's F4 and F5 tornadoes do their damage in the United States, most of them on the Great Plains between the Rocky Mountains and the Gulf of Mexico.[57]

The melting pot of air masses

Why is North America the playground for three fourths of the world's tornadoes? It is not just because of the cold, dry air coming over the Rocky Mountains and the warm, moist air from the Gulf of Mexico. Rather, the United States is a melting pot, not only of diverse cultures and ethnicities, but of air masses. No other land mass in the world sees the coming and going of so many different temperatures and moistures of air so routinely. Besides the cold air coming over the Rockies and the warm air sweeping up from the Gulf, a third kind of mass slips across the border from Mexico, hot and dry. And, just like cultural assimilation, this air mass diversity creates turbulence, which generates frequent tornadoes and sometimes destruction and death.[58]

The cold, dry air coming over the Rocky Mountains and the warm, moist air coming up from the Gulf of Mexico are likely to meet over Oklahoma, or somewhere close by. The warm, moist air from the Gulf is like a yeast that spawns thunderstorms,[59] but this does not always create tornadoes, of course. The warm, moist air will be pushed up by the cold, dry air, just like the warm, moist air that comes out of a tea kettle rises straight up. This steamy air will settle high in the chilly atmosphere, where it will form clouds out of droplets of water, like the tea kettle steam against a cold spoon. Then it will rain, and there might be lightning and thunder, but the rain itself will kill the thundercloud and soon it will be gone.

If just those two masses meet in Oklahoma, residents will probably be safe from tornadoes. Across the world, 45,000 thunderstorms occur each day, and right now as you read these words, there are about 2,000 thunderstorms raging around the world.[60] In fact, like a diplomat standing between two diverse groups, a thunderstorm helps settle the difference between the two air masses by equalizing the pressures. Thunderstorms resolve the tension between the cold air and the warm air, or the dry air and the moist air. They have been called "nature's admirable ability to restore order by force." After a bit of storming and swirling, the confusion is over and peace returns.[61]

The situation gets dangerous, however, when the third mass of air slips across the border from Mexico, hot and dry, and joins the meeting over Oklahoma. The hot, dry air sits on top of the warm, moist air. The warm, moist air wants to rise, but now the hot, dry air is blocking the tea kettle's vent, and the warm, moist air cannot get out. The hot, dry air is like a cap, refusing to let the warm, moist air blast up into the chilly atmosphere high above the earth to form clouds out of droplets of water.[62]

Because the hot, dry air keeps the warm, moist air from rising and forming clouds, people on the ground might say the weather is beautiful, with hardly a cloud in the sky. As the day wears on, though, they will notice that it is so hot and sticky they almost feel suffocated. The warm, moist air is pressing down on everyone, building up pressure, trying to blow through the cap of hot, dry air above.

By afternoon, the sun has been beating down on the earth all day, and the warm earth is making the warm, moist air even warmer. Storms most often occur in the afternoon and evening, because by that time of day, the trapped air is so warm and sticky that something has to give. Finally, the breaking point is reached and a hole is blown through the cap of hot, dry air, quickly forming a thunderstorm.

Blowing its top

Only one in a thousand thunderstorms is the more dangerous kind of storm called a *supercell*. Even then, only one in four or five supercells create tornadoes. No one agrees entirely on what ingredients it takes to turn a storm into a really bad storm, but besides the meeting of several different air masses, the storm must also have unstable winds that change speed and direction.[63]

Every storm starts as a cloud, but supercells start as *really big* clouds. The warm, moist air, bursting through the cap, may rise eight or ten miles high.[64] As this air ices, its water droplets form a huge cloud like an anvil, pressing against the layer of air beneath it. The anvil may stretch, pointing out far ahead of the storm, tipping forward. This huge tipping action is what makes a storm dangerous. If the cloud were not tipped, the rain from the top would slow the air that is rushing up like steam. Now, because the cloud is tipped forward, it will not kill itself with its own rain. Instead, the rain will go out ahead, and the air rushing out of the tea kettle will keep right on going up, making an even bigger cloud.[65]

In a 60,000-foot high supercell, the motion of the air shooting up and the air coming down and the temperamental winds all join together to create a whirling motion up to six miles wide. This is a mesocyclone—not a tornado, but it means that a tornado might be coming. The mesocyclone is like a drinking straw in the middle of the supercell. The air rushing up this straw begins to curl and swirl.[66] Next, a strong downdraft of air also blasts to the ground at the back of the supercell. Some people think that tornadoes form when this strong downdraft bumps against the mesocyclone.[67] Regardless of how exactly it happens, scientists know that something happens to the mesocyclone to make it spin faster and tighter. On radar, weather forecasters see an ominous "hook echo."

On the ground, watchers will probably not see anything yet except a low gray cloud that Mr. Fujita named a "wall cloud." Above the wall cloud there might be a "collar cloud." Some people describe the wall cloud as an upside down birthday cake, with the collar cloud as the cake platter.[68] The very worst tornadoes ever have been described not as funnels but as boiling masses of clouds.[69] "It's like a huge hill turned upside down with the peak facing down," said an Alabama man in the 1974 outbreak.[70]

In the Bible, Ezekiel describes "a whirlwind [that] came out of the north, a great cloud, and a fire infolding itself, and a brightness was about it" (Ezekiel 1:4). Tornado skies have been described as "the color and texture of aluminum foil." Observers might also see "lightning that makes the eye ache."[71] Watchers have reported rainbows of color: purple, red, orange, green, and yellow, dancing in the lightning.[72] Some night tornadoes have been reported as "beautiful, fire-spinning columns."[73] Usually during the day, tornadoes are white from the water droplets they contain, until they become choked with dust and debris.[74]

PART TWO:
RINGGOLD, GEORGIA

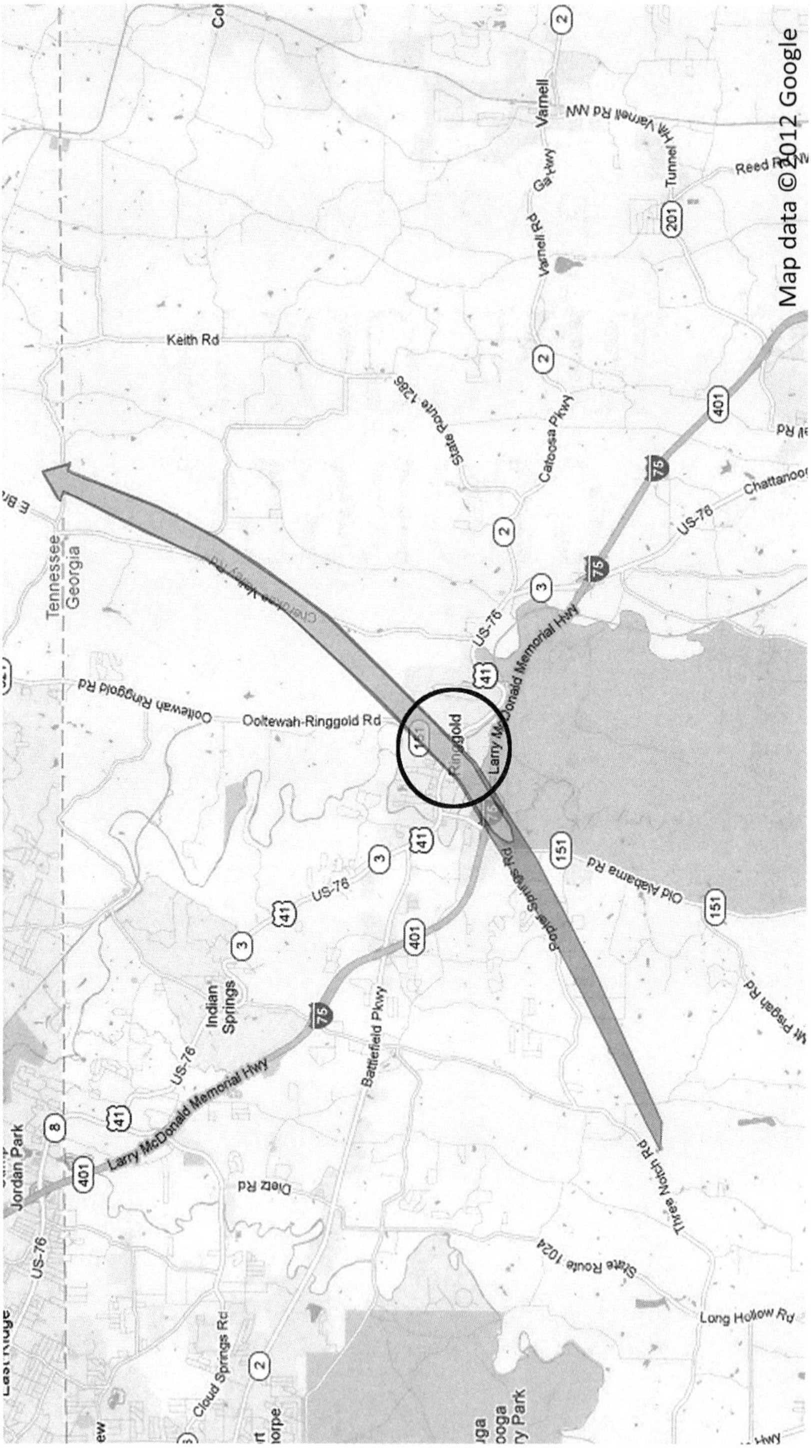
Map data ©2012 Google
Tennessee
Georgia
Keith Rd
Varnell
Varnell Rd
Varnell Rd NW
Ga Pkwy
Tunnel Hill Varnell Rd NW
Reed Rd
State Route 1265
Catoosa Pkwy
US-76
Chattanooga
Ooltewah Ringgold Rd
Ooltewah-Ringgold Rd
Ringgold
Larry McDonald Memorial Hwy
Old Alabama Rd
Poplar Springs Rd
Mt Pisgah Rd
Indian Springs
Battlefield Pkwy
Jordan Park
Dietz Rd
Three Notch Rd
State Route 1024
Long Hollow Rd
Cloud Springs Rd

Ringgold, Georgia

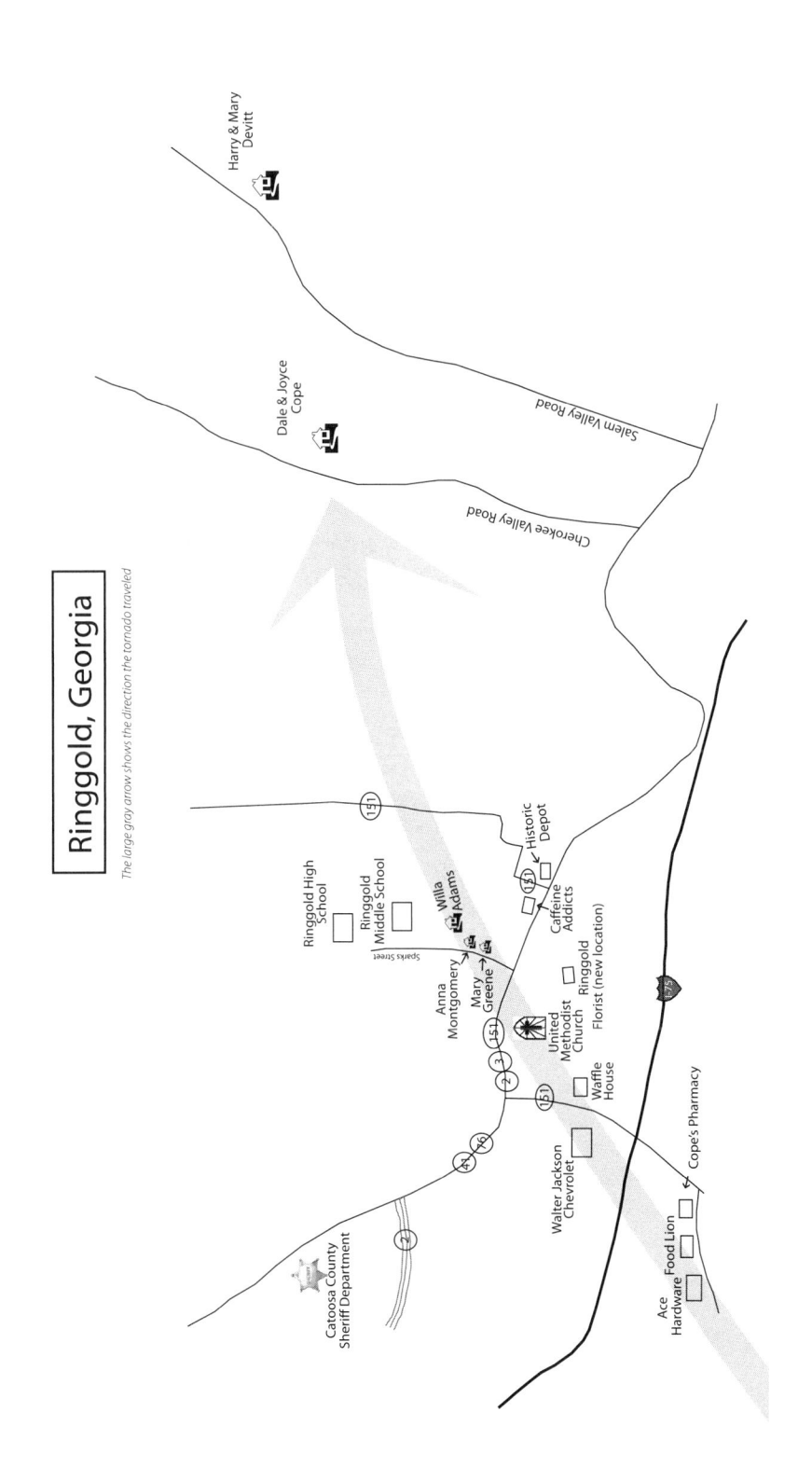

The large gray arrow shows the direction the tornado traveled

Frequently encountered characters

Residents:

—Mary Greene, weather enthusiast, Sparks Street

—Anna Montgomery and twin grandchildren, Sparks Street

—Willa Adams, Shady Place

—Dale and Joy Cope and sons, Cherokee Valley

—Harry and Mary Devitt, Salem Valley

Business Owners/Personnel:

—Jan Henry and grandson Dakota, Caffeine Addicts Coffee Shop

—Selina Riley, owner of Ringgold Florist

—Ryan Jackson, general manager at Walter Jackson Chevrolet

—Lana Duff and Clint Shoemaker, Angel Emergency Medical Services

—Major Gary Sisk, Catoosa County Sheriff's Department

1
Before the Nightmare

The moments prior to disaster slip into the inaccessible past.
—Mark Levine, *F5*

Ringgold, Georgia, fastens like a bulb on the cord of I-75, which plugs Chattanooga, Tennessee, into Atlanta, Georgia. Although Ringgold is in Georgia, it is part of the metropolitan area of Chattanooga. Southeast of Chattanooga, I-75 comes to a series of mountain ridges running from north to south, reminding tourists that they are still in Appalachia. Ringgold sits in the corner, trimmed off to the south by I-75 and insulated on the east by the first beautiful mountain ridge. Still, with Chattanooga only fifteen miles away, urban energy pulses downstream to the little town.

"It's basically a bedroom community," says a local. For those employed in Chattanooga, it's cheaper to sleep in Ringgold.

Arriving at the Ringgold exit, you will see houses balanced on the top of a ridge against the sky. Ringgold is safe from tornadoes, people say, because of the White Oak Mountain ridge.

Overflow from Chattanooga has sparked a blaze of hotel chains and fast food restaurants to handle the extra traffic. McDonald's, Ruby Tuesday, Waffle House, and Taco Bell attract interstate travelers far from home or locals tired of Chattanooga. On the other side of the interstate, Food Lion, Ace Hardware, and a pharmacy provide necessities to the locals.

Walter Jackson Chevrolet sits across from Waffle House. Walter is no longer living, but his son has taken over the business, and his grandson Ryan Jackson is the general manager.

Ringgold Florist, housed in a low white building, shows off bouquets through large glass windows. It's a busy time of year, so owner Selina has 150 ribbons and bows carefully placed on shelves. Now all she has to do is stick in the flowers. The coolers are also bursting with early Mother's Day flowers.

Farther into town is Ingles grocery store. It sits in a retail strip with a Dollar Tree and several empty stores.

Not far down the road is Spencer B's Barbecue. In a tiny shack that somehow manages to serve both dine-in and drive-through customers, customers purchase pork or beef barbecue with potato salad or fries. The lady at the window catches Northerners off guard with, "Would you like coleslaw on that barbecue sandwich?"

A few blocks away is historic Ringgold. A sidewalk leads pedestrians to the city center. The sidewalk passes a landscaped creek with paths dropping to its edge. Park benches invite couples to sit and talk for a while beside the gurgling water as they take a break from the bustle of life. The water tempts children to take off their shoes and see how far out they can walk without slipping on the algae and ruining their clothes.

Across the road from the creek is a playground with a jungle gym and plastic tunnels and slides. A composed black neighborhood cat steps over the playground chips, as if on a security beat. A few steps away, walkers come to an old cemetery of blackened tablets guarded by a Confederate flag.

Lafayette Street takes pedestrians to the doorstep of a historic depot and a coffee shop named Caffeine Addicts. Visitors can be identified by their mispronunciation of Lafayette, which is supposed to be said with the accent on the second syllable: "luh FAY et." When the depot was built in 1849, Ringgold was a larger town than Chattanooga.[1]

The top bricks of the depot are limestone, a different color from the bricks at the base. The depot was badly damaged in the Civil War, and the mismatching limestone was the only thing on hand with which to rebuild. The Great Locomotive Chase of the Civil War ended with the train's Union hijackers being captured by Confederate soldiers just north of Ringgold. In World War II the depot was also an important departure point, and soldiers signed their names on the depot's massive door.

The depot is now used for community events, and a Saturday night might find residents dropping by the depot for a banjo and harmonica performance. Dexter, a city worker with a wonderful sense of humor, runs the concession stand at the depot. He sells coffee, packaged cookies, and microwave popcorn to guests.

Caffeine Addicts, a long, two-room coffee shop run by Jan Henry, buzzes with life on the average Tuesday evening. One section of Caffeine Addicts is devoted to couches and chairs for students pretending to do homework and people wanting to read. The couch corner alone can comfortably hold ten people. In the other room, ten tables and a long bar with outlets provide lots of space for people on computers. Framed news articles about Caffeine Addicts and books about Ringgold history invite the curious.

Jan's grandson Dakota helps her run the coffee shop. Dakota is working his way through college. He has a special place in his heart for people who drink their coffee black. He's pretty sure that northwest Georgia's trouble with diabetes could be related to the amount of sugar and creamer that gets dumped into the coffee.

Similarly, grits in Ringgold have unhealthy additions, he informs. In Chattanooga, people might serve shrimp and grits, in Mississippi you can find fish and grits, and in southern Georgia salt-and-pepper grits. But in Ringgold, grits are cooked with salt and butter and then blasted with generous spoonfuls of sugar.

When school dismisses for the day, the younger crowd pours over to Caffeine Addicts, armed with computers, science projects, or textbooks. Jan, mixing drinks behind the counter or delivering a bowl of Brunswick stew to a businessman's table, sometimes has to quiet down the young people. On the busiest days, Jan describes Caffeine Addicts as "wall-to-wall kids." At some tables, they actually do homework; at others, they just chat.

For those who haven't gotten permission to drink caffeine yet, Jan churns up frozen hot chocolates. No one can tell they're not loaded with espresso. Little people beam from ear to ear over the tall glasses that turn wet with condensation even in April.

At 5:30 or so the school crowd drags itself away. The supper crowd arrives—parents trying to catch a few moments alone or people who just can't go another night without Jan's legendary chicken salad, stuffed with red grapes and celery. Potato salad, pasta salad, and egg salad are other homemade delicacies Jan serves, along with typical coffee shop sandwiches. Tonight she's also serving Brunswick stew packed with ham and chicken, swimming with spices and small vegetables in a dreamy barbecue sauce.

With the ample seating at Caffeine Addicts, it's an attractive destination for Bible studies, book clubs, or get-togethers with old friends. These groups arrive after supper and order drinks or pastries. The espresso machine steams and whines, dishes clatter, and people laugh.

\\\\\\\\\\\\\V/////////

Angel Emergency Medical Services has an ambulance station in Ringgold. Lana Duff, paramedic and operations manager, works from the main office several miles away. Lana can keep an eye on calls, ambulances, or weather on two screens at her desk.

Angel EMS is equipped with two disaster buses, a luxury that many ambulance services do not have. One holds ten stretchers, and the other four. Much of their disaster work has involved flooding in wet weather, such as heavy storms in 2009.

Major Gary Sisk sits at his desk in the Catoosa County sheriff's office. The office is in a sturdy block building that also houses the jail. If disasters threaten, an Emergency Operations Center (EOC) forms at the sheriff's office. The purpose of the EOC is to get all key emergency and government people in the same room so that if there is a disaster, they can plan strategy with as little confusion as possible.

The EOC can convene at a moment's notice.

\\\\\\\\\\V//////////

Sparks Street, a few blocks north of the coffee shop, is lined with a pleasant row of houses. Tuesday evenings are calm and tranquil, with children biking on the streets and residents weed eating and mowing grass. They nod to each other when they meet.

It's not quite like it used to be, people say. There was a time when everyone, black or white, knew everyone else. In those days, people got along and people also knew each other's aunts, in-laws, and embarrassing stories. In fact, chances were that the two people meeting on the street might be related, since so many people had intermarried. Now Ringgold has grown, and people simply don't know everyone anymore.

Mary Greene lives on Sparks Street along with two other unmarried sisters and one brother. Their house is shaded by trees. A maple tree curves to the side, creating an artistic overhang. There's also a pecan tree nearby. In the fall they harvest pecans, and the curving maple turns to gold.

Most mornings find Mary heading over to the high school to exercise by walking the track on the football field. Often while she's out there, she meets her former high school science teacher, now an elderly man, who also exercises on the track in the morning. He was a favorite teacher of hers, the man who would get his students' attention by walking through the classroom doorway shouting, "An object in motion remains in motion unless acted on by an outside force," or some other scientific bellow.

Mary is a weather enthusiast who feels a tinge of regret that she didn't go to school to be a meteorologist. If she had the chance to ride an airplane into the eye of a hurricane, she would do it. She stays up to date on the weather, making sure she gets weather alerts on her phone.

Mary's brother has a little house out back where he stays most of the time. He has a bit of a mental handicap, but he's not helpless. He likes to walk to downtown Ringgold.

It's not hard to find Mary because she is just a few steps from a brilliant purple house on the next cross street. It's impossible to miss. Like a politician, the purple house has its supporters and its opponents. Some people love its bright splash of color in the neighborhood, and others think it's too much.

\\\\\\\\\\\V/////////

Anna Montgomery has lived in the Ringgold area all her life. When she was thirteen years old, she was down the street at her grandmother's house when she heard a terrific *BOOM*. She ran up the street. Her family's home was in ruins, blown up by dynamite. She remembers her older brother running and screaming and pulling people out, including her baby brother Larry, who survived the explosion. She remembers the house torn to pieces, the splintered wood, the rubble. She remembers their clothes hanging high on the electric lines and trees.

The explosion killed her mother.

As she weaned Larry off his pacifier and made meals for her other brothers and sisters, Anna heard the grown-ups discussing how the house had been destroyed. She remembers that, although there was no way to prove it, everyone knew it was the Ku Klux Klan. That was reality in Georgia in 1963.

Technically the case is still active, and Anna respects the FBI investigator in charge, but the case has grown cold. The men suspected of blowing up the house are old now. One man did confess to the crime on his death bed, after being admitted to a mental hospital.

Anna's father held the family together.

"We had a good daddy," Anna says. "He was always doing stuff with us."

Anna's twin grandchildren, a boy and a girl, are staying with her for the evening. They are thirteen, just the age Anna was when her childhood home got blown to the sky.

Anna keeps a beautiful house. It has a wrought iron table and matching cushioned chairs. A round glass table topper sits on the heavy table, resting on rubber circles to keep it from scratching. On a shelf, Anna keeps a memorial scrapbook of her father, who has passed away.

\\\\\\\\\\\V//////////

Willa Adams, eighty-three years old, lives just a few blocks from Mary and Anna, right across from Ringgold High School's tennis courts and parking lots. The name of the street is Shady Place because of its many oaks, pines, and cedars. Her mobile home rests under the protection of tall trees. Next door is a brick house.

Willa is confined to a wheelchair, but the wheelchair doesn't limit her soul. She reads her Bible and prays when she wakes up in the morning and again before bed at night.

It's just been a month since Willa buried her husband of nearly fifty years. It's still strange for her to be the only one at home. She welcomes visits from her children. Her son lives close by, so he drops in now and then.

\\\\\\\\\\\V//////////

Drivers headed south out of Ringgold pass White Oak Mountain and arrive at Cherokee Valley Road. A left turn on this road plunges a person between two beautiful mountain ridges with cozy woodland homes dotting their broad sides. Some of the homes are almost invisible, lost behind rows and rows of beautiful old trees, thick with leaves and needles.

Here on the side of a ridge, Dale and Joy Cope's home rises. It's a beautiful house overlooking the Cherokee Valley. The pharmacy they own sits on the opposite side of Ringgold. A balcony wraps around the first story of the house and descends to the ground by way of a staircase with turns and platforms. A hundred-foot oak stretches past the deck and towers above the cathedral ceiling of the living room.

Joy loves the privacy provided by the eighty or so trees on their property. The trees were one reason they chose to live here when they moved from Birmingham, Alabama, five years before. When they are cozily settled in for the evening, it's like they've stepped behind a curtain. No one can tell by looking up the ridge if they are home or not. They can eat watermelon on the balcony and spit the seeds over the side in complete privacy. Sometimes the seeds sprout and grow more watermelons.

Inside, a spacious room with windows from the floor to the cathedral ceiling overlooks the valley, and staircases that turn corners travel from the basement to the upstairs. There's a large painting on the wall that they purchased in the Virgin Islands.

On the average evening, Dale and Joy's sons come home from school, climb the stairs to their rooms, drop on their beds with their homework, and listen to music, oblivious to the world.

\\\\\\\\\\V/////////

On the other side of the same ridge, Harry and Mary Devitt live in Salem Valley. Their ranch-themed log house sits on a slope surrounded by eighteen acres of trees. The trees are so tall and thick that the road, the opposite ridge, and the neighboring houses are all invisible. If cars buzz by on the road, Harry and Mary never see them from their house. Like the Cope family, they live in their own private corner of the world.

Their two dogs, Brutus and Muffy, roam the place. Brutus, a giant Great Dane that makes humans feel like game pieces, would appear to be in charge of the pile of curls called Muffy. But Muffy the English sheep dog is ten years old, and Brutus is only three. And Muffy is definitely the boss.

Mary keeps a photo of a young girl with radiant blonde hair. It's her daughter, who spoke French and Japanese and was planning to attend foreign language school in California. When she was seventeen, she went driving with a friend. It was raining and the car hydroplaned. The friend lost control and the car slammed into three trees. Her friend walked away from the accident, but Mary's daughter was killed.

Although Mary had been raised in a religious setting, she didn't walk into a church for seven years after her daughter's death. She could not mention the girl's name for two years, and she avoided girls with blonde hair or girls who wore dresses like her daughter's.

She remembers the day that she came to realize that God also loved His child, yet He was willing to send Him to die. "I still didn't understand why," says Mary, "but I finally realized that God understood the pain."

According to doctors, Harry should have died in 2004. He was diagnosed with cancer and given two months to live. The doctors were wrong.

2
The Storm Approaches

*Aw, we'll be fine—you know how it is.
Doesn't nothin' ever happen here in Ringgold.*
—Ringgold city worker

One advantage Georgia has on April 27, 2011, is not being first. Stories are coming over from Alabama. Warnings crackle through radios and television, and orange alerts flash on computers.

The storms are coming to northwest Georgia.

The National Weather Service puts this corner of Georgia, so close to Chattanooga, into a rare high-risk forecast category. As the afternoon grows old, a tornado watch is announced with an extra phrase: "particularly dangerous situation."

At Angel EMS headquarters, Lana Duff is watching the weather forecast. At 8:00 a.m., she reaches for her phone and brings up the roster of numbers for the off-duty paramedics. She dials down the list, asking each of them if they would be available to come in if there were a weather-related disaster.

Another emergency service borrows the Angel EMS disaster buses early in the day but returns them by evening. At 5:00 p.m., Lana calls the backup workers. They arrive, doubling the ambulance force. With the extra help, Angel EMS will be able to staff ten ambulances instead of five, plus the two buses.

They sit and wait in the storm shelter.

\\\\\\\\\\\\V//////////

Major Sisk and the fire chief across town have been watching the weather all day. They've heard about the tornado that decimated Hackleburg and the other severe weather that's been happening in Alabama.

Major Sisk and the rest of the staff leave work, but they are still on the alert. At 6:00, news is worse, not better. Major Sisk consults the fire chief again, and they decide to start the Emergency Operations Center.

\\\\\\\\\\\\V//////////

Churches cancel Wednesday night prayer meetings. Ace Hardware and Ringgold Florist close early. Worried about hail, Walter Jackson Chevrolet pulls as many vehicles as possible into the service bay.

At Caffeine Addicts, Jan plans to close shop early. The forecasts have been ominous all day. Other Main Street merchants have closed, so sales have been slow since 2 p.m. Jan is working alone, keeping the soup warm and doing a little bookwork, kept company by dozens of empty chairs, tables, and couches. Wednesday is usually a little slower because many people go to church, but this is even slower than usual.

Dakota is not working today. He's at school, sitting through Spanish and chemistry. Two days ago on Monday, when the college had a tornado drill, the students mocked it. Yes, the weather was bad, but tornadoes didn't happen here, they said. They weren't happy about wasting time locked in the ugliest building on campus.

Now, on Wednesday, Dakota's last class is canceled because of high winds.

He's glad for the break, but he's still not worried, because this particular teacher has canceled before. He goes to a friend's house to wait out the rain.

Back at Caffeine Addicts, the phone rings.

"Jan, we need to lock up and go home." It's her friend from the Ringgold Art and Frame Gallery next door. "My husband just called, and he says there's another storm coming our way. I told him, 'Jan's the only other one down here, and I'm not leaving without her.'"

"Well, I am planning to go early," Jan replies.

"No, we need to go now," says her friend. "I'm locking my doors right now."

"Well, I can't leave *right* now, because I have the soup on," says Jan hesitantly, glancing around the kitchen area of the shop. "It won't take long to wrap up..."

"Okay, well, I'm not leaving without you," says her friend. "I'll be right over to help you pack it up."

With the help of her friend, Jan packs the leftover tomato bisque into the refrigerator and lightly cleans. At 5:30 they leave, and Jan drives the fifteen minutes to her home.

With her husband she stands on the porch, watching the sky. It's not raining here, but there's some wind.

"Look at that cloud!" says her husband. "That's called a wall cloud, I think. The kind that turns into a tornado."

The cloud is moving so quickly that it looks like a car traveling down a road.

\\\\\\\\\\\\V/////////

Ringgold city workers are closing down for the day. Besides running the concession stand at the depot, Dexter is also a street employee. As they prepare to end their work, he discusses the weather with a trash disposal worker.

"Aw, we'll be fine—you know how it is," the disposal worker says. "Doesn't nothin' ever happen here in Ringgold."

SHATTERPROOF // RINGGOLD, GEORGIA

3
Danger in the Air

Pray! Just pray!
—Anna Montgomery

With the eye of a weather enthusiast, Mary Greene keeps close watch on the weather all day as announcers predict trouble in the atmosphere. She tells her handicapped brother to stay home today, but he wanders off to town anyway. A kind man brings him back.

In between moments of gazing at the weather, Mary steps outside with her broom. A woodpecker has been working on building a nest to start a little family. Now, blackbirds are swooping in to take over.

"I wouldn't like building a house and having it destroyed," Mary says, so she goes on the warpath with her broom, chasing the blackbirds off. Then she studies the weather again. She also dresses herself in clothes that would be comfortable if she had to spend the night somewhere other than in her bed. She takes the weather seriously. Anything could happen.

It's late afternoon when Mary gets a call from another brother. He's at work, and all the employees have just been sent to the basement.

"I've got work to do, and here they have me in the basement," he complains to Mary.

"You just be glad you have a basement to go to," Mary tells him. "You cool your heels and leave that macho stuff for someone else."

The afternoon turns to evening. The sky gets dark, but the sun hasn't gone down yet. It begins to rain. Mary's sisters are both home by now, and they grill hamburgers outside. As they put supper away, it grows even darker.

"If it doesn't hit us, it's going to hit close by," Mary predicts. She's glad she's wearing the go-anywhere clothes.

When the dishes are put away, Mary's sisters go to the living room to watch TV. Their brother stays outside in his little house. Mary heads straight to her closet with a weather radio in one hand and a cell phone in the other. In the top of the closet, comforters and sheets are bagged in black plastic garbage bags.

"You need to take shelter!" she tells her sisters, but they are content to keep relaxing.

Her radio comes alive.

"Ringgold, you need to take cover," the announcer says. He reports winds of 77 miles per hour, moments later changing the number to 80 miles per hour.

The house goes black.

"Where are you?" Mary's sisters call.

"Just take cover and stay where you are!" Mary hollers. It's too late for them to join her, so they run to a hallway. It's not very safe, because both ends are open. They protect their heads with couch cushions.

In the closet, Mary reaches up and jerks down the garbage-bag-wrapped blankets and pulls them on top of herself. She curls into the fetal position under the pile of blankets, but the weather enthusiast in her is still alive.

She pokes the closet door open, peering through the crack.

\\\\\\\\\\\\V//////////

Normally, Anna Montgomery and her twin grandchildren attend prayer meeting across the street on Wednesday nights. Tonight church is canceled.

Anna tells her grandchildren that tornadoes do not come here.

"If a tornado would come, it would probably tear us up, though," she admits, "because it would get trapped between the ridges."

Anna tries to distract the twins. The forecasts have been going all day, but nothing has happened, so she isn't too concerned. She goes to the game cupboard and picks out a cardboard box of Phase 10 cards. They don't know how to play. All the better; she will teach them. They sit at a table and Anna deals cards.

Anna doesn't hear the tornado coming. They are playing Phase 10 when a window explodes. The curtain stands straight out and the roof begins to disintegrate.

Anna's grandchildren scream. They run to the hall closet. They scream so loud that Anna can feel the terror of their screams as a physical pain in her heart.

Anna—once thirteen years old too, staying at *her* grandmother's, screaming and running when her house exploded—runs after them.

One of the twins had prepared, dragging the mattress off his bed and into the hallway. They step together into the closet. It's Anna's utility closet in the middle of the house, the one with shelves of cleaning supplies on one side. There's a box on the closet floor, and Anna and the children drag it out to make room. They pull the mattress in front of the closet door for more protection. They clutch each other in the darkness with the smell of cleaning supplies in their noses.

"Pray, just pray!" Anna yells above the racket.

They're having Wednesday night prayer meeting after all.

\\\\\\\\\\\\\\\V///////////

On this stormy afternoon, Willa's neighbors come over to see if she would like to stay with them until the weather clears. She agrees, and they help her over to their house in her wheelchair.

When Willa's son gets off work, he picks up his girlfriend so they can spend the evening together at his mom's house. Everyone at work has been repeating, "There's a tornado coming!"

When they reach her house, Willa is gone. Her son makes a few phone calls. He finds out that his mom is at a neighbor's house, and he heads over to get her. There's no place like home when it's stormy.

Back in the trailer they watch the news and the updates on the storm from the living room. Willa heads her wheelchair back to her bedroom. While she settles in for her nightly Bible reading, her son opens the windows.

The trailer goes black. It's quiet, and they don't hear any sirens, just a deep, threatening stillness, like something from a bad dream that can't be described the next morning. Outside in the dimness, the nearby trees bow their heads in a sudden, severe wind. Willa's son closes the living room windows. He's running to close the kitchen windows when the trailer explodes.

\\\\\\\\\\V/////////

Dale and Joy Cope lock up their pharmacy and head home. There have been storms all day, but they aren't particularly worried. They turn off Cherokee Valley Road into their subdivision and climb the steep lane home.

Dale is weary from a day behind the counter of the pharmacy, and he debates going directly to bed. Instead, he drops on a couch in the front room with the cathedral ceiling and the floor-to-ceiling windows. Joy brings him a plate of chicken and green beans.

After Dale finishes the meal, he sets the plate aside. Suddenly he hears a rumbling sound. He gets up and walks out onto the balcony. The hundred-foot oak tree bobs and bends like an inflatable toy. There's a black storm heading their way.

He rushes back in. He looks back out through the big windows and thinks of Birmingham.

Dale was studying to be a pharmacist in Birmingham, Alabama, when

Hurricane Ivan made landfall. A number of massive trees fell near his house. He remembers running from one side of the house to the other to escape. In the end, the top of the one tree was only six feet from the house. Ever since, he's had respect for trees in storms.

He looks at the oak again, and now it is bent even farther than before. He knows it can't go much farther without breaking, and it could land right on their house.

"Go to the basement!" he shouts from the living room. In the kitchen, Joy hears his voice and runs. It's not his words that make her run so much as the tone of his voice. In their bedrooms upstairs, their sons hear this voice too. They race down the turning staircase as well, all the way to the basement. They sit on a couch, away from the basement windows.

\\\\\\\\\\V/////////

Over in Salem Valley, Harry and Mary Devitt are sitting in their cozy, western-themed home watching the news. Mary knows there's word about bad weather.

In preparation Mary puts a quilt in the bathtub. The bathroom matches the rest of the house, with cast iron horseshoe towel racks and a framed print of a galloping band of horses.

She continues to prepare the tub. She adds important bills she needs to pay. She gets her most valuable belongings and puts them in. She thinks of everything.

"Better put on some clothes that you don't mind being seen in," Harry warns. Mary agrees and soon lies down for a little nap.

"If you are living in Salem Valley, take cover *now*," the TV announcer says.

"Come on, come on!" Harry yells at her.

Mary jumps up. She dashes into the bathroom, past the galloping horses on the wall, and slides into the bathtub with the quilt and valuables. Harry dives in after her.

SHATTERPROOF // RINGGOLD, GEORGIA

4
8:15 P.M.

Being alive is not what it used to be.
—Mark Levine, *F5*

The cold front sweeping across the Mississippi Valley, pushing moist air from the Gulf of Mexico, leaves Alabama and arrives in Georgia. When it does, it's a black cloud, vibrating with atomic bursts of lightning that rip through thousands of feet of writhing storm.

    The tornado touches down at 8:15 p.m. in Ringgold as an EF1 but soon escalates in force. It wraps Ace Hardware in ribbons of silver aluminum siding. It steals 80 percent of the roof metal and blows out the walls. It breaks open the A and the E of the big red letters that spell ACE on the front of the store. It reaches inside the hardware store and upends rows of paint and tools, and spills bins of bolts, nuts, and washers. It activates the sprinklers, soaking the inventory. Amazingly, it leaves the aisle of cleaning supplies standing as neatly as undisturbed dominoes. On its way out the front door, it scatters a stack of bright blue pallets like a deck of cards. Several of the ceiling lights, running on backup battery power, glow weakly over the sodden waste.

The tornado destroys Dale Cope's pharmacy. It whacks the front off the Food Lion grocery store as the eleven people inside race back between aisles of baking supplies, barely making it to the coolers at the back of the store. It flips over a white SUV in the parking lot.

The tornado crosses I-75 and blasts into the Exit 348 hotel and restaurant area, whisking away the red lights and the signs that tell drivers where to turn. It hits Taco Bell, Kentucky Fried Chicken, Ruby Tuesday, Day's Inn, Quality Inn, and Baymont Inn and Suites. Only the Holiday Inn Express gets missed. Diners at Ruby Tuesday hide in the kitchen before the building collapses.

The tornado mows over McDonald's and the nearby McDonald's billboard on I-75. Once spit out of the whirl, McDonald's looks like a colorful plastic toy house run over by a careless older brother mowing lawn. The red curly slide in the play area still stands amid the wreckage. The colorful letters spelling PLAY PLACE are crooked, and some are gone. The billboard, scarred and nearly unreadable, matches the building.

The tornado hits Waffle House and Walter Jackson Chevrolet, throwing a stoplight and an interstate sign into the showroom beside a 1978 model car. From his home on a hill above Ringgold, Walter Jackson's grandson Ryan, now the general manager at the dealership, watches the tornado. He sees flashes of green blasting through the sky, higher and wider and more powerful than anything man could invent. The destructive mass is moving slowly.

The tornado ruins Ringgold Florist, wiping out the entire room where 150 ribbons are waiting for their flowers. A wall clock in the flower shop stops at 8:26.

The sheriff is just pulling into the parking lot to join the Emergency Operations Center at the county sheriff's office when he receives word that a tornado has touched down in Ringgold. He does a u-turn and heads toward town. At the same time, Major Sisk rushes EOC members to the training room. He brings in extra phones. Most of the members of the

EOC bring their own laptops and smartphones with them.

\\\\\\\\\\\V/////////

The tornado increases in strength and charges down Sparks Street to where Mary Greene is crouched in the closet, her sisters in the hallway, and her brother outside in his little house. In the dimness of the closet, Mary sees dirt and leaves flying. The window air conditioner unit disappears as if removed by a speedy looter. She hears the popping noises of trees crunching and cracking open. Her woodpecker friend in the front yard is losing his carefully built home—but not to the blackbirds. She hears loud noises, and the only thing she can think of is that it sounds like a war zone.

She's still peering out the closet door when she sees a tree jutting through the side of her house. Even for a weather enthusiast, this is too much. She stops peeking. She pulls the closet door in on herself and curls deeper under the blankets, still clutching her cell phone and radio.

The tornado churns into Anna's house, where Anna and her twin grandchildren have just made it to the closet. It whirls around it, knocking over the walls, just like the dynamite knocked over her family's house so many years before. It strews clothes, splinters wood, and creates rubble. It snatches the rubber protectors from under the glass table topper but leaves the heavy round table unharmed otherwise. It whips around the bathroom door, which crashes toward the closet, but it's blocked by a huge blue mattress. Behind the blue mattress, Anna and her thirteen-year-old twin grandchildren are safe.

The tornado whips into the tree-shaded lot where Willa's trailer sits on Shady Place. With a violent twisting motion, it tears the trailer open. It throws Willa like a rag doll and uproots the toilet, which slams against her. It plucks up a tree like a twig and tosses it into the middle of the exploding trailer, into the kitchen where Willa's son is headed to close the windows. He turns and watches his girlfriend flying through the split-open roof.

By now the tornado is surging out of downtown Ringgold. It climbs White Oak Mountain, one of those ridges that was supposed to keep tornadoes out of Ringgold. It leaves a path like a lawnmower pushing through tall grass, except that this lawnmower is spitting out trees, not blades of grass. As it crests the ridge and dashes down the other side, the tornado strengthens even more, turning into an EF3, and then an EF4. The tornado plows down Cherokee Valley and bounces against the next tornado-preventing ridge. It's almost as if the raging, whirling machine is trapped by the mountain, like a lawnmower turned loose in a ditch.

The tornado hits the house of Dale and Joy, who are huddled on a couch in the basement with their sons. Dale is still thinking about the tree, not about tornadoes. The family hears rumbling, breaking noises, the sound of wood twisting and limbs striking the house. The tornado acts like a knife, chopping the house in half. Then, the one half disappears, as if brushed off the cutting board.

At the beginning of its path, the tornado destroys Dale's pharmacy. Five miles later, before leaving Catoosa County, it destroys his house.

From an aerial view, the whirling blades of wind seem to ride down the side of the mountain, flattening houses, chewing trees, destroying life. When it finally disappears, Cherokee Valley is flat. From a distance, the trees that remain look like perfect twigs for roasting marshmallows over a campfire. They're stripped of branches, and some of bark. A few have even been whittled to a pencil-tip point at the top.

The tornado tops the ridge and now it's rushing down into Salem Valley. It crosses Ware Road and charges up the slope to the house of Harry and Mary Devitt, knocking over fences and snapping thousands of trees like dandelion stems. It races past Brutus, the Great Dane, and Muffy, the English sheep dog, and over the bathtub into which Harry and Mary have both plunged. Like many people who live through tornadoes, Mary does not remember hearing anything. Harry hears a whooshing sound like a vacuum cleaner gulping something.

When the tornado evaporates into thin air, it leaves behind a thirteen-mile track, one-third mile wide.[2]

The Death of a Tornado

There's not much to say about the death of tornadoes. They simply become wispy and ropy and disappear. Some seem to lift off the ground, but really, the bottom of the tornado has disintegrated, perhaps because of the friction from hitting objects on the ground. "Towns usually destroy tornadoes this way, although not before suffering damage."[3]

Sometimes a kind of tornado hand-off takes place, in which one tornado stops and another one starts. Mostly though, the tornado just departs in peace, leaving the wreckage behind for someone else to deal with.

SHATTERPROOF // RINGGOLD, GEORGIA

5
Like a War Zone

We were homeless in two minutes.
—Joy Cope, Cherokee Valley

Dexter, the concession stand clerk and city worker, lives outside the destruction zone. He gets a call from Ringgold.

"You're not going to believe this," says the voice on the other end. "Ringgold's been wiped out by a massive tornado. You have to get back in here."

Dexter holds the phone silently, staring straight ahead at his living room wall, giving the caller a chance to say the punch line and apologize for the bad joke. After all, Dexter is famous for jokes himself, and it wouldn't be surprising if someone tried to trick him. When nothing comes, Dexter realizes the message is not a joke.

"I'll be right there," he promises.

He runs outside and climbs into his four-wheel-drive Jeep Wrangler. He heads down the road until he can go no farther, and then he turns into a field. The sturdy Wrangler proves its endurance tonight, climbing over trees, plunging through pools of water, maneuvering in and out of fields and on and off roads. Dexter knows that keeping the roads clear is his responsibility, and he knows it's going to be a long night. Maybe a long week—or month.

When he finally arrives in Ringgold, he finds that the Angel EMS station in Ringgold has been demolished. They need a temporary place to park ambulances immediately, and Dexter is the man for the problem. He finds a building to use and changes the locks for security.

He wonders if his co-worker, the trash disposal worker, has changed his mind about nothing ever happening in Ringgold.

\\\\\\\\\\V/////////

At her house, Jan Henry is getting calls from her family.

"Mom, are you all right?" asks her son, his voice thick with worry.

"We're fine," she assures him.

A few minutes later, the phone rings again.

"Mom, are you all right?" queries her daughter's husband.

"We're fine," she says again.

The phone rings again.

"Mom, are you all okay?" It's her son again.

This time, Jan laughs. "Well, of course we are. Why did you call again?"

"Well, I just had to be sure," he says. "We keep hearing that things are terrible in Ringgold."

\\\\\\\\\\V/////////

Jan's grandson Dakota is heading for Ringgold, but he hasn't heard about the tornado yet. The traffic is a nightmare, so he knows something is wrong, but he assumes there must have been an accident. He gets to a traffic light that is out of service and is being treated as a four-way stop except by some people who are jetting through it. He finally makes it to an intersection not far from the Methodist church. The traffic is stopped, and a trucker calls to him from the side of the road.

"You know what happened?"

Dakota's face is blank. "No . . ."

"A tornado just came through."

As the news sinks in, Dakota peers ahead and sees Ringgold Florist. Even in the near-darkness, he can see the building is destroyed.

Suddenly in panic mode, Dakota realizes that the tornado may have hit his fiancée's house. He tries to reach her on his dying cell phone as he hurries over to Caffeine Addicts. Service is terrible, but he manages to talk to his fiancée for about two seconds, long enough to know she's okay.

Caffeine Addicts is all right as well, but the power is out. Numbly, Dakota moves milk jugs from the refrigerator to the freezer, hoping that will keep them colder longer. He steps out the back door where trash cans have blown over. After righting them, he heads to his fiancée's house.

\\\\\\\\\\\V/////////

"Where are you? Are you all right?" Mary Greene calls from the closet to her sisters when everything is quiet.

"Yes, I'm coming!" one of her sisters calls back.

"No, don't! Stay where you are!" She hollers back. She knows that tornadoes sometimes travel in pairs, and she thinks they'd better lay low. Finally she pushes off the bags of blankets, uncurls herself, and crawls out of the closet. She feels the crackle of a raincoat in the closet, so she puts that on over her sweatshirt. It's dark inside the house, and she feels her way carefully along to the hallway where her sisters are. Insulation and ceiling materials are lying everywhere, dangling from what is left of the ceiling. She needs to use the bathroom, so she heads that way, but the bathroom door will not open. Whether from the pressure or from the force of flying objects, the frame of the house has shifted and the door won't budge.

Mary's handicapped brother crawls into the house through a new opening.

"Are you okay?" Mary asks him. His little house has taken a tumble in the tornado, with him inside it, but all he has is a scratch on his head.

Looking outside, Mary sees that the brick duplexes across the street have lost their tops. Firefighters are beginning to move up the street, checking on people. The street is a maze, choked with debris, crisscrossed with trees, and laced with power lines. Bright flashes spark into the night sky as transformers die and power lines hit the ground.

Mary calls her other brother, the one who just complained about being in the basement.

"The tornado hit us," Mary informs him.

"What? Are you sure?" he asks.

A firefighter comes to the door. He's there to help them to safety, but he also wonders if they have any water on hand.

Mary finds a one-liter bottle in her refrigerator. The firefighter drinks it all without stopping.

As their rescuer leads the way, Mary takes stock of her surroundings. It's not too dark to see that everything is a colossal mess. The pecan and maple trees in the front yard are wrapped around the house, along with aluminum siding from some business down the road. Trees and power lines are everywhere.

"These lines are hot!" the firefighter yells suddenly, and they can see sparks flying not far away. "You walk where I walk, step where I step, and don't touch anything." He has a light, and he's panning it this way and that, looking in every direction.

Mary's emotions are as messed up as her front yard, but she clings to one thought. *We've come through the storm, and we're okay. We made it.*

\\\\\\\\\V/////////

Anna and her twin grandchildren pry at the closet door and the blue mattress. As they crawl into the darkness and rain, Anna hears her name.

"Anna! Anna! Are you all right! Anna, where are you?!"

Anna calls back.

"We're all right!" she says. "We're right here!"

She looks around her and realizes why people are yelling.

Houses are shredded and possessions are strewn. For the second time in her life, her house is in ruins. The walls are gone. The roof is gone. Only the part in the middle with the utility closet stands.

They stay with a neighbor that night. One of the twins wants to sleep in the neighbor's closet. No one blames him. Another friend his age joins him, and they sleep on the floor right outside the closet door.

\\\\\\\\\\\V/////////

Willa's son finds himself in a puddle outside. The last thing he remembers is running to close the kitchen window, the tree flying toward him, and his girlfriend getting sucked through the roof.

He sits up in the puddle. His left arm is sticky, and in the lightning flashes, he sees that the arm is cut and bleeding. He gets to his feet, dripping, sticky with mud and blood, and walks through the eerie flashes. He sees the pile of rubble that was his mother's trailer just five minutes ago. He's pretty sure that the screaming he hears is coming from his girlfriend. He finds her under pieces of the trailer. She seems okay.

"I've got to go find Mom!" he shouts to her, turning, looking.

"I'm going with you!" she screams, crawling out. "Don't leave me!"

He helps his girlfriend to her feet. They find Willa. She's quiet, her eyes closed, blood covering her face, the toilet on top of her. Her son grabs the heavy white bowl and shoves it away. Rain is pouring down now as he leans over his mother. Her chest moves in and out.

"She's alive!" he hollers.

He picks Willa up and walks down the littered street.

Next door, a woman lies twisted, screaming in pain, and her husband calls for help. Fire trucks pull in closer. Firemen bring blankets and gurneys.

"Over here!" Willa's son yells, directing the rescue personnel toward the woman and his mother.

He helps settle his mother onto a gurney and covers her with blankets. Other people lift the woman from next door onto another gurney. There's no time to do everything right. The little procession starts off toward the ambulances, which are unable to get through. The gurneys bounce over pieces of lumber and slide through puddles and crunch over glass. They tip and rock despite the hands of family members and firefighters. As they wheel around a corner, they see two men, just staring.

"Grab hold and help us!" Willa's son says to them, and they lurch forward, just in time to keep one of the gurneys from tipping. Everyone is glad to help.

By this time Willa is soaking wet and stunned, but alert. She doesn't seem to be critically wounded, and they begin to hope she might be okay.[4]

\\\\\\\\\\V/////////

On the couch in the basement, Dale and Joy and the boys realize the noise has passed. Water begins dripping onto their heads through the basement ceiling. Dale thinks that the tree must have hit the house, maybe breaking a water pipe.

They get up dizzily and walk toward the wooden stairs. As they turn the first corner, they see daylight. Their shock intensifies with every step until they arrive at the top and realize half the house is gone.

The room with the floor-to-ceiling windows has disappeared. The large painting purchased from the Virgin Islands has vanished. One of the boys' bedrooms is gone. The master bedroom has been wiped away.

As the reality of the situation dawns on them, they see they are not the only ones who have been devastated. For the first time, they can see Cherokee Valley from their house, but it is now a valley of horror. Their neighbors' houses have been demolished.

They stand at the edge of their house and holler, "Are you all right down there? Can you hear us? Are you okay?"

Their two closest neighbors answer. They are okay.

There's another neighbor at the very top of the ridge, the house bumping against the sky. The boys holler until their throats are sore, but no one responds. Since it takes the boys thirty minutes to take a few steps over the rubble to turn off the water, climbing to the top of the ridge is unthinkable.

The feeling of desolation is complete. "We were homeless in two minutes," Joy reflects. Everything they had worked for was gone.

Dale, Joy, and the boys each grab a suitcase and try to find things they need. Then they wait for someone to rescue them. It starts pouring rain.

"It seems like an eternity when you don't know what you're waiting for," says Joy.

After two and a half hours, a cousin arrives and takes them to his house. Before they leave, they are relieved to discover that the family at the top of the ridge is safe.

\\\\\\\\\\\V//////////

In Salem Valley, Harry and Mary Devitt climb out of the bathtub. They walk outside to investigate, but it's getting dark. Their house doesn't seem to be damaged. Mary dimly sees a tree with its head on the ground.

"Oh, it looks like there's a tree down," Mary says. It's murky, as if ink had been poured over the neighborhood. They do not see the extent of what has just happened. The power is gone, and they know there is nothing to do now. They go to bed.

\\\\\\\\\\\V//////////

The Angel EMS ambulance crew gets its first 9-1-1 call: a tractor trailer has blown over and someone is trapped inside. Clint Shoemaker heads out to answer the call, but trees, power lines, and debris are blocking the roads.

Lana Duff, the Angel EMS operations manager, is headed toward

Ringgold along with the two disaster buses. She's also keeping watch on the calls coming in. In the first twenty minutes, there are a hundred 9-1-1 calls from the city of Ringgold. She calls for mutual aid from other services. Within an hour, twenty-three ambulances have arrived from eleven departments.

Clint's crew heads one way, and another ambulance heads another way. Again, Clint is forced to turn around while the other ambulance goes on. He stops at a cluster of apartment buildings near the Methodist church, and he and his partner begin a door-to-door search. Children are screaming. The injuries are minor, but the terror is major. Clint works to spread calm, but he can spend only a few moments with each person.

People ask, "What can we do? Can we help with anything?"

Clint knows that responsibility helps people relax. Because there are so many children in this apartment, it's easy to assign jobs. Clint directs adults to take the children to a safe place away from wires and shaky structures.

"Is anyone in here?" he hollers grim-faced into the darkness again and again.

On the other side of the street, firefighters are working their way up Sparks Street to Mary Greene, Anna and the twins, and Willa Adams. Only the heavy fire trucks can be trusted to drive over the power lines and debris.

Lana is helping establish a command center where injured people can be evaluated. At first, the center springs up in the middle of the road between the ruined McDonald's and Walter Jackson Chevrolet.

Hotel occupants mill in the road, dazed. They step gingerly across the littered pavement and the yellow lines shiny from rain and reflected lights. Many of these people had just been going to their rooms or driving back from restaurants when the tornado tore off the hotel roofs.

"It was like a war zone," a paramedic reflects. "People were walking around, bleeding."

Down in the training room at the county sheriff's office, the Emergency Operations Center sounds like a telemarketer's call center, but the babble is controlled. According to policy, disaster response is managed in twelve-hour sections of time. This means that some people, as soon as the tornado hit, were assigned to planning the *next* twelve hours. Others are talking to the state officials, letting them know what Ringgold needs now. The biggest need is for a crew trained in search and rescue. Ringgold doesn't have its own specialized unit, so they have to find one. The state officials know where to find extra help throughout the state, and they quickly send it toward Ringgold.

Although the tornado has passed, forecasts show that another storm is moving in. Planting the command center in the middle of a road is not a good idea if another tornado arrives. The ambulances and police move to the Ingles parking lot. There's a row of smaller buildings beside Ingles. Dollar Tree is in the center space, but the other two are empty. The crowds need a place to get out of the storm, but there's no one to give permission. Police force entry into the empty building between Ingles and Dollar Tree.

The command center will stay at Ingles for a number of days. Lana knows how many ambulances are present and where the others are, and she receives and dispatches all the calls from the 9-1-1 Center.

The Emergency Operations Center functions throughout the night. Major Sisk is trying to find a better building for the people who have no place to stay. When they find one, it must be prepared with resources like blankets and bottled water. A thorough registration system must also be put in place, which will take quite some time.

6
Night With No Rest

*The reality of what happened didn't sink in
for days because we were so busy.*
—Clint Shoemaker, Angel EMS

In Ringgold, firefighters take people to the city hall to get out of the rain and storm. The beauty of the strong brick building with its golden dome and white pillars is lost in the darkness as the people struggle in. Many are soaking wet. Mary Greene is better off than most with her raincoat. She's also fortunate because her cell phone and her sister's phone are both fully charged. They loan their phones throughout the night.

The flashlights of rescue workers reflect off the aluminum of Sprite and Coke cans from the break room fridge. Mary and her sisters help pass out drinks to the nervous crowd.

The visitors from the hotels are lost in a broken town they can't call home, sheltered at a city hall they've never seen before. Images of hotel roofs being flung into parking lots replay in their minds. They get on their cell phones, trying to gain strength by sharing the nightmare.

A man who was at the Laundromat when the tornado hit admits, "My wife told me not to go. She told me if I go do my laundry in this storm, I'm a dead man." Now he can't get through to his wife, and he's sure that she thinks he *is* a dead man.

He and another man talk about their experience at the Laundromat. They took shelter under the metal tables used for folding clothes. The tables had been bolted to the floor. When the ceiling crashed down, the tables stood strong and saved their lives.

"Well, this is no good," the other man says with a wry smile. "Now my clothes are all down there in that ruined building, and all I have is what I have on my back."

The men's humor is good for the others in the shelter.

"Did your house get destroyed?" someone asks Mary.

"Yes," she replies.

"Did it get the purple house?" he asks.

"I don't know," she says.

"I hope it didn't," he replies.

Soon another man approaches Mary in the dusk.

"How is your house?" he asks.

"Pretty bad," Mary replies.

"Did it get the purple house?" he asks.

"I don't know," she says.

"I hope so," he grins.

When morning comes, they see the brilliant purple house—still standing.

As the night wears on, another front moves in, and it looks like there's more bad weather coming.

"Look, we have to have a plan if another tornado comes," Mary says. She's already inspected the restrooms and decided they would not make a good shelter. Instead, if another tornado comes, they will meet in the large hall in the center of the building. Some people will go outside and tell the people idling there to come in, and others will close the doors.

Thankfully, the danger passes, and the plan is not needed.

A man from out of town stops by the shelter and asks if anyone needs a ride.

"I'd like to go to the hospital where my mom is," Willa's son says. "Some friends are trying to come get us, but they can't make it all the way here." He has been using Mary's cell phone to call these friends, because his has vanished.

As Willa's son and his girlfriend leave with their ride, they have no way of knowing that they will not be allowed back into Ringgold for several days.

Mary doesn't sleep a wink. In the spacious and stately front foyer of the city hall, she lounges with a few others on the couches under the chandeliers. She feels calm, but her frequent trips to the restroom seem to indicate otherwise.

Finally, before the night is over, a bus arrives to move them all to an official shelter, the Lakeview Fort Oglethorpe High School. Fort Oglethorpe High School and Ringgold High School have long been rivals. "I'd rather be dead than red" is a Ringgold saying, referring to Fort Oglethorpe's school color. Now, the citizens of Ringgold are being taken—perish the thought—to dreaded "enemy" territory.

The taut emotions of the night once more turn to giddy laughter. "I mean, do you have to take us *there?*" someone complains to the bus driver, and everyone laughs, with the exception of the out-of-towners who don't know the joke.

\\\\\\\V////////

It's about midnight, and Jan's children have stopped calling to make sure she's okay. She's on the Internet, staring at pictures of the damage. She can't stop wondering about all the people she knows, many of them faces across the counter at Caffeine Addicts. The man who always orders a chicken salad croissant. The little girl who pays for her frozen hot chocolate with exact change.

The practical questions rankle too. How long will the freezers at Caffeine Addicts stay cold without power? She thinks they might last forty-eight hours, and she wonders if the power will be on by then.

There's a knock on the door. Jan goes to answer it, expecting to find her son. Instead, it's her grandson Dakota. Before she can speak, he wraps her in his arms in an enormous hug.

\\\\\\\\\\\V//////////

Down at the County Sheriff's office, the night has just begun. Major Sisk, in the Emergency Operations Center, is managing the resources and men pouring in. Lana Duff of Angel EMS is doing the same thing with medical personnel in the Ingles parking lot.

It will be a long night. Most workers won't stop until the next afternoon or evening. Even then, they may not rest for long.

"The reality of what happened didn't sink in for days, because we were so busy," says Clint from Angel EMS. "You run on adrenaline. You're not thinking about the magnitude of what happened. It really sinks in four months later when you drive by the same destroyed properties every day, and you remember what it was like before."

"The Catoosa County men were amazing. They worked all night," says Anna Montgomery.

Although the story is different in Cherokee Valley, there is just one fatality in the city of Ringgold. It's Mary Greene's 86-year-old former science teacher, the one who would enter the high school classroom spouting scientific facts. Mary suspects he went to bed before the tornado hit so he could get up early to go walking as always.

7
The Aftermath

The next day was worse than that night, because [the night] was dark and you didn't really have time to stop and think.
—A Catoosa County sheriff

When the curtain of darkness rises to reveal April 28, 2011, reality hits Ringgold. A student desk and chair lie mangled in a pile of cement chunks outside the school. A gas pump is on its side, huge utility poles down behind it. Restaurants are collapsed like fallen books. A cloth doll with plastic feet and hands lies among the shards of glass on the carpet of a church, a stainless steel fork a few feet away. A folding chair holds up a line of yellow police tape. On the chair, someone has taped a red poster with black letters: THERE IS ALWAYS HOPE.

Circling through the town are emergency workers from throughout the state, including a K-9 team. No one wants to think about what the dogs might be trained to find. People with hard hats and official uniforms peer into ruined homes. The faces of rescue workers are somber and strained. Most of them have just worked through the night without sleep.

\\\\\\\\\\\\\V/////////

When Harry and Mary Devitt wake up in Salem Valley, they can't believe what they see. The landscape is so changed that for a moment they wonder if their house has been moved. Hundreds of trees lie in piles. At the top of the hill, the trees are twisted even more.

They don't recognize their property. They step out of the house and see their garage split open and daylight pouring in.

They find their concrete driveway. This ribbon of pavement, snaking down the long slope to the road, is the only thing that has stayed the same. As they crawl over and under the forest of fallen trees, they keep their eyes on the concrete to keep from getting lost.

They begin to hear machinery below them. They can't see, but they begin to holler.

"We're coming!" voices shout. They are people from church, with chainsaws and a bobcat, chewing a path up the narrow driveway. For a while the church people had not even been able to find the mouth of the driveway beneath the wreckage of the trees.

"To this day, I remember those words, 'we're coming,'" Mary says with tears in her eyes. "The care from our friends touched us deeply in our time of need."

\\\\\\\\\\\\\V/////////

The Emergency Operations Center operates twenty-four hours a day for the first days after the tornado. The personnel have many tasks. Major Sisk's job includes visiting the high school shelter so he can give information to the displaced people there. Here he finds out that many of the people in the shelter are from the hotels and do not even live in the area. He arranges for buses to take them back to find their cars.

"So many power lines and trees were down, you couldn't even get up the road," Major Sisk recalls. "The trees were crossed and laced with power lines, so for a while the best mode of transportation was on foot."

Georgia Power agrees to work twenty-four hours a day if the city is closed. During a closing, all the roads are barricaded to prevent people from going out or coming in. This makes it easier not only to repair power lines but also to prevent injury and looting. When locals are finally permitted entry, passes are made for residents and business owners.

Georgia Power gets the power back in just a few days.

There is plenty of pressure to open the city, so there is a trial run on Sunday. The city opens at 7 a.m., and things go fine until after lunch, when people get out of church, or perhaps out of bed. The early afternoon rush is so crazy that the city closes again for several more days.

Lana Duff and the medical command center give tetanus shots and treat injuries received during debris cleanup. Help pours in from all over. Off-duty doctors come from as far as Atlanta to volunteer. Retired EMS personnel with still-active licenses join the effort.

"It's amazing how much support we got," Angel EMS employees say. "We spent six years planning for disaster, with continual training, and then it came."

Clint oversees the food department along with his medical tasks. Food donations pour in from all directions. Food Lion opens their doors immediately. Krystal's, a southern version of White Castle, donates their specialty sandwiches called Sunrisers. Little Caesars shows up with pizza.

Carabba's, an Italian restaurant, sets up in the Ingles parking lot too, grilling chicken and vegetables. They take meals door to door and also serve them in the parking lot, donating all the food. People do not go through a line. Carabba's asks guests to sit down and be served.

The health department monitors the food. All food must be kept at safe temperatures, so Ingles pitches in with cooler space and food warmers.

"Food was coming out of the woodwork," says Clint. "We served 350 people three times a day."

\\\\\\\\\\\V//////////

ACE Hardware hires a salvage company. The salvage company cleans out the store and sells what is still usable to a discount store. The manager of ACE Hardware has a friend in Gulf Port, Mississippi, who notices that his local discount store is selling ACE hardware items. The manager suspects they are from his ruined Ringgold store.

The store front is still standing, and so is the sign, despite the broken A and E. The building doesn't look ruined. But on closer inspection, the manager realizes the only usable part is the steel frame. The building is otherwise unstable.

ACE Hardware spends the summer rebuilding. However, they are not completely closed. A small glass building in their garden center survived the storm without damage, and they operate from this greenhouse all summer with a small quantity of new merchandise.[5]

\\\\\\\\\\\V//////////

Parts of Ringgold Florist have vanished completely. The front ceiling is precariously balancing on top of a Styrofoam arch. The coolers are packed with Mother's Day flowers that will go to waste.

Selina Riley looks in on the coolers and has an idea. She's not sure how people will respond, but she takes a bucket full of flowers, and steps out onto the street.

"Would you like a flower? Would you like a flower?" she asks. The flowers are stressed, but she offers them anyway.

It works.

Taking the flowers, some of the people break into tears.

"This is the most beautiful flower I've ever seen," one person says. Selina calls to a helper to bring her more buckets.

When the insurance company tells her that the Ringgold Florist building is not a complete loss, Selina can hardly believe it. They ask her to crawl into the building to take pictures, but the building is not safe.

"Do you see those cases of vases holding up the debris?" she wants to ask them. "Do you see the Styrofoam arch holding up the ceiling?"

The Styrofoam arch has caught one woman's eye. She calls Selina, explaining that she decorates for weddings. She asks if Selina is planning to save the arch. If not, she would like to have it. Selina tries to explain that rescuing the arch will probably bring the ceiling down on the rescuer, which would not be worth the free arch.

Selina needs a new place of business. She considers the building for sale across the street from the United Methodist Church. At first she's sure it's too small, and she pursues another building. Then she drives back to the small brick building and changes her mind. It has a cozy porch and large glass windows in front. She buys it.

\\\\\\\\\\\\\\V/////////

"You kept wanting to wake up from a nightmare," says an employee at Walter Jackson Chevrolet. "I remember sitting on the couch thinking, *What in the world. Am I going to have a job?* You can't sell autos if you don't have power, if you don't have inventory."

Ryan Jackson's father breaks down when he first sees the family business. Except for the cars in the service bays, windows are broken out of every vehicle. The large windows in the front showroom have disappeared. Except for the I-beams dripping with insulation, the showroom is destroyed. A traffic light rests inside.

The Jacksons call a Thursday morning meeting with their more than forty employees. The employees are assured that the dealership will be rebuilt and that they will get back to work as soon as possible.

Volunteers, employees, and friends help clean up the auto dealership.

Just three days after Wednesday's tornado, the cleanup is finished. Power returns on Monday, and the business re-opens on Tuesday. They operate out of a trailer.

At first, business is slow, but Ryan and his father are glad that the men are at least able to work. A glass company repairs the outside vehicles, which are sold as is. People line up to purchase the marked-down vehicles, with some $41,000 trucks selling for $15,000. By the end of May, sales are up 300 percent from the previous May.

8
Down to the Bare Bones

Why be mad? I'm alive!
—Anna Montgomery

After staying one night at the high school, Mary Greene and her brother and sisters move to a nephew's home.

Spectators bother Mary when she returns to Ringgold. People drive through, snapping pictures. It's as though they're visiting a zoo. Mary prefers to talk to people who have been through the tornado. She wants to be with people who have experienced the same thing she has. "I don't want to be famous," she says.

Nor does she feel the need to see all the damage there is. "I just want to be able to go to my house and work in my yard. People ask me if I've been to Cherokee Valley, and I say no," she explains. "I don't want to go down there."

Storms still have an effect on Mary. She remembers the storm that came not long after the tornado.

She was in a vehicle with her sister, who was driving. Her sister's knuckles gripped the wheel in terror, her veins standing out. The wind was blowing hard, driving rain and debris. When they arrived home, their nephew noticed their panic and teased them. "What's going on? The sky's not falling." He stopped laughing when a tree snapped.

A few months later Christian Aid Ministries hires Mary to drive Amish construction volunteers. One day Mary is driving a twenty-passenger van with eighteen volunteers. Again, the wind blows strong and it begins to rain.

It's not tornado season, Mary tells herself.

She clutches the steering wheel. She sees the faces of the young men in the rearview mirror.

You've got to pull it together, Mary.

In several storms since the tornado, Mary has pulled over beside the road to cry. But she can't do that this time. She wants to stay strong. She doesn't think the volunteers know she is upset.

Mary's handicapped brother who survived a tumble in his little house is more easily frustrated since the tornado.

"Is it going to tornado?" he asks.

"All in all," says Mary, "it's been a struggle." The hardest struggle of her life, she thinks.

"Your father's passing and your mother's passing—you expect those things to happen," Mary says. "But with a storm, the warnings come and go as usual, and you think you'll go on as always. When you get taken out of the home where you lived, you are stripped down to the bare bones. You're at the infant stage, and you have to come back again."

Fear

Because tornadoes strike so suddenly, people fear they will be surprised again. Fear becomes anticipatory. The threat of being a victim controls them.

Victims might eat their meals or spend a night in the basement or storm cellar if there is any indication of bad weather. Storm cellar manufacturers do well after destructive tornadoes; no one wants to take another risk. No one cares if they are ridiculed about their extra precautions.

Humans are not the only ones to experience fear. Richard Bedard describes a heifer he saw after a 1993 Oklahoma tornado. At the time of day when the tornado had struck, the animal became "fearfully still," as if bracing itself.[6]

1947: When teased about her new storm shelter, a woman says, "I lost one child; I'm not losing another one." Despite her neighbors' teasing about her "bunker," the woman found that in bad weather her new storm shelter was full—with her neighbors.[7]

1965: Some children in the Palm Sunday tornado hid in a coal bin. Although a flower pot tumbled down the coal chute toward them, it did not injure them. When asked for their opinion on the design of their new house, they had only one request. They wanted a coal bin.[8]

1974: A young man in Alabama said that just hearing the word *tornado* upset him.[9]

Anna is out in the streets with the rest of Ringgold when the sun rises on April 28, 2011. She and her grandchildren assess the damage and find out if everyone around them is okay.

The entrance to the town is strictly guarded; curious onlookers are not admitted. As the freeway into Ringgold slowly opens, however, help begins to arrive. Besides Georgia Power Company, people appear with cartons of bottled water, canned food, and hot sandwiches. Church groups arrive, handing out warm supper plates. Eventually, there are so many people out and about that the city announces that volunteers must be at least eighteen years old.

The news media swarm Anna with questions.

"Do you feel angry about the tornado? You lost everything, right?"

Anna seems genuinely puzzled. "Why be mad? I'm alive!"

She agrees that it hurt to lose almost everything. "I was worried about finding pictures," she admits. "But I was able to find the majority of my family pictures."

Some of Anna's pictures flew across the railroad track, but she reclaimed them at the United Methodist Church. The church, even though it received some damage, has become a disaster center.

Anna's trampoline has disappeared without a trace. She rejoices to find the memorial scrapbook she made for her father, the man who had raised the motherless family so well. Anna also finds her camera and recovers the beautiful ornate round table with the matching cushioned chairs.

In the coming days, volunteers bring Anna seven full plastic totes. Some contain canned goods, like chili and vegetables. Some are filled with pasta. Others hold cleaning supplies, a mop head, and a miniature broom and dust pan.

Anna stays close to her thirteen-year-old twin grandchildren. Although the tornado isn't the worst thing that ever happened to *her*, she realizes it was the worst thing that ever happened to her grandchildren. She knows

Anger

After the tornado disappears into dust, the story line becomes as complex as the boiling and churning in the supercell before touchdown. But here in the tornado's footprint, there is no one to blame. There is no one to forgive. There is no way that the storm, 60,000 feet high, could have been stopped. There will be no way to stop a future tornado. The misty shadow that caused all the trouble is gone.

Perhaps this is why anger is not a common tornado response.

> The *Huntsville Times* discusses anger based on interviews from Limestone County, Alabama, in 2011. This same county was also hit hard in 1974. The article says that all along the tornado's path, people who had nothing left and who were healing from fresh wounds still expressed joy, even giddiness, at being alive. Those who lost less actually showed less gratitude. They were often angry, like the man who hurled objects against the crumpled walls of his mini-storage unit.[10]

from experience that the exploded house will stay in their minds for years and years.

In the coming days Anna sympathizes with her grandchildren's fear. Sometimes they come home from school before their mother comes home from work. If the weather looks threatening on these days, Anna picks them up and takes them home with her.

It bothers Anna when people who lost only a few shingles say they were "in the tornado."

"You weren't in the tornado," Anna wants to say. "We were there bumping around in the closet like a roller coaster, with the floor rising right there in that closet behind that mattress."

Some people think the twins should go for counseling, but her grandson isn't sure about that. "Grandma, what did you tell us that night of the tornado? Didn't you tell us that we were supposed to pray? That's what we're supposed to do now too."

When Anna is asked to take someone to Cherokee Valley, she agrees reluctantly. When she arrives and sees the blue tarps, the destroyed forests, and the people living in tents to fend off looters, she wants to leave. She can't stand seeing the nightmare all over again.

"I can't do it; I'm going back," she says.

One night as Anna and two of her friends sit on the porch, it begins to get a bit stormy. All three of the ladies sit up straight and crane their necks, peering at the clouds. Suddenly, they begin to laugh.

"Look at us!" they say. "Sitting here with our necks stretched out!"

But they are not alone. When the weather gets bad, Ringgold porches are full of people with their necks stretched out, peering at the sky.

\\\\\\\\\\V/////////

The hospital pronounces Willa Adams ready for release. Her son wishes his mother could stay and rest at the hospital a few more days, since she has no home to return to and her walker and wheelchair have both been destroyed by the tornado.

"My mother was just in a tornado," he protests. "She just lost everything, and you want to send her to a shelter?" However, Willa is fine and the hospital needs the space. Her son knows there must be other people who need her bed.

Willa's son states that it was definitely the worst experience he's ever been through. "People say you should write stuff down to remember it. What happened there is engraved in my memory, and I won't ever forget it," he says. "There's a big difference between hearing about tornadoes and actually being in one. When you face death—when a tree crashes toward you and just brushes you instead of nailing your chest, you're never the same. You don't cheat death. When it's your time to go, it's your time to go—but we were spared."

A relative offers Willa a place to stay. She gratefully accepts.[11]

\\\\\\\\\\V/////////

Down in Cherokee Valley, where the tornado turned into an EF4 and where most of the fatalities occurred, Dale and Joy Cope are picking up the pieces and starting the process of rebuilding. One morning they arrive at their home and find that they have been visited by looters. A chain saw and a large four-wheeler are missing.

"A massive tornado throws a huge task in front of you," Dale says, "but you can get through it because it's a natural disaster, even though it's hard. Then looters steal the tools that you need to put your life together."

At church Dale shares the story of the looting with the congregation, asking them to pray for the thieves. They definitely need it, he tells the church.

Two weeks later the looters return, completely cleaning the job site of all tools and a brand new $1,000 generator Dale has borrowed from his cousin. Chain saws, drills, and even a five-gallon gas can are gone.

In the midst of the pressures of building, Dale is forced to spend the entire next day buying new tools, filing a police report, and trying to control his frustration. He talks to God all day long.

The same day, Dale's neighbor Chris calls to say that a team of volunteers has arrived from Atlanta, and he offers their assistance to Dale.

Dale listens skeptically. "By the way, Chris, we were robbed again, and they got *all* my tools this time." He breaks down on the phone.

"You're kidding."

The next morning the volunteers from Atlanta show up. The mission pastor meets Dale.

"I hear you were robbed recently," he says.

"Yes, sir," Dale replies.

"They took a lot of your stuff?"

"Yes, sir."

"We brought some money with us, and we'd like to help you out a little if we can," says the pastor. "What do you need?"

Dale shakes his head, trying to think what to say.

"Well, I'm definitely going to buy a new generator, because I was borrowing it from my cousin," he finally says. "So if you could put anything toward that..."

"Sure, we'll do that," says the pastor.

Because Dale is needed at the job site, Joy goes along on the shopping trip. They discover that the money is exactly enough for not only one but two generators: one to return to Dale's cousin, and one for Dale and Joy.

Joy doesn't struggle with anger about the tornado. It's God's work, and no one on earth can prevent it.

"One thing I never wanted to be was homeless, and we are definitely homeless and jobless. But that's the only way God sees how faithful we are through trials. God moves in mysterious ways—what He gives, He can take," Joy says. "I feel that I shouldn't tie myself to material things."

Joy does remember storms that came up in the days following the tornado.

"The word is *alert*," says Joy with a serious laugh. "We were out trying to figure out where the wind was coming from. We tied down our vehicles."

One of the storms came through around 1:00 a.m. The boys woke up and stayed awake, watching and listening.

"I'm not sure if they ever went back to sleep that night, and Dale didn't either," Joy says. She did, though, because she figured that if she weren't sleeping, she'd just be worrying.

Harry and Mary Devitt get $25,000 from their insurance company for their outbuildings, shed, garage, and pool. The spa on their deck looks as though it's been picked up with large hands and set back down hard. There's a "fault line" starting on the deck and running into the house. It's just a slight hump in the floor, but you can feel it in the dining room and all the way across the house to the bathroom. The sewage line is damaged. All the windows in the house need to be changed. Two more storms hit with strong winds, doing more damage. *What else could go wrong?* they wonder. The $25,000 is long gone before the repairs are all made.

Not long after the tornado, Mary notices a sensation in her ear. Then her eye begins to swell. She goes to the doctor, and he sends her home with medicine. When things do not improve, she goes to another doctor. Before long, she has a temperature of 103 degrees.

Mary is hospitalized for several days. Nurses keep her on steady morphine to combat the pain, which feels like a paring knife slicing into her head. The doctors tell her the stress of the tornado has brought on a bout of shingles in her head. Shingles, a rash that is possible in anyone who has had chicken pox, is most common on the body. But Mary says that shingles on the body is nothing like shingles in the head.

For about a month after the tornado, she stays in bed in a dark room, fearful of the light that hurts her eyes. At one point she tells her son she just doesn't want to live any longer. After that, the pharmacist increases her medication, and Mary experiences some relief. Doctors tell her it will take about a year to completely recover. In the meantime she takes medication and deals with occasional confusion.

Still, the tornado with all its baggage doesn't compare to losing a golden-haired daughter.

9
Grace Enough

*If I were to say one word ... of all the things we've gone through ...
the single word would probably be "grace."*
—Dale Cope

Ringgold in October 2011 is a study in contrasts. Sitting in the shiny new Waffle House with its bright red chairs and glistening black tile, it's easy to think things are back to normal and even better than before. The parking lot is jammed with cars, and the kitchen is swarming with workers. Waitresses circle, crying "hello" to everyone who walks in the door and asking repeatedly, "Would you like some coffee, honey?" The UPS man, the county sheriffs, and the manager of ACE Hardware are here eating sandwich melts and hash browns, waffles and bacon. Across the street is a glistening new Pizza Hut that is "coming soon."

Glancing out the window, however, diners also see rafters still bleaching in the sun above a broken hotel. Its windows are printed with phrases such as "NO TRESPASSING" and "STAY OUT." After months of exposure to the weather, the ruined hotel is even more depressing than it was in May.

Down at the Food Lion, customers are busy shopping. It's hard to tell that anything ever happened, but over by the customer service counter is a framed memorial. Six photos, four newspaper clippings, and a receipt dated May 3, 2011, are framed by a dark blue mat. The receipt shows that after six days of cleaning insulation, sweeping broken glass, and picking up dropped ceiling tiles, the grocery store was back in business.

On October 7, 2011, ACE Hardware anchors strings of red and white triangle flags to its sign, which says "GRAND RE-OPENING SALE." Blue, red, and green wheelbarrows surround the entrance, with yellow and orange mums at their feet. The store is floating with shiny red helium balloons, and customers get a free five-gallon bucket and 20 percent off their purchase. Everything in the store is glistening, from the piles of colorful extension cords to the shiny metal washers, bolts, and screws in long rows of bins.

Ringgold Florist has relocated to the brick building Selina purchased. It belonged to another florist fifteen years before. It has wide front windows and a charming red screen door that bangs cheerily whenever anyone goes in or out. Bins of colored balloons are stacked inside on a cabinet. Nearby, spools of colorful ribbon and a helium tank are ready to add flair and bounce to the balloons.

Selina tells about a special moment during cleanup at the old building. One of her workers called her and told her she had to come and look at something. Near the telephones in the back, there had been a miscellaneous shelf holding beaded crosses. The tornado had hung one of the crosses on a nail in the wall by the phone jacks.

Now the new building is bristling with life and beauty. Behind the counter, wreaths hang full of flowers that breathe fall and Thanksgiving. Above the counter, candles hang from the ceiling in flower-decked glass jars. Selina touches a bowl of floating yellow rose heads on the counter.

"These are getting old," she says, testing one of the floating roses like a pianist touching keys. "They were just a little too full for bouquets, so we thought we'd at least put them out on the counter for people to enjoy."

"Selina, I hate to interrupt you," a worker comes from the back. "But there's a man on the phone who wants to put a twenty-word verse on his card." That's a few too many words to cram comfortably onto a florist card.

Selina laughs and picks up the phone to help the man clarify his request.

\\\\\\\\\\\\\\\\\\////////////

Across the top of Walter Jackson Chevrolet, a banner reads "OPEN FOR BUSINESS." Inside the showroom, everything glistens. Salesmen are still using temporary offices, but the remodeling and repairs will be done soon.

In an interview with *Dealer* magazine, Ryan's father expresses surprise at the support he received from customers and, more notably, from competitors.

"There was never a doubt in my mind that I was going to get back up and running once I got calls from my competitors," he says. "The people rallied around us in the community."[12]

\\\\\\\\\\\\\\\\\\////////////

United Methodist Church has suffered roof damage, but it still serves as an aid center.

Unlike many disaster workers, the United Methodist case workers are volunteers. They have volunteered for five months, seven days a week in the beginning, and now down to three days a week. Their office is tightly packed with computers, files, and copiers. Large maps of Ringgold and the entire state of Georgia are fastened to the wall with borders of heavy tape. News clippings are pinned to a bulletin board.

"FEMA came, did not conquer, and left," the *Catoosa Weekly* quotes local citizen Ruby Adams-Johnson in one of the clippings on the board.[13] The case workers came and stayed.

United Methodist also makes room in the crowded office for Cheryl Troyer, a secretary for Christian Aid Ministries' Disaster Response

Services. Cheryl finds a place for her computer and books in front of the Ringgold maps. She sleeps in a corner of a church storage room.

Cheryl is more than a secretary. As volunteers show up to build houses, Cheryl shows them which houses need to be built. She drives Amish workers and runs to get supplies. She oversees inventory counts, cleanup, and schedules. Some days she takes care of problems all day. But from her confidence and focus, her co-workers are assured that she knows what she's doing.

There in the United Methodist office, the conversation is purposeful and focused. Phones ring. Snatches of one-sided conversations mingle in the air. "I question whether she'll be able to get a loan . . . SBAs are hard to get anymore. He's the executor of the will, so he could force her off the land."

"Have I let anything drop yet?" case worker Jeanne Abdy teases in a busy moment. "You know what they say—if you want to get something done, find a busy woman."

Donna Greeson, another volunteer case manager, is transforming tragedy to triumph not only in Ringgold but also in her own backyard. Donna has lived in Ringgold for forty-three years. When the tornado came, she heard the roar, and her husband heard the trees popping.

Losing the trees in her yard was hard, but Donna has come up with a plan. Instead of the shady yard she had before, she is now going to have a sun and butterfly garden.

"It's my therapy these days," she says of working on the garden.

\\\\\\\\\\V///////

The fatalities are difficult to talk about. Fewer than ten people died as a result of the Catoosa County tornado, but each life leaves a large hole. Ringgold High School lost two of its students in the tornado. Mary Greene's former science teacher left a living legacy. "A lot of him is alive in us," she says. She remembers how he never simply sat in his chair during class. He would stand on a chair sometimes, or sit down and prop his feet dramatically on his desk. Of course, she will always remember walking with him around the track the day before the storm. She hasn't gone back yet to walk that track alone.

Mary feels people have learned from the tornado. She points to Anna as an example.

"I asked Anna when she took cover," Mary says. "She said, 'When the roof came off.'" Mary knows Anna will find refuge sooner the next time.

Mary continues, "For years, we've had tornado warnings, and people get complacent. If I could send a message to people, I'd tell them it doesn't hurt to take extra caution. Get a blanket, get a pillow, take cover before it's too late. You have to respect storms."

Mary is pretty sure she will always be fascinated with the weather. And she's not angry either.

"Who would I be angry at? I'm just thankful. I appreciate the people I live around. Maybe it's God's decision, waking us up to think. It has been an exhausting experience and I don't wish it on anyone." She pauses, wiping away tears. "I have days when I wish it had never happened to us. But then I go driving in the city, and there's a point on the hill where you look down on all those cars and all those subdivisions and streetlights, and I think, *What if the tornado had hit here?* I'm okay, and it's better that it hit where it hit."

Anna Montgomery senses a difference in people's attitudes. "We have a different outlook on things now," she says. "Before the tornado, people kept to themselves and minded their own business and didn't think about what was happening with their neighbors. You didn't think about what was going to happen tomorrow. Now, you think about these things. You want to help people out, you want to share, and you want to give—because you don't know what's going to happen tomorrow. We're alive! God kept us safe!" she asserts joyfully.

Anna watches as houses spring up in Ringgold by the end of the summer. A new house is going up for her and will be finished in December, in time for Christmas.

During the cleanup process, the FBI agent in charge of the case of Anna's exploded childhood home comes to check on her to see if she is all right. He also admits to her that there has been no progress on the case.

"It's okay," Anna says. She doesn't like to talk about it much, and she's not going to let it rule her life.

"I'm confident that God's going to do the right thing," she says. "God is good. He brought us through."

\\\\\\\\\\\V//////////

Mary Devitt begins to recover from her shingles and is able to work on the cleanup, but the task is overwhelming. She and Harry are grateful for all the volunteers. Mary remembers one day when there were thirty-six volunteers on her place at once and they had to be split into groups. She remembers a group of men and women, all sixty years old and older. She remembers a woman who brought her children to help one day.

While repairs are made at Harry and Mary's house, Brutus the Great Dane is allowed to live in a section of the house that is functioning as the garage. He stretches his expansive form on the rug. Mary is sure that he's planning to stay in this room for the rest of his life, and he will be shocked when he has to move. Outside, Muffy naps unconcernedly—just a pile of curls, but she's still the boss. A neighbor reported seeing Muffy escort Brutus down the long lane to the mailbox, as if showing him how far he's allowed to go.

One day Mary and a group of volunteers stop to pray on the deck. Brutus saunters over and shoulders his way into the middle of the prayer meeting. He lowers himself to the deck and crosses his feet reverently.

\\\\\\\\\\\V//////////

Jan is back at her coffee shop, which was not damaged. As customers pour sugar and creamer into their coffee, she hears story after story.

Her favorite memory is seeing Joy Cope again for the first time.

"Oh, I've just got to hug you!" Joy says.

"Are you okay?" Jan asks.

"It's okay, we're still alive, and we have our sons!" she says. Then she tells Jan the story. Had she and Dale not been at home to warn their sons, they may never have heard the tornado coming, because they were in their rooms with their headphones on. Joy's eyes still get big when she thinks about one of those bedrooms lying in pieces in the mountains.

\\\\\\\V////////

At Dale and Joy Cope's house site, there are smells of sawdust and varnish and the sounds of repair. The busy tools signify hope. Hammers pound, skill saws whine, and construction lingo flies around.

"We've got to untie this . . ."

"Did you say you wanted this scaffold in the back of the house?"

"Two and seven-eighths . . ."

There's a table piled with bananas and grapes and a cooler of bottled water and Gatorade for the workers. The volunteers have come from all over: Ohio, Vermont, Washington, Michigan, Missouri, and Virginia. College students from Texas are joined by a man from North Carolina who is eighty-six years old.

The October sun is shining. It shines on the watermelon plants that sprouted from seeds spit over the side of the balcony. Joy encouraged two fat fruits by watering them through the summer when the rains refused to come. Now one of the fat ones is gone, its tasty sweetness recently devoured. Standing in the shadows of the basement, Dale pauses from the construction work for a moment, thinking back over the drama of the summer.

"If I were to say one word . . ." He pauses. "Of all the things we've gone through . . . the single word would probably be *grace*." His voice falters, and it's clear that images are flashing through his mind. A ruined pharmacy on one end of town. A ruined home on the other. Looters. Looters again. Volunteers.

Dale speaks of God's grace as he looks around at his house crawling with out-of-state volunteers. He feels their love in concrete ways, and he is grateful. Although he's always been a believer in hard work and responsibility, Dale admits that in the aftermath of the tornado he just couldn't get going. How do you pick up the pieces of a house and a business both at once?

This is bigger than me, he realized. He recalls telling Joy that he just didn't think they would have the funds to finish repairing their home to its former state.

Then he met a volunteer who wanted to talk to him about his house.

"I have someone who wants to donate the roof to you," the man said.

A crew of volunteers from Maryland arrived and "happened" to have a roofer with them. They went right to work on the roof with the donated materials.

Dale and Joy accept their help with humility, knowing it is a gift from God. "If it weren't for God's grace, I would be a broken man. Grace is what we learn so much of with such an event," Dale shares.

"God gave us life, and we still have it," Joy says. "God left us here for a purpose, because we still have things to do."

Dale and Joy's story reflects the strength that God gives to people who accept His mysterious working in their splintered lives. His grace is shatterproof.

PART THREE:
JOPLIN, MISSOURI

208

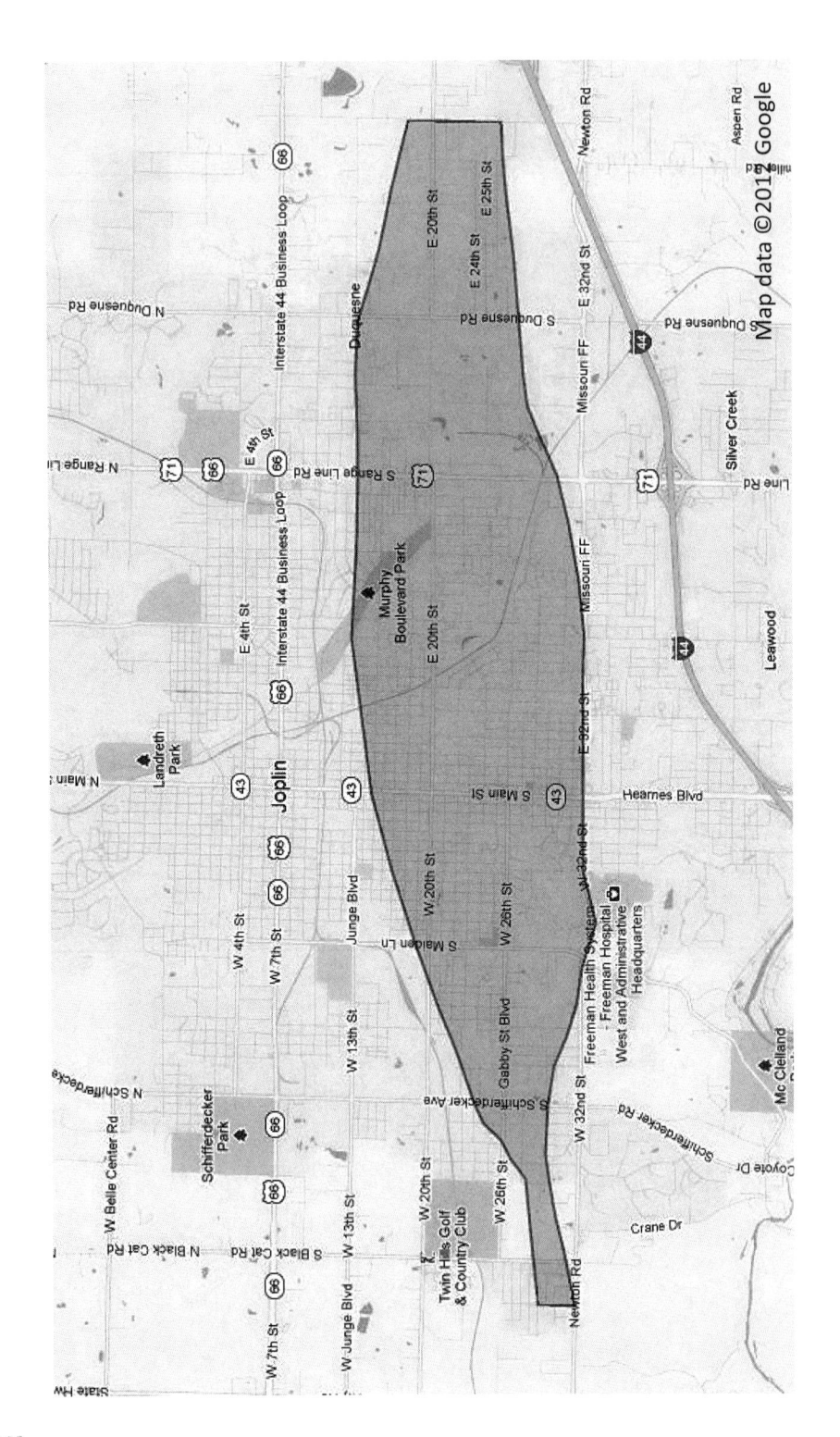

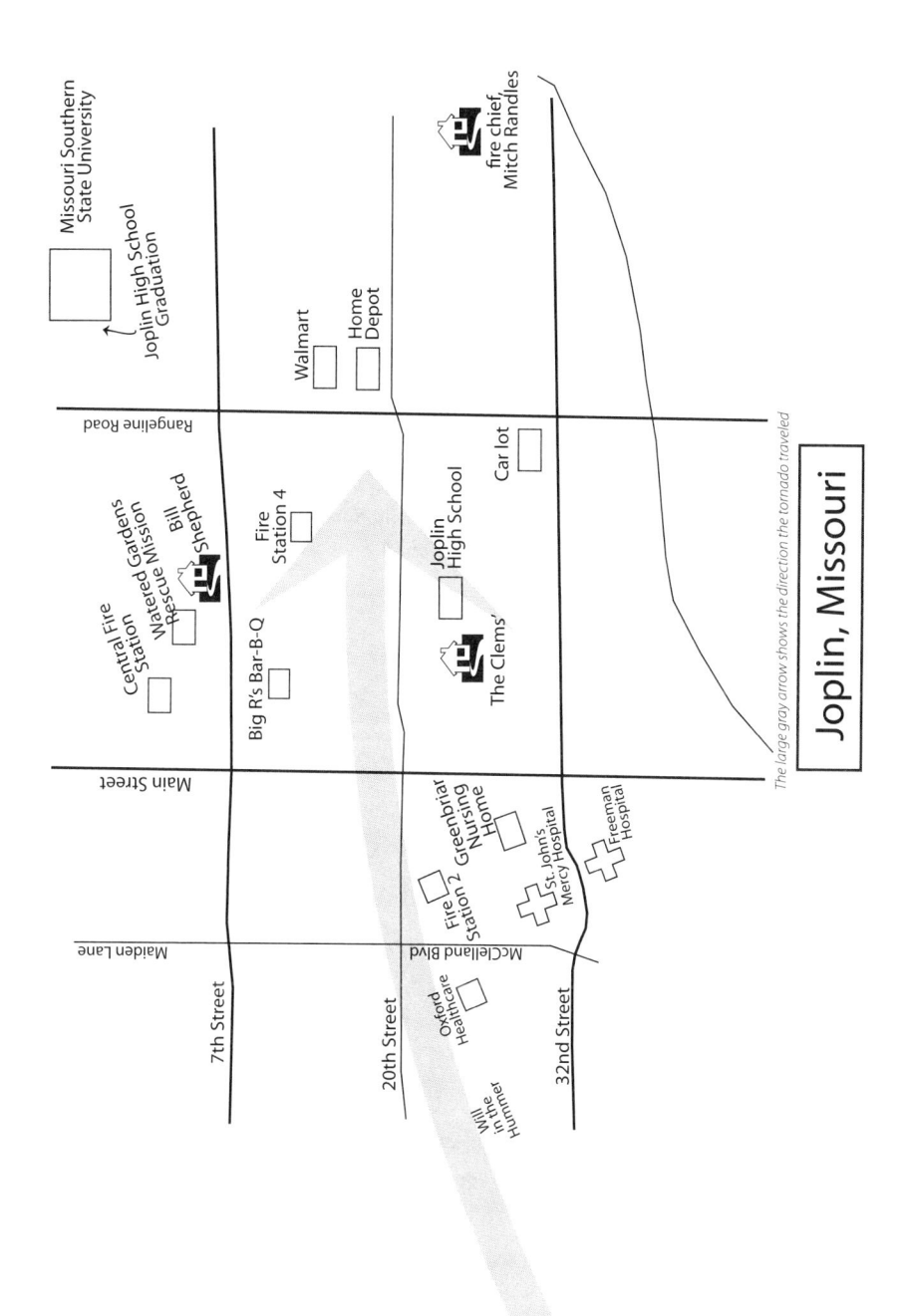

Frequently encountered characters

Residents:

—Will, Keegan, and Griffin, Joplin high school graduates
—Rob Hargis
—Lee and Tenika Clem and son Jackson, Minnesota Avenue
—Bill Shepherd, freelance photographer

Business Owners/Emergency Personnel:

—Mitch Randles, Joplin fire chief
—Keith Stammer, Emergency Management Agency (EMA), director
—Cheryl Fitch, Oxford HealthCare, vice-president
—Dennis Manley, St. John's Mercy Hospital, safety director
—James Whitford, Watered Gardens Gospel Rescue Mission, director
—Bob and Renee Denton, Freeman Hospital, directors of nursing
—Chris Newby, Action Missions, field coordinator

1
On the Grid

The combination of watches and warnings and the dissemination of information through schools and the media has seemingly eliminated the massive single-tornado death tolls that once plagued the United States.
—Thomas Grazulis, *The Tornado*

With 50,000 residents, Joplin is big enough to show up on the map, yet it's dwarfed by giant neighbors—Kansas City, St. Louis, and Oklahoma City—all several hundred miles away. Joplin's daytime population swells to 240,000.[1] Joplin is in the bottom left-hand corner of Missouri, just a few miles from where the Oklahoma/Kansas line meets Missouri. In fact, looking at a map of the United States, Joplin seems to be almost in the center. It would be hard to say in which part of the United States Joplin resides—north, south, east, or west.

Joplin is nestled in the crook of the interstate arm formed by I-44 and U.S. Highway 71, but these roads are outside the city. Joplin itself contains four main roads. Running east and west are 7th Street and 32nd Street. Main Street and Rangeline Road run north and south. The four roads create a perfect grid, as if the city's founders thrived on extreme tic-tac-toe.

Rangeline Road, the up and down crossbar on the right, hosts well-known chains such as Chick-fil-A, Home Depot, Walmart, and Aldi. Just before Rangeline hits I-44, several hotels gather at the bottom right of the tic-tac-toe grid.

Remains of a prairie mining town are still present on Main Street, the left bar in the grid. The farther north it goes, the higher the false fronts rise, climbing to ten stories. At the top, the Joplin Public Library, the *Joplin Globe* newspaper office, and the central fire department and police station pin the town in place.

The top horizontal bar is named 7th Street and crowns the main part of the city. It hosts another Walmart, only five miles from the Rangeline Road Walmart.

The bottom horizontal bar is 32nd Street, and it divides St. John's Mercy Hospital above it from Freeman Hospital below.

Most of the businesses in Joplin are posted along these four main roads. The people of Joplin live in thousands of houses, many of which occupy the center of the tic-tac-toe between 7th and 32nd. Joplin High School also sits in the center box of the grid along with the houses, some of them crowded fourteen or sixteen to a block.

Since it was an important lead- and zinc-mining town, Joplin already has a reputation for grit and grime, hard work and helpfulness. When a mine exploded in the old days, the other miners dropped what they were doing and banded together to free their trapped friends.

In 1908, a small tornado destroyed four mining plants. In 1971, one Missouri Southern State University student was killed in a large tornado that damaged more than a thousand Joplin buildings. No sirens sounded before the tornado touched down. In a small book called *The Joplin Tornado,* an article entitled "The Case for an Adequate Tornado Warning System" addresses the problem.[2] At that time, the National Weather Service was not as highly organized as it is today.

In 1973, three people were killed in a Joplin tornado. From there, Joplin's tornado history dulls for more than thirty-five years.[3]

The offices for Oxford HealthCare, a home health agency, sit on the west of town close to St. John's Mercy Hospital. Cheryl Fitch, vice-president of Oxford HealthCare, says the company barely needs a building because the real work with the patients happens in their homes. However, the Joplin office is a base for the employees. It's also home to heavy black filing cabinets filled with patient information.

During the seasons that are especially prone to dangerous weather, Oxford employees receive weather fliers with their payroll checks, reminding them to take safety steps. Oxford employees are also asked to always carry their Oxford picture ID with them. With the ID, they are able to reach patients even if police block roads.

With computer technology, the home office is able to tell where the employees are. Employees call in when they arrive at and leave a house, and the computer keeps track of everyone. Oxford drop boxes have been stationed all over Joplin to save employees extra miles. Employees turn in their timecards at these drop boxes.

Little Oxford cars, equipped with GPS, buzz all over Joplin and its back roads in all kinds of weather. Besides ice and snow, Cheryl worries about rain. Rain turns dirt roads to mud and floods low bridges.

In home healthcare there is no such thing as, "I can't get there today." Employees need to know that, no matter what the weather is like, they are responsible to get to their patients. Oxford owns several heavy-duty vehicles with deep traction tires, able to pick up stranded employees in the worst weather. New employees are also taught to ask each patient if they have a safe place in their home in the event of a tornado.[4]

St. John's Mercy, a 367-bed hospital, rises to nine stories just west of Main Street and north of 32nd Street on the tic-tac-toe grid. On several sides, large trees block the view of the hospital. Parking lots sprawl far across the grounds, promising a cardio warm-up for people walking to the entrance. Small trees and striped flowerbeds add to the peaceful atmosphere of the landscape. The backs of St. John's Mercy business cards announce the hospital's mission statement: "As the Sisters of Mercy before us, we bring to life the healing ministry of Jesus through our compassionate care and exceptional service."

A nine-story tower was built in the 1960s, and a six-story tower was built in the 1980s. St. John's has been part of the Joplin landscape for years and has opened its emergency room doors to victims of Joplin tornadoes in the past.

St. John's shiny red helicopter is home today, resting on its landing pad. When severe weather threatens, the helicopter pilot normally takes it up to the Joplin Regional Airport for safekeeping. St. John's is also equipped with a disaster trailer. In an emergency, patients can be treated in this trailer, which is equipped with communication technology.

Three weeks ago St. John's switched to computer charting. Nurses are still getting used to completing the right progress reports and selecting the proper files. Doctors have barely begun trying.

With the extra challenge of a new charting program, drills are annoying.

"Do you really want us to move the patients into the hall?" nurses ask Dennis Manley, St. John's safety director.

"Yes, I do," says Dennis.

When "Code Gray" is called over the speakers, nurses take action. They close drapes in the rooms and move patients into the halls, away from the windows. Even when it's not a drill, it's a lot of work to respond to yet another tornado forecast. The workers have some doubts about whether the drills are necessary, thinking that hospitals are big and strong enough to withstand most tornadoes.

A few blocks away, Greenbriar Nursing Home is practically in the shadow of St. John's. Like many nursing homes, Greenbriar seeks to provide a home-like atmosphere. Residents do not wear identification bracelets and are treated as though they are family members.

Joplin's central fire station looks down over the town from the top of the tic-tac-toe grid like a watchful father. It is located in the city administration building, which includes offices for both the fire department and emergency management. In the police department area, glass display cases house fire and police souvenirs, including a yellowed brochure labeled "Tornado Safety" on the bottom shelf of one case.

Joplin's fire trucks park in the spacious engine room. To the side of the trucks, uniforms lay ready for action. Fire coats and gear hang in red wire racks, where they can air out between uses.

Fire Chief Mitch Randles' office is a short walk down the hall from the engine room, past the firehouse kitchen. On the chief's desk, an industrial-sized mug of coffee is usually on duty beside his computer screen.

Chief Randles is forty-five years old. He has twenty years of experience, but he has been fire chief for only seven months. Like the rest of Joplin, he's been through many storms.

\\\\\\\\\\\\\\V/////////

In the basement beneath the central fire department, Keith Stammer manages the city's emergencies. Among many tasks, it's his job to decide when to set off the city's storm sirens. A large poster by his desk shows the locations of the twenty-five storm sirens and the section of the city that should hear that siren. The sirens are meant to warn people outside to take cover. For this reason, parks, golf courses, and walking trails are given extra coverage.

The National Weather Service radar base is just sixty miles away in Springfield. Keith watches their radar images on a screen in his office. He also chats online with other emergency personnel when the weather grows ominous.

Keith's office and the dispatch office share the basement with fire and police training rooms. The basement, built in 1967 during the heart of the Cold War, was meant to be a fallout shelter. For a while it was stocked with food and supplies to sustain over a hundred people for a month. Keith displays one of the orange Fallout Shelter signs in his basement as a memorial to those days.

No longer a nuclear shelter, the basement's three-foot-thick cement walls make it a great tornado shelter. In the event of a tornado warning, neither Keith nor the four dispatchers across the hall need to move.

At the bottom of town, just below 32nd Street, Freeman Hospital's steady gaze meets the eyes of its competitor, St. John's Mercy. Thirty-Second Street divides the two Joplin hospitals by a matter of yards, as well as placing them in separate counties. None of these distinctions are important to the average eye, which sees two hospitals across the street from each other.

Freeman Hospital has expanded upward with a blue and brown tower, only five years old. Its emergency department has forty-three rooms and a wide entrance with white pillars supporting the roof of the bay. Freeman's EMERGENCY/TRAUMA sign is red letters on white, opposite of St. John's.

Freeman Hospital has just completed a week of disaster training. Japan's massive earthquake has made American healthcare anxious, so this week's training focused on mass casualties. In the process, Freeman realizes their ham radios need to be repaired, which is done Friday night. Freeman seeks to be prepared to fulfill its mission statement: "Taking care of Joplin with our hearts and our hands."

The Stormy History of the National Weather Service

The Bureau Handoff

The National Weather Service began as the Weather Bureau in 1870, part of the War Department. It was the bureau's job to find out about the weather in the West and to send that information east before the air masses got there.

In 1891 the Weather Bureau became part of the Department of Agriculture. With telegraph use, forecasting became advanced beyond a race to beat the weather.

In the early 1900s the Weather Bureau made a law forbidding the use of the word *tornado,* so that their forecasts would not scare people. Although the ban ended in 1938, tornado warnings were not publicly forecasted until the 1950s.[5] There was no tornado warning for the 1947 storm in Woodward, Oklahoma.

The events surrounding the deadly 1925 Tri-State Tornado, which claimed 695 lives, were disturbing. Although the weather patterns on that day were nearly identical to another horrible tornado outbreak in 1884, no tornado forecast had been made.

In 1940 Franklin Roosevelt moved the Weather Bureau to the Department of Commerce.

Tornado research and forecasting took a turn for the better when a tornado hit an Oklahoma Air Force base and blew away $10 million of unprotected airplanes. When the army began research to protect its property, the public demanded to be warned as well.[6] In 1945 Congress gave the U.S. Weather Bureau permission to study thunderstorms. In 1946 Horace Byers started the Thunderstorm Project at the University of Chicago.[7]

Radar had improved dramatically during World War II and had

become commonplace for weather forecasters. But government weather stations did not yet have the new Doppler radar machines, which made radar more accessible. At this point, only specialized weathermen were able to make sense of the radar.

Forecasting Struggles at the Time of Joplin's 1973 Tornado

In 1970 the National Oceanic and Atmospheric Administration (NOAA) was created. The Weather Bureau became NOAA's National Weather Service, still part of the Department of Commerce.[8] A 1971 handout read, "The human eye is still the only positive detector of tornadoes."[9]

Gary England, a TV spokesman in Oklahoma in the 1970s, mocked the National Weather Service forecasts. "You could warn Henry down the street," he said, "but only if John's house blew away first."[10] Mr. England finally ordered his own Doppler unit, something the National Weather Service did not have yet. He ruined his relationship with them for good when he beat one of their forecasts by fifteen minutes. Other TV stations followed him. It became a contest to see who could predict weather first and most accurately.

Mistakes and Advances

In 1993 an Oklahoma channel announced a fearful warning to the people of Ryan, Oklahoma, based on the urgent update from a storm chaser in town. The next day, the channel writhed in embarrassment when they found out that there had actually been no tornado in Ryan.

The storm chaser was probably embarrassed too.[11] However, he redeemed himself in May of 2011 by shooting chilling footage of the Joplin tornado, which became a big hit on his website, www.twister-chasers.com. Probably no one remembers Ryan, Oklahoma, anymore.

The National Weather Service eventually got their own Doppler radar units and gained back the people's confidence. Today, although they issues warnings, each local government has its own policy about warning the people and sounding sirens.[12]

For some people, only the sirens stand between them and death. Unlike hurricanes or floods, which can often be seen for days in advance, there is no time for preparation in a tornado. Even if there were time, sandbags and storm windows won't help. As Richard Bedard says, the "best hope is for a timely alarm and a chance to escape."[13]

2
Life—As It Was

Keep in mind, I drive a Hummer. So really, I shouldn't have any reason to be scared.
—Will Norton, May 2009

"I'm graduating today!" Will Norton types into his Twitter account on Sunday, May 22, 2011. The message flashes out to the many followers drawn to Will's lightning wit, warm smile, and laughing eyes. Even though Will drives a charcoal Hummer and stands six foot three without his thick brown hair, he does not intimidate people.

The friends he graduates with today remember his open-invitation party, where he prepared his basement to host two hundred classmates. They know he is a young man of faith. He is not ashamed to share Bible verses on his Twitter account. Friday, May 20, 2011, Will typed, "But about that day or hour no one knows, not even the angels in heaven, nor the Son, but only the Father" (Matthew 24:36).

Today, he will say goodbye to his high school years and look ahead to college. Will enjoys documenting events and has been filming himself and his friends for years.

Two years ago, Will recorded his thoughts after a windy day. It was May 12, 2009.

> Keep in mind, I drive a Hummer. So really, I shouldn't have any reason to be scared. I turned onto the main road of my town, and the wind was so crazy. I was having trouble keeping my car on the road. This should not be happening. I drive a Hummer!
>
> It reminded me of the last tornado I was in—it was that type of feeling. Anyway, I made it safely home, and I think I'm just going to take a nap for the rest of my life, because I didn't die.
>
> I'm done. I. Am. Done. I'm never driving in [such] weather again. Ever.[14]

Two years later, in 2011, Will is still the gifted storyteller, sharing his love for every topic from his pets to his trip to Africa with the family. Will owns a parakeet, gerbils, sugar gliders, and fish.

There are three others in Will's family: his parents and his sister Sara. Will and his family are best friends, often going to Sonic or Starbucks for drinks after school. Will likes to order a grande white mocha.

Now on May 22, 2011, Will's thoughts are on graduation, not on his pets, Starbucks, or the weather. A tornado watch has been announced, but that is almost as common as a spring afternoon in Joplin.

"Hey, I don't have to be there for a little bit, but you should go on and get your seats," Will tells his parents and sister.

Sara and her parents drive across town to Missouri Southern State University where the Joplin High School graduation will be held. Will follows a little later.

When he arrives on campus, Will joins his friends, Keegan and Griffin, and the rest of the 450 graduates robed in maroon gowns. Will, Keegan, and Griffin, also known as the "Three Amigos," attended private schools before enrolling in Joplin High School. Although Keegan and Griffin play football,

Will doesn't enjoy sports. He plays some tennis, but it's not a passion.

Keegan has just graduated from EMT training. He wants to be an emergency room doctor, joining the medical field like most of his family. His father is the administrator for Newton County Ambulance. His mother is a nurse practitioner. Two of his sisters are ER techs, one at St. John's Mercy Hospital and one at Freeman Hospital.

As Joplin High School students cross the stage and hurl their caps in the air, their teachers cheer the maroon student body. They remember the good and bad times.

One teacher, Kristi McGowen, has just won the Golden Apple Award for excellence in teaching. She remembers how Will and his mother nominated her. She also remembers her photo in the newspaper after the award ceremony. As the students passed her picture around the classroom, she lamented that the camera shot made her arm look huge.

"But Mrs. McGowen," Will teased, "look how small it makes your body look!"[15]

\\\\\\\\\\V//////////

Rob Hargis moves silently along the familiar streets of his dog-walking route. A pit bull and a white Scottish terrier trot at his side. Neither dog belongs to Rob, but because he walks them, feeds them, and pets them more than anyone else in the house, they are attached to him. The pit bull in particular refuses to leave Rob's side.

Rob, a quiet man with a receding hair line, is caretaker not of just the dogs, but also of the others in the house. He's a natural in the kitchen. He answers the door.

These things are important in a house of drug users.

For fifteen years Rob fought off drug addiction. Finally he gave up the exhausting fight in 2005 and settled back into the habit, finding a place to stay with other addicts. He avoids the more dangerous drugs. But, like the others, he's addicted.

Sleep is not a priority here. Some occupants of the house stay awake for days at a time, depending on which drug they are pushing into their veins. Only Rob refuses to use IV drugs. He sleeps on the living room couch. The pit bull sleeps beside him.

Before Rob's arrival, food was not a priority either. Empty boxes from frozen meals littered the house.

Then Rob moved in and made fried chicken and mashed potatoes. The people of the house actually sat down at the table for a meal. Rob can also make salmon patties and grilled asparagus. He's a man they hope to keep for a long time.

\\\\\\\\\V/////////

Lee and Tenika Clem and their son Jackson live in the center of the tic-tac-toe. Their neighborhood, close to Joplin High School, is full of old and young residents, swimming pools, and backyard barbecues. The aroma of grilled chicken and barbecue sauce waft through the air often, inspiring others to pull out their grills. Fresh landscaping with flower gardens, patios, retaining walls, ivy, and hanging pots reveals the creative side of the residents. A neighbor weed-eating around a fence waves to another neighbor driving home from the grocery store. Children chase each other up and down the quiet streets on bikes, breaking the peace with their shrieks of laughter.

Jackson plays in the shade of giant oaks with Freya, the family's black Doberman, darting in and out of the blue and white house through its bright red door. All down Minnesota Avenue, the oak trees and their relatives keep people cool, shading the neat rows of houses.

Inside the Clems' house is a 150-year-old china hutch. This family heirloom is full of the teapots Tenika has collected since sixth grade. She thinks she has around thirty. There's a rabbit-shaped teapot from

Australia, brought across the ocean by Tenika's traveling grandparents. They have also brought her teapots from Germany, New Zealand, Ireland, Switzerland, Hawaii, and Holland.

Lee enjoys music and is singing in the living room as Tenika lays out clothes for the morning.

Four-year-old Jackson runs through the house from his mother to his father. Saturday night means it's almost Sunday morning, and Sunday morning means going to church. After spending the day with Freya and the oak trees, Jackson is fresh and clean after his bath.

"It's time for bed," Tenika says.

Tenika and Jackson join Lee, and the three of them sing a good-night song. Tenika is grateful that her youth pastor husband is able to be home tonight. She pats the blond head of her four-year-old son. As she sings, "They are weak, but He is strong. Yes, Jesus loves me," the nagging question creeps across her mind: *Jesus loves children, but . . . ?* She knows all the right answers to that question, but after years of battling depression, she is exhausted by the advice from books and friends.

Although her phone rings, her parents never call. The relationship is broken, and they simply don't talk. This is just one patch of the suffocating mental fog. Another piece of the fog is her weakness in stressful situations. She gets hysterical about small things. Although the fog is heavy sometimes, and lighter sometimes, it always comes back. The denser it grows, the less she is able to reach for the right sources of help.

\\\\\\\\\\\\\V//////////

A few blocks north of Lee and Tenika's house, Big R's Bar-B-Q restaurant advertises, "We have the meat you can't beat." A sign over the windowless wooden front door says, "Entrance to the best food in town." In the middle square of the tic-tac-toe, surrounded by churches and apartment buildings, Big R's is out of the typical restaurant zone.

The location fits, though, because the restaurant doesn't want to be like other restaurants. The doors have no glass and no knobs. The bathroom door locks only with a heavy metal latch. The bathroom sink is a replica of an old-fashioned wash basin. It looks so authentic that the drain at the bottom is surprising. In the dining room a rowboat with a stuffed man hangs upside down from the ceiling, the man's head dangling among the light fixtures that have aluminum pails as shades. Waitresses bring icy drinks in quart-sized glass jars.

In the entryway a cooler is stacked with cream pies. Big R's offers thirty-five kinds of cream pies. The artisan carefully rolls out the crust by hand, baking it in deep dish pie pans. Some pies are crowned with peanuts, some with caramel and cinnamon, some with marshmallows and chocolate chips, and some with candy bar pieces.

Just a few blocks from Big R's, Parr Hill Park invites diners full of barbecue to walk along its paths. There's a wooden bridge, clean cement paths, and playground equipment for the younger generation. Trees shade the park and anchor their roots in the banks beside the park's pond and waterways.

\\\\\\\\\\\V//////////

While the horizontal streets are neatly numbered in Joplin, starting with 1st Street in the north and working south to 32nd, many of the vertical streets are named after states. Tenika lives on Minnesota. Big R's is on the corner of Michigan and 15th.

A barber lives in the residential part of the grid with his wife and two children. He enjoys Starbucks and newspapers. He has a gift for words.

Like everyone else in Joplin, the barber and his family have been through storm warnings many times before. He hasn't lived in Joplin his entire life. He's lived in Las Vegas as well, near a large airport where he got used to the sound of planes constantly coming and going. On May 22 he has a heightened awareness of the weather but figures that in the end it will be no big deal, like always.

\\\\\\\\\\\V//////////

Freelance photographer Bill Shepherd loves nature and backpacking. He combines his passions, capturing wonderful photos of the Rocky Mountains and his home region in the Ozarks.

He lives with his wife and three-year-old son at the top of the tic-tac-toe grid, just east of the fire station. He hopes to start a studio in his home someday, displaying his photos.

\\\\\\\\\\\V//////////

Light streams into Watered Gardens Rescue Mission on Kentucky Street just a few blocks from the fire station. On the average morning, men cross the hardwood floor and fill their mugs at coffee pump pots. As they dump in sugar and creamer to taste, it's easy to think that this is a comfortable and cozy coffee shop, not a homeless shelter. A loaded bookcase against a brick wall adds to this feel, and evergreens outside the window wave at the men. Volunteers from local churches come in each morning with their arms full of omelet casseroles and breakfast rolls. James Whitford, the director, walks them in, smiling cheer. He stands taller than most of the men. He speaks with confidence, walking the fine boundary line between friendship and authority.

Inside, the volunteers set up shop in a small corner of the kitchen lined with little plastic boxes of spices and towers of canned green beans.

An older man comes up to James with a request.

"Only if you pray for us," James replies with a grin. Then he calls to the gathered bunch, "Carl's going to pray for us this morning." All heads bow and Carl prays.

Watered Gardens started as a day center, connecting Joplin's needy families to supplies such as furniture, shoes, and air conditioner units. The center then became a men's nighttime shelter as well, with homeless men arriving in the evenings and checking out in the mornings. The men sleep on the second floor, folding their sleeping bags in a storage area during the day. The shelter offers classes called "worthshops," aimed at helping people out of their cycles of despair and dependency. The shelter men make art notebooks for children in Ghana who are rescued from child slavery. Addicts are offered twelve-step programs similar to Alcoholics and Narcotics Anonymous.

The vision of James and his wife is to help the church serve the poor, thus benefiting both. The very name of the shelter is borrowed from Isaiah 58, which pictures the church as a watered garden, reaching out to those in need. The shelter has chapel services on Friday and Sunday, and Scripture plays from speakers above the front door.

3
Pressure Builds

Tornadoes break every rule that might allow scientists to build a complete explanation of their behavior.
—Michael Allaby, *Tornadoes*

May 22, 2011, is unlike April 27 in Hackleburg and Ringgold. No dire storm predictions are sounded for Joplin today. The *Joplin Globe* quotes Greg Carbin, a meteorologist from the Storm Prediction Center. "The forecast leading to the April 27 tornado outbreak across the Deep South and the forecast for Joplin on May 22 were fundamentally different.... It was a typical day in May for widespread severe weather. This day in May in Joplin is what you would expect. Nothing really stood out."[16]

As 5:00 p.m. draws near, hundreds of students receive their diplomas at Missouri Southern State University. Chief Randles' mind is not entirely on the graduation. He communicates with Keith Stammer, back in the cement basement under the fire department, by texting. They know the weather is a bit unstable, but Keith reports that the storms seem to dissipate before becoming full-blown. Neither of them feels uneasy.

At 5:09 p.m. the National Weather Service in Springfield issues a tornado warning for the area north of Joplin that appears at risk. Keith sees the supercell moving in on the radar screen from the west. He suspects it will go north of Joplin, maybe catching the top corner close to the airport. However, according to policy, the sirens are to be activated when any portion of the city is at risk for tornadic activity.

At 5:11 Keith crosses the hall and steps into the dispatch room. He moves to the spot in front of the black filing cabinets where he can lean over the divider and see everyone in the room.

"Spin 'em, log the time, and call Jasco." He says "spin 'em" because the sirens in Joplin are rotating sirens. He reminds them to log the time because pressing the button on the computer does not automatically log the time. He says "call Jasco," the sister 9-1-1 Call Center, so that both locations will be on the same page.

Those words are all it takes. The dispatchers hover over their computer mice and touch screens. All twenty-five of Joplin's rotating storm sirens begin their three-minute blaring into the Sunday evening air.

By 5:17 something ominous has taken place on the radar screen, where the storm clouds appear as masses of yellow and dark red. A smaller supercell to the south of the main storm is joining the larger storm. Also, the large storm appears to be inching to the right. If it keeps tipping, it will threaten not just the airport north of Joplin. It will be aimed for the heart of Joplin, the center of the grid.

Things are still not clear to the National Weather Service team at the Springfield office. Although they see rotation in the supercell, the classic tornado hook echo is not appearing. Still, the meteorologist on duty makes the call to issue the 5:17 warning for all of Joplin.

\\\\\\\\\\\\\\V///////////

At Missouri Southern State University, Chief Randles and the rest of the parents and families have been dismissed from the graduation. The ceremony has just ended. The chief hears Keith's 5:11 sirens wailing. At

5:17 he receives the National Weather Service tornado warning alert for the entire city.

He knows he needs to get into the fire station. He heads south out of the university campus. This will take him first to his home, where he will drop off his family. From there, he plans to take his normal route to work, heading into the center of Joplin on 20th Street. He will then turn north to the fire station.

He's talking to Keith and watching the radar on his phone.

The chief drives south past a College Station Donuts and Coffee, a Kum and Go gas station, and a number of other shops. The road home is straight ahead, but Chief Randles pulls into the right turning lane.

"Look, I'm going in," he says to his wife and two children. "You're just going to have to be bored and sit down at the fire station with me."

His wife does not say it at the time, but later she recalls the feeling too, right before they pulled up to 7th Street. "I got this feeling, 'I can't go home,'" she tells him later.

The 9-1-1 Call Center receives a complaint call. It's a woman, and she's frustrated that the sirens have been sounded when there is no storm activity. She thinks the sirens should be saved for the worst storms only, not for pleasant Sunday evenings like this one.

Keith is not laughing about the call. He's chatting online with storm spotters and watching the radar. Keith sees rotating activity west of Joplin, and he frowns. Certainly, the storm is not over; in fact, it doesn't seem to have arrived yet. But it's been nearly twenty minutes since the sirens were set off, and what if people think the danger is past?

\\\\\\\\\V/////////

Chief Randles and his family arrive at the station in a torrent of rain and hail. They rush inside through the painful attacks of hail and the stunning explosions of lightning. With the rest of the staff on duty, they hurry to the basement with the three-foot-thick walls.

As they usher everyone downstairs, Keith and Chief Randles gratefully talk face to face. They stare at the radar. Most of the tornadoes in Keith's experience have been EF0 or EF1. These tornadoes provide about seven to ten minutes of warning, and by the time the sirens have screamed for three minutes, the tornado has arrived. Besides the fact that there's usually no time to set the sirens a second time, there's a danger that people could think the second siren is an all-clear signal.

But this time feels different, and Keith and the chief think it would be better to err on the safe side. This one isn't going away. Keith steps back toward the cubicles of his office staff, busily clicking their computer keyboards. They see his lean face and graying hair re-appear by the black filing cabinets.

"Spin 'em, log the time, and call Jasco," he says again.

Click, click, click. They follow his unusual directions. The twenty-five rotating sirens begin to scream again, probably to the great annoyance of the caller who had complained earlier.

The time is 5:31.

Keith and Chief Randles also agree it's time to suspend responses at all fire stations.

"Tell everyone to take cover in their pre-assigned safety rooms," the chief announces. Any 9-1-1 calls that ring in will be held until the danger is past.

4
Code Gray

I will fly to places yet unseen.
—Joplin High School graduation song

As students emerge from Joplin High School's graduation, all 450 of them stand in a maroon line, waiting for the official copy of their diploma. As they wait, they snap photos of each other. Will, Keegan, and Griffin pose together.

The first round of tornado sirens is blaring in the background, but people are not worried. Although they try to get inside before bad weather, tornado sirens are normal springtime music in Joplin. Keegan's mom keeps snapping pictures.

Keegan's father, the administrator for Newton County Ambulance, is ready to go. He thinks he should get to his radio and make sure everything is going okay back at the ambulance station. Keegan's family leaves.

Will's mother and sister Sara leave, heading home for Will's graduation party. Lightning is beginning to shake the atmosphere. Will's father waits to ride with Will in the Hummer.

Keegan leaves in his white Chevy Avalanche about ten minutes after his family. He drops off a friend. He's not in a big hurry until his father calls.

"Get home," his dad says.

Keegan heads down Rangeline Road to his house south of Joplin. He cannot see the road well because of blinding wind and rain. He has lived in Joplin all his life, so he keeps going. Other drivers pull to the side of the road and park.

Don't pull over, don't pull over, something tells Keegan. He barrels on, sometimes hitting 80 miles per hour in the 45-miles-per-hour zone. Other times he has to slow down when he's unable even to see the brush guard on the front of the Avalanche. At home he finds his dad where he expects him—in the garage, watching the sky, waiting for his son.

\\\\\\\\\\V//////////

Sara and her mother hurry home down Rangeline Road, then across on 32nd Street to their home on the west side of town. Sara is driving her mom's car, hoping to get home before it hails. The sky is growing black. Sara is usually a careful driver, but now she's in a hurry.

She gets a call from her father. Will chose to turn onto 15th Street, heading west across town. Once across town, they will turn south to their home. Will is driving the Hummer, his father in the passenger's seat.

"We'll be home in about twenty minutes," he says. "Just make sure you open the garage door for us. We're going to pull right in."

As the sky grows even darker, Sara comes to a red light. For the first time in her life, she deliberately runs a red light. She races up the hill to their house. Like Keegan, she hits 80 miles per hour.

She pulls up to the garage. The power, which has gone out, flashes back on for just a moment. In that flash, the garage door opens and she drives in. After them, pieces of trees blow into the garage and crash onto her mother's car. The power quits, and the garage door is stuck open.

Again, Sara gets a call from her father.

"Dad, I can't open [your] garage door," she says. "Just pull up outside and run in. Mom's garage door won't close."

They are having trouble hearing each other.

"Dad, are you there, can you just answer me? Please, are you there? Are you there?"

Before the phone goes dead, Sara hears her father's voice, but he's not talking to her.

"Will, pull over, pull over. There's the tornado. Pull over!"

Sara hears tremendous wind, and glass shattering.

"Dad, can you hear me? Just tell me you're okay . . . I love you! Can you hear me?"

The phone is dead.

Will's mother calls her son's name as the tornado roars by close to their house. For some reason, she's calling only Will's name, not her husband's. Sara watches her. Why is she worried only about Will?[17]

\\\\\\\\V/////////

Cheryl Fitch is not at the home healthcare office on Sunday afternoon. She goes on a bike ride with her husband.

"It's almost too pretty today," she comments. It's easy to be suspicious in tornado season.

Many of her employees are with patients as the tornado sirens begin to wail.

At St. John's Mercy Hospital, it's a quiet evening with 183 patients. Sunday evenings tend to be slow, with few patients in surgery. One hip surgery is in progress in St. John's operating room.

Although severe weather is expected, St. John's helicopter pilot hears that the storm is expected to head north of town toward the airport. It will be safer to leave the chopper at home, he concludes.

When "Code Gray" is announced at St. John's right before shift change, no one is thrilled. However, personnel circle through the units, closing drapes and helping patients to the hall. The nurses continue to prepare medications, check blood sugars, and record interventions in the new computer charts. Although the power may go out in a storm, they know the hospital is equipped with a small army of backup generators.

It's 5:42.

In the emergency room, Dr. Kevin Kitka hears a security guard shout.

"Take cover! We are about to get hit by a tornado!"

Dr. Kitka rushes to a small doctor's office with no windows and dives under a desk.[18]

\\\\\\\\\\\V//////////

Next door at Greenbriar Nursing Home, employees have a harder time. It's suppertime, and many residents have dementia. How will they understand that they need to leave their rooms or their suppers and go to a safe place? Many of the residents cannot walk by themselves, and some can barely move at all. According to policy, measures will be taken to defend residents where they are if they cannot move. Moving at all is traumatic for some of them. Rapid response to tornado alarms is a nightmare.

\\\\\\\\\\\V//////////

Rob Hargis hails from northern Kansas and doesn't get excited about tornado warnings. When the warning comes, he is barefoot and wearing a T-shirt and a pair of jeans. He is about to shower and figures he will go ahead with his plans.

He glances out the window and notices the sky is a deep grayish green, something like an old moss-stained rock. He postpones the shower, but is reluctant to join the others in the basement. Two members of the house are looking out the back door.

"There it is!" one of them says, and they head for the basement.

Rob is standing at the top of the steps holding onto the basement door when the windows explode. He feels his ears begin to pop. He feels dirt in his hair. He dives down the stairs, joining seven other men and two dogs.

\\\\\\\\\\\\V//////////

It's Sunday afternoon, so Lee Clem, the youth pastor, has gone to church. Tenika and four-year-old Jackson are at home when they hear a tornado siren at 5:11. Tenika knows the weather is unstable, but in Missouri, storm sirens come around about as often as Sunday.

Just a few weeks before, Tenika had been thinking about tornadoes as she cleaned the green tile above their bathtub. She remembered her father telling her to hide in a bathtub if a tornado comes. Thinking about that, she had asked Lee where he thought it would be best to hide. He said that in their house, the closet would be the best option. At the time, Tenika filed the thought in her brain like a fire escape plan: good to know, but unlikely to ever be needed.

Now, three weeks later, it's 5:31, and Tenika hears a second siren.

A second siren is *not* a weekly occurrence. Tenika slips on her tennis shoes and takes Jackson's hand.

"Come on, honey, let's go," she says evenly. She can't believe the calm voice she hears is her own.

Tenika and Jackson slip into the closet. Freya, the black Doberman, chooses the green bathroom.

"What are we doing?" Jackson asks.

Tenika begins singing, "Jesus Loves Me."

They finish the song, and Tenika quotes Scripture and prays.

"Jesus is my Rock and my Salvation," she breathes into her son's blond hair.

\\\\\\\\\\\\V//////////

The barber takes a forgotten backpack to the next-door neighbor's child. That's when he hears the thunder that won't quit. It seems to come and go, like the sounds he remembers hearing by the Las Vegas airport—planes taking off and landing in a series.

In shock, he hurries his family toward their closets. *I think we're going to die,* he realizes. The two children fit in one closet, and he and his wife fit in the other, and all he can think is, *I hope I put them in the right closet.* He's not afraid to die, but he hopes he made the right choice for his children.

\\\\\\\\\\\V/////////

Photographer Bill Shepherd is home with his wife and three-year-old son. When the sirens sound at 5:11, the three of them head for the basement. The minutes pass, and Bill and his wife head back upstairs. They hear the second siren. Bill steps out onto the porch.

"Get back down into the basement!" says his wife. She returns to the basement with their son.

Still upstairs, Bill sees horror in the air.

"Hon, there's the tornado!" he says. "Prepare for a direct hit!"

He quickly joins his family in the basement.

\\\\\\\\\\\V/////////

Big R's Bar-B-Q is closed on Sundays, so the building is empty. To the east, the business district on Rangeline Road is open with the exception of Chick-fil-A, also closed on Sundays. New graduates are going out for supper. People are running errands.

James, the director of Watered Gardens Rescue Mission, is at home when the weather reports start. He hears one that gets his attention. It's a live reporter on scene, and everything is crackling, the static breaking up the sound.

"There's debris raining from the sky," he says.

James pauses and stares at the radio as if it should answer questions. Then he gets into his truck to head to the shelter. He has to see if the men are okay.

Storm Chasers

"Few life experiences can compare with the anticipation of a chaser while standing in the path of a big storm in the gusty inflow of warm, moist gulf wind sweeping up into a lowering, darkening cloud base, grumbling with thunder as a great engine begins to turn."[19]

When the sirens wail, most people will take cover. Those who stay to see the funnel know they might sacrifice their lives. A Kansas farmer named Will Keller is one of the few people who lived to tell about his close-up view of a funnel. He is quoted by many tornado books as the man who saw "right into the heart of the tornado," as it lifted up just in time to avoid hitting him.[20]

Then there are storm chasers. These are the people who head toward the storm instead of away from it. One man describes tornado chasing as a "deep human yearning—or is it just a male yearning?—to get very, very close to something that could kill you."[21]

Most people feel a deep human alarm about anyone intentionally endangering his own life. But most of the scientific storm chasers, the ones who travel thousands of miles from April to June, are outfitted with equipment needed to stay alive. Their storm-chasing trucks have been dented by giant hail, but they are built from the sturdiest materials.[22] They are loaded with devices to help them record the phenomena they are chasing. Four or five computers with Internet access and radar screens crowd inside the vehicles. There might be some paper maps too, just in case the electronics fail. After all, electronics cannot be depended upon at all times. Even when the devices are working, the human eye is the best tool.[23]

Some chasers are researchers, slipping weather instruments into the path of the tornado. One of the reasons that scientists chase tornadoes is because Doppler radar cannot read what is happening in the lowest thirty feet of the storm. This section, the dangerous "bear's cage," is the least understood portion of the tornado. "Why does this lower region matter? Because that's where we all live," say the storm chasers.[24]

The men featured in *National Geographic*'s April 2004 article dropped 45-pound "turtles" into the path of tornadoes. These turtles have weather instruments to measure speed and direction of wind, air pressure, humidity, and temperature. It was with just such a turtle that a 100-millibar pressure drop was discovered inside a tornado. In common terms, this drop is "like stepping in an elevator and hurtling up a thousand feet in ten seconds."

Other chasers just want the thrill of seeing how close they can get to something dangerous. Some are tourists who pay for "tornado safaris" that take them as close to tornadoes as possible.[25] People who are bored with normal life describe a super-charged aliveness out on the Great Plains when faced with the question, not of whether they have money to pay their bills, but of whether they will live or die—and if they die, how?

Even the storm chasers admit this. "Chasing tornadoes is like hunting grizzlies. You want to get close, but not on the same side of the river."[26]

HACKLEBURG, ALABAMA

Dr. Morrow and his staff treated patients from a temporary clinic in a semitrailer and two army tents.

This sign spoke volumes about the resilience of the victims.

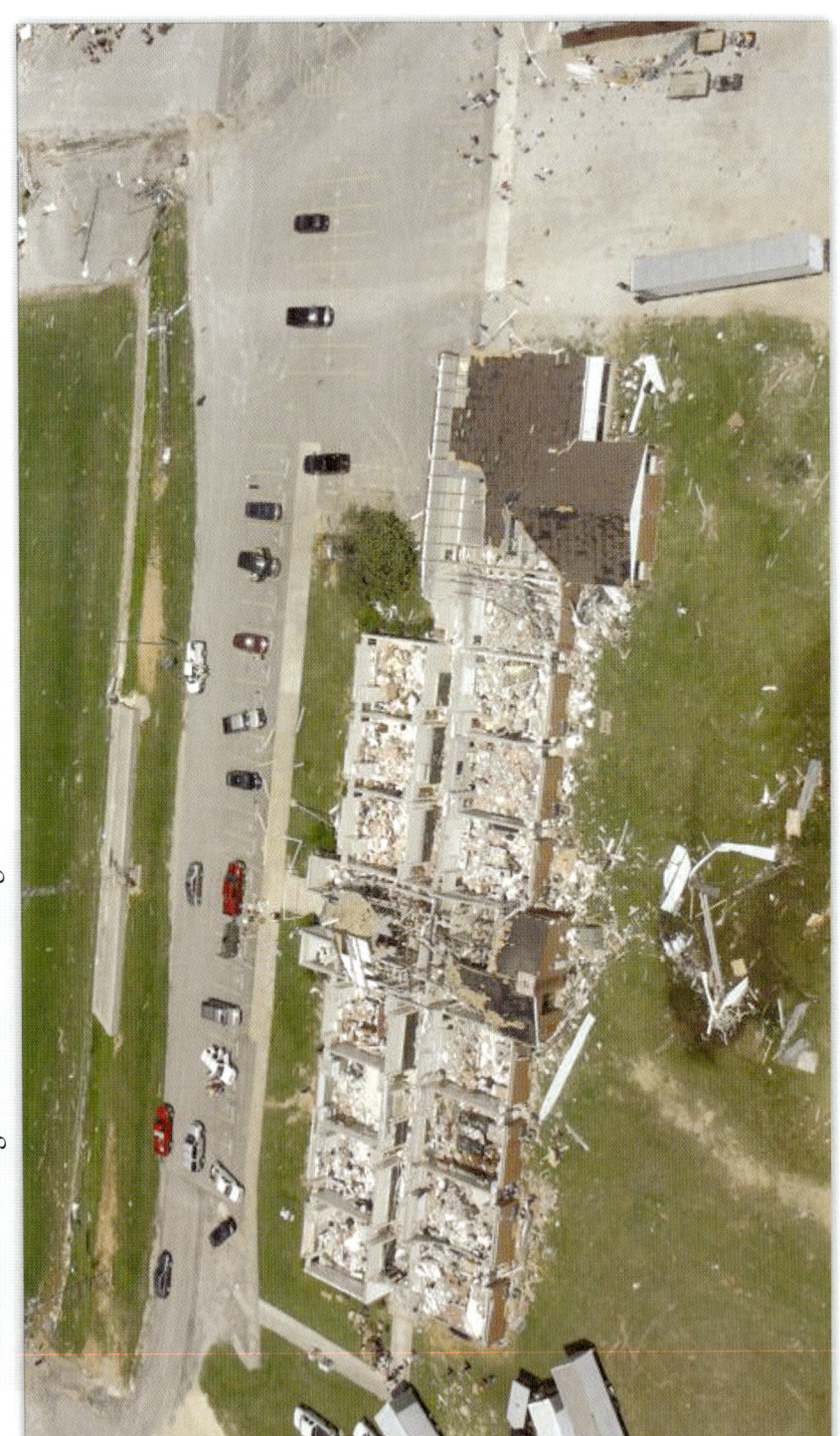

The demolished high school in Hackleburg.

Before the F5 tornado: Leah Philips' house.

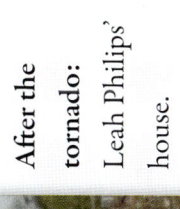

After the tornado: Leah Philips' house.

The Hackleburg Piggly-Wiggly store (also known as "The Pig") after the F5 tornado.

The glass door of the fire department building.

The Hackleburg Police Department building.

One landmark that did not change in Hackleburg.

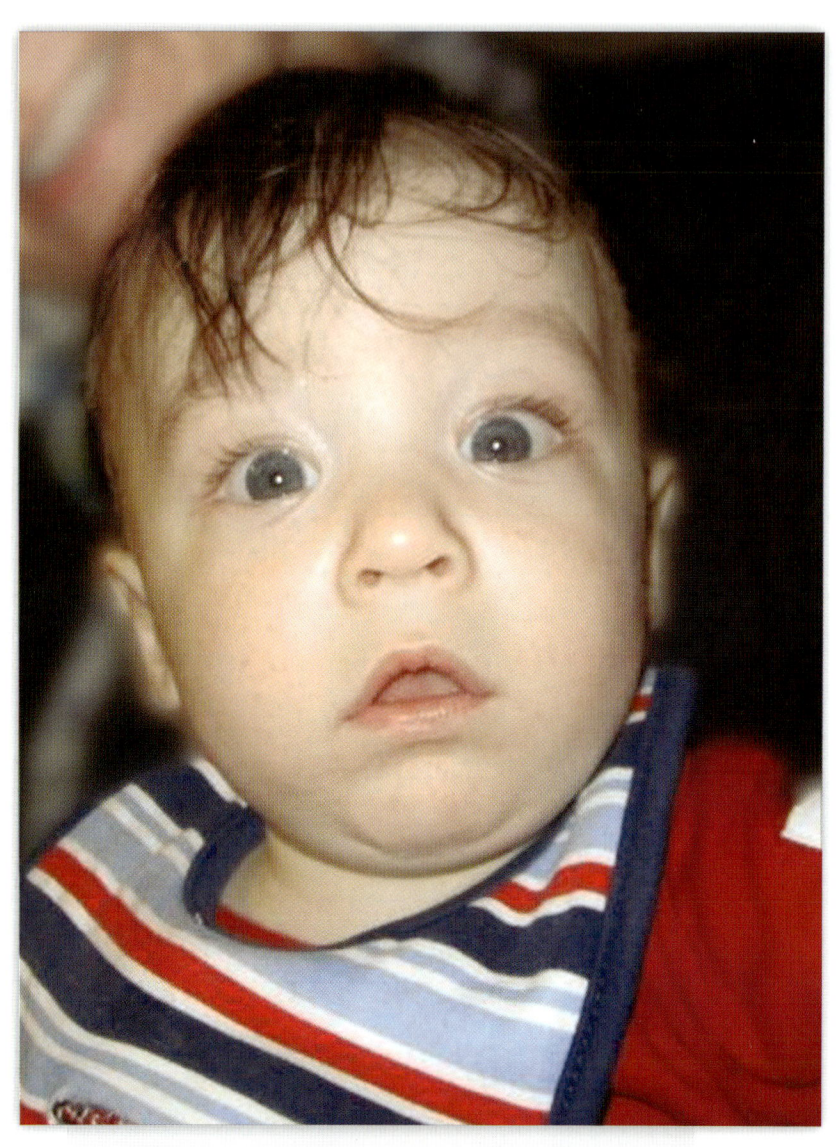

Seven-month-old Mitchell survived the tornado, while his mother did not.

BEFORE

The Wrangler warehouse, before and after the tornado.

AFTER

A pair of Wrangler jeans found months after the storm.

RINGGOLD, GEORGIA

The F4 tornado left a barren path on the ridge rising above Cherokee Valley.

Remains in Ringgold.

A devastating scene in Ringgold, Georgia.

On left, weather enthusiast Mary Greene, with her sister and new house in Ringgold, Georgia.

JOPLIN, MISSOURI

The 2011 tornado moved St. John's Mercy Hospital, a nine-story building, several inches off its foundation.

Lonely closets left standing.

Disaster in the closet.

Emergency relief work started soon after the F5 storm.

The "blue fish" sketched originally by Chief Randles while on a chopper in the air. With night vision goggles, he and another city leader stared down at the path of destruction through the rain.

The Hampshire Terrace Apartments in downtown Joplin, MO, along 20th Street at 7:01 p.m., May 22, 2011. A building burns in the background as the sun shines through the smoke.

© B. W. Shepherd/Ozarkjournalist

The Joplin High School, where Will Norton attended.

Photo taken at 6:28 a.m. on May 23, 2011: The residential neighborhood directly across from St. John's Hospital along 26th Street lay in total destruction the morning after the tornado.

© B. W. Shepherd/Ozarkjournalist

Keith Stammer, director of Emergency Management Agency (EMA), in his basement office.

Rob Hargis at Watered Gardens Rescue Mission.

Shattered world, resilient hearts.

5
The Vacuum Cleaner

Though most tornadoes last fifteen minutes or less, the phenomenal wind speeds and pressures at the center of the cyclone make it a place where the laws of physics of ordinary Earth life seem to be repealed.
—Stefan Bechtel and Tim Samaras, *Tornado Hunter*

At 5:41 the National Weather Service states, "NUMEROUS REPORTS OF TORNADO ON THE GROUND WEST OF JOPLIN AND POWER FLASHES."[27] This damage is still off the tic-tac-toe grid, about two miles away from Joplin's hospitals.

Several storm chasers catch the formation of the tornado on camera. Looking through the camera, the sky in front of them seems to be split in half horizontally, with a dark gray cloud above and clear sky beneath. This bank of ashy gray kicks pieces of itself down into the clear sky. Powerful lightning electrocutes the air again and again. Then the gray pieces explode and multiply.

This sudden mass of darkness, still framed by a clear background, reaches the ground and tears across it like a giant sweeper head across the carpet of southwest Missouri. It even sounds like a giant vacuum cleaner. "Listen to it!" a man behind the camera says. Even the lightning ripping through its middle doesn't faze this sucking monster that no one can turn off.

A storm-chasing husband and wife drive with the storm. Besides watching out the window, they watch the radar screen inside their van.

They see a giant cloud forming, sprinkling debris. They meet two policemen at the corner of 7th Street and Black Cat Road. The husband rolls down his window and tells them what he's seeing.

"The tornadoes are trying to come down right here!" he says. "Get the sirens going!" Minutes later they hear the second sirens screaming through the howling wind, set off at Keith Stammer's command.

The husband drives while his wife captures footage of the giant cloud and begs him to be safe. The wind and rain swirl around them. Light objects whip past their windshield. Lightning explodes in the wild gloom. Each bolt is a brutal surprise, a blast of untamable power going wild, trying to even out the charges in the terrible supercell. Hardened storm chasers though they are, the couple's tension rises as they watch destruction break over the city of 50,000.

"It's tearing up the entire city of Joplin on the south side right now," the husband reports urgently into his radio. "It's a massive tornado doing massive destruction."[28]

\\\\\\\\\\\V//////////

The tornado's mouth is still narrow when it descends on Schifferdecker Road like a vacuum cleaner in a toy box. It zips right toward the spot of road where Will has just pulled over about a block from home.

It snatches the Hummer. The driver's side window explodes. As the other windows shatter and the sunroof rips away, Will and his father wrap their arms around each other. Will begins to shout Scripture verses.

Then his seat belt breaks.

"I love you!" his father shouts. He's hanging on to his son with all his might. His bicep tears. His other forearm breaks.

Will is sucked through the hole where the sunroof was.

When the tornado spits the heavy vehicle out of the storm, crumpled like a cheap toy, Will has disappeared. His father is alone, a large section of skin peeled back across his head.

\\\\\\\\\\\\V/////////

The tornado rushes over the Oxford HealthCare office building, ripping off its beautiful new roof and scattering the black filing cabinets.

Roaring into St. John's Mercy parking lot, the blast piles cars against the building like a bank of fall leaves. Dr. Kitka's car disappears. The tornado pounds against the hospital windows, breaking out the glass. On the fifth floor psychiatric unit, the shatterproof glass windows are the only ones that hold.

The shrieking mass peels off roofing material and whirls ceiling tiles out of their place. It blows doors off their hinges and piles debris against the doors that hold. It blasts debris into the hallways, turning the patients' safe place into a wind tunnel. Nurses dive on top of patients and under stretchers. Patients curl under blankets.

The tornado twists the helicopter and grinds off its shine. It demolishes the disaster response trailer, taking tires and trailer pieces with it and throwing them into a basement two blocks away.

Gas and sewer pipes break. The hospital sprinklers turn on. The tornado destroys the hospital's backup generators, removing all electric power. It shuts off the emergency lighting in the stairwells. In the operating room, the hip surgery is plunged into darkness, and water begins to rise around the ankles of the surgery staff.

Under the desk in the ER, Dr. Kitka feels a terrible force slam into the building. He hears screams, glass shattering, and light bulbs popping. Water lines break and water pours into the room. The ceiling caves in. Dr. Kitka feels a tight pressure in his head.[29]

Oxygen tanks begin to spew into the air. When the tornado finally leaves, the 367-bed hospital has moved 4 inches off its foundation.[30]

The tornado lunges on, just far enough north to miss a direct hit on Freeman Hospital, where patients are also gathered in the halls. Roofing is damaged at Freeman, however, allowing rain to seep in.

Roaring on, the tornado hits Greenbriar, where a nursing assistant leans over two elderly people, protecting them with his body. The tornado tosses cars into the nursing home. The nursing assistant and the two residents are crushed.

\\\\\\\\\\\\V//////////

The tornado reaches Rob and his seven friends and two dogs in the basement of the group house. As he stands on the basement steps with dirt in his hair, Rob hears the terrifying vacuum and hears the house collapsing over their heads.

It's just like my addiction, Rob realizes in the midst of the roar and the flying dirt and the shattering glass and the popping pressure in his ears. *The roof and my drug addiction—they're both coming down over my head, and I have to escape.*

\\\\\\\\\\\\V//////////

The tornado comes to Tenika's closet, where she clutches her son Jackson and shouts Bible verses and prayers. It rips into the 150-year-old wooden china hutch, splitting it open. It grabs Tenika's teapots. The rabbit teapot from Australia blends with all the rest, spraying the whirlwind with sparkling colors.

The tornado roars against the green bathroom, yanking it off its foundation and dropping it into the living room, filling with debris the bathtub that Tenika might have chosen to hide in but for her husband's recent suggestion.

Tenika hears shattering and snapping, and the *click-click-click* of a train on the tracks, a train that must be charging right over their house.

Tenika should be hysterical and sobbing, but she's not.

6
Snapshots

It seems inevitable, however, that a killer tornado with a death toll of one hundred or more people will strike the United States sometime in the future.
—Thomas Grazulis, *The Tornado*

At Joplin High School, security cameras above entrance doors capture ceiling tiles breaking loose. Glass doors burst open and debris pours in. Cafeteria tables shudder and scatter. Then the view dulls to a fuzzy haze of white as the cameras themselves are overcome.

The massive tornado barges in on the barber and his wife and children hiding in their closets. They hear glass breaking and heavy hail, and something goes *boom-boom-boom;* then faster, *boomboom-boomboom-boomboom. Is this machine gun fire? It must be bricks,* he thinks grimly. He feels vibrating, as if the whole house is getting an electric massage.

The machine gun fire in his mind is just one sentence: *Are the children okay? Are the children okay? Are the children okay?* Shouting to them is so out of the question that he doesn't even consider it. Even if he had the loudest voice in the country, he knows they could not possibly hear him above this deafening din.

The noise, the vibrating brain overload, goes on and on.

"It didn't just seem long, it *was* long," he says.

The closet where he and his wife are clutching each other begins to collapse, but a chest of drawers smashes against the closet door, changing the airflow, and the walls remain standing.

\\\\\\\\\\\\V/////////

As the wind howls over the empty Chick-fil-A, the curly red letters that spell its name slide off the restaurant, still attached to bricks. The A breaks off the end and lands in another pile of bricks. Inside, the arching sign announcing, "Dessert at Chick-fil-A: how sweet it is," stands strong over a dining area churning with mangled chairs, silvery duct work, insulation, and muddy booths. The gray letters that say "HOME OF THE ORIGINAL CHICKEN SANDWICH" blur under clouds of sticky dust.

\\\\\\\\\\\\V/////////

Heroes emerge in their own homes and at businesses. What St. John's nurses and Greenbriar Nursing Home's staff began, the rest of Joplin continues. A man sacrifices his life for his wife by leaping on top of her. At Pizza Hut, an employee takes people to safety in a cooler and then leaves the safe room to find a bungee strap to fasten the door. He never makes it back.

At Home Depot, an employee is leading two girls to safety when a wall crashes down on him. A customer at Walmart sees a baby in a car seat and dives on top of it. Steel beams and shelves rain down on them, but both survive.[31]

\\\\\\\\\\\\V/////////

The tornado rages straight through the corridor of town between 7th Street and 32nd Street. Had Chief Randles been driving toward work on 20th Street, he would have had a head-on collision with the monster.

Oxford HealthCare boxes are scattered throughout town, the employee time cards whirling into the storm. All across town, Oxford employees hide with their patients. No employees leave their patients.

\\\\\\\\\\V//////////

One Joplin family eats premium fast food at Culver's this Sunday afternoon. After leaving the world of ButterBurgers and caramel cashew sundaes, they head home. They hear sirens, but everything looks clear, and they stop at the Kum and Go for gas. That's when the golf-ball-sized hail starts.

"We've got to get home," the father yells, pulling out of the station without filling up.

At home, they park and run into the house. The back door is swinging wildly, and they try to shut it four times. The last thing they see as they run for hiding is sheet metal the size of a U-haul landing in a tree. In the background is a gray-brown pincushion wall that wasn't there before, half as wide as the city and stuck full of debris, roaring toward them. It doesn't just sound like a freight train; it sounds like a freight train in a megaphone.

A tree falls on their house, and a 2 x 4 impales the driver's side windshield of the vehicle they just parked. The pressure is intense. Ears are popping as if they were climbing a mountain or riding a roller coaster. The mother feels like her eardrums are about to burst, and it's hard to breathe. They are crouching on the floor when their child begins to vomit. The mother grabs for towels. Later she learns that children up and down their block vomited during the tornado. She herself battles a migraine the next day from the massive pressure on her brain.

\\\\\\\\\\V//////////

The tornado meets a young girl driving in Joplin. When the giant vacuum blows out her vehicle's windows, she decides it's time to unbuckle and find a ditch. But before she can take her seat belt off, the force sucks her *out* of the seat belt and into the street. Down the street she careens, like just a piece of debris or brush. But unlike many people whose stories begin this way, she does not die.

\\\\\\\\\V////////

When the tornado did its disappearing act, it left behind itself a path one-half to three-quarter mile wide and approximately thirteen miles long.[32] It was a slow tornado, hugging the ground for thirty-two minutes. With winds of over 200 miles per hour, it came to be classified as the rarest of all tornadoes, an EF5. It became the deadliest U.S. tornado since modern record-keeping began in 1950.[33] At the final count several months afterward, 161 people are found to have been killed due to either the tornado itself or related injuries.[34]

Killer Tornado

In his 2001 book, *The Tornado,* Thomas P. Grazulis makes this statement in his closing chapter:

> The last tornado that killed one hundred people was at Flint, Michigan, in 1953, the first full year of tornado forecasting. Since that time the combination of watches and warnings and the dissemination of information through schools and the media has seemingly eliminated the massive single-tornado death tolls that once plagued the United States.

Grazulis looks at history and concludes that the deadly single tornado might not be gone forever. He adds, "It seems inevitable, however, that a killer tornado with a death toll of one hundred or more people will strike the United States sometime in the future."[35]

7
After 5:41 P.M.

Our world changed from color to black-and-white in just five minutes.
—Joplin barber

Back at home, Sara and her mother don't know what to do. Mrs. Norton isn't about to let Sara out of the house, but other people volunteer to go looking for Will and Mr. Norton. Many of those who try get turned back by blocked roads or flat tires.

Finally, Sara's aunt and uncle recognize the remains of the charcoal Hummer. They quietly pull the registration papers out of the glove compartment. The rest of the vehicle is empty. They snap some photos and then return to the Norton home.

"They couldn't have survived that," they say.

Despite their tears, Sara and her mother head to Freeman Hospital with their support group. They have to find out for sure.

The hospital is chaotic, lined with patients with broken bones and peeled skin. They go to the desk and give the names of the two people they are seeking.

"They were driving, and they're not in their car," they explain.

The hospital staff tells them that many patients have arrived unconscious, without identification. Also, many of the patients have been transferred to other hospitals. However, they ask Sara and her mother to wait in the chapel and promise to tell them if anything is discovered.

Without much confidence but with nothing else to do, they go to the chapel. An hour later a volunteer comes to them with the news that Mr. Norton is in the operating room.

They both feel a rush of relief, but the volunteer goes on.

"But he kept saying that your son's dead," she says, looking at Sara's mother.

When they finally get to see Mr. Norton, he has one question.

"Where's Will?"

"We can't find him," Sara tells him. "We're looking really hard."

"I don't think he made it," her father replies. "I saw him fly out the sunroof."

Sara tries to convince her dad and herself. "Will could have been picked up by an ambulance. He could be at a hospital in Springfield, Kansas City, or Tulsa. There is no proof that he's dead."

\\\\\\\\\\\V////////

Rob emerges barefoot from the basement. His head begins to swim. Usually he can't see the houses across the road because of all the trees. Now everything is flat, and there are no trees. The oaks that were there moments ago are gone, and in their place are white splintered stumps.

I need shoes, he thinks. He picks his way toward what used to be the living room, where he slept on the couch, but he can't find his shoes. He looks out toward the east, and he can see Rangeline Road thirty blocks away—something he could never have seen before.

Dazed and overloaded, he heads down the street, not sure where he is going. He checks on a family he knows. They are okay. He looks around. He can't choke back the sobs that wrench his body, and now the tears are coming from the sky too. Everything is getting soaked, the road is full of power lines and glass, and Rob is walking down it barefoot. He smells natural gas. He sees water shooting twenty feet in the air from broken hydrants. He tears his eyes away from the horror and looks away, only to see something worse.

He meets a man, dazed and bug-eyed. "I just saw a dead body," the man gasps.

Rob keeps going, and he turns west, still stepping over the lines and around sharp objects. He's walked the dogs through here all the time, but he's not sure where he is now. The landmarks are gone; everything is changed. Nothing is normal.

He meets someone else.

"You need to find shoes," the person says, staring at Rob's bare feet.

It is almost surprising that someone notices. Most of the people Rob meets are walking in a daze, noticing nothing. Their faces are blank. He sees an elderly man with a walker, picking his way through the rubble, pale and expressionless.

Rob turns south and walks down the yellow line of this larger street. He passes a couple with two boys. One of them is clutching a teddy bear.

"I know he's dead. I know he's dead," the boy is saying over and over, and none of the family even looks at Rob.

Someone is driving a car around carefully. "Are you all right?" he asks Rob.

Rob shakes his head, trying to clear his thoughts. His sister's house is the place to go.

"Can you take me south to 15th Street?" Rob asks.

He forgets that 15th Street isn't south; it's north.

But he gets a ride.

When the soundtrack of fear ends, Tenika looks into the face of her son. "We're alive!" she says.

She feels deep joy surging through her.

She hears whimpering. *Freya is alive!* Tenika peers out the closet door carefully. She sees the black Doberman, so she slips out and brings her into the closet. Freya's fur is matted and powdered with gray, but she's okay.

In a daze she picks up her son, holding him tightly, and steps out of the closet. Freya refuses to leave the closet.

Everything is dripping and the bedroom certainly doesn't look safe. She takes a step forward, and part of the bedroom roof collapses on the bed.

She stops. She shakes her head in disbelief. The world is suddenly a place with different rules, a place she's never been before, a place where roofs fall in on beds. She heads outside.

The world outside is even more foreign. Tenika is glad for the tennis shoes on her feet as she stares at the rubbish: broken lumber, her yellow broom, Jackson's toy car, concrete, glass, and insulation. What was a street of beautiful old shade trees moments ago is now a petrified toothpick forest. Two of the giant front yard oaks have been pulled out of the ground, their roots where their branches were minutes before.

Tenika looks to the west and sees the hospital, something she's never seen from her house before. She looks north and sees the mangled high school. In disbelief, she asks herself what kind of world twists steel like pretzels and knots tin around trees.

Her ears are worse messengers than her eyes. The houses are making noises—children screaming, people crying for help. She smells natural gas and sees flames. Somewhere houses catch fire. She shivers in horror.

"Are you okay?" asks a man, someone she doesn't know.

"Yes, we're fine," replies Tenika. She's shivering, holding Jackson in a sopping blanket, but these things aren't important.

"Do you have a cell phone?" she asks.

He pulls his out and she calls Lee at the church, but he doesn't answer. She leaves a message. "Honey, it's me. We're okay, but the house is gone." She explains that she's using someone else's phone, so he won't be able to get back to her.

She hands the cell phone back to the man she has never seen before. In reply, he takes off his coat and puts it around her shoulders.

"You'll need it more than me," he says, and then he's gone.

A few minutes later Lee gets Tenika's message. He wonders what she means by the word *gone*. There are so many different levels of *gone*. Which meaning was she trying to use? Surely if the house were really gone, Tenika would have been hysterical and sobbing.

Lee fights traffic, but it's such a mess. Random people are directing traffic, and chaos is reigning. Dazed faces are seen through the windows of passing cars.

As he gets closer, Tenika's use of the word *gone* becomes more chilling. Maybe she really did mean *gone*. All around him he sees horror, and he isn't even sure where he is. The stoplight he always turned at, the Pizza Hut, the big line of trees, the huge house on the hill . . . everything really is gone, and he has to rely on his wits. Whether the surroundings have changed or not, the streets must still be the same.

He passes the high school and takes the last leg on foot. He knows where his house should be, but it's not there. Instead, there's broken lumber, uprooted oak trees, and a yellow broom. He sees the bright red front door leaning over a stack of broken lumber—he knows he's home.

\\\\\\\\\V////////

The barber and his wife stare at each other as they realize that the roaring has gone and they are crammed in a closet that's about to collapse. They carefully maneuver their way out, thinking of nothing but their two children.

With great relief, they see that the closet the children are in is still standing and actually held up better than theirs did. Their daughter is calmly helping her younger brother climb out. They all throw their arms around each other. It's so good to be alive and well!

They look around. "Even a healthy mind can't comprehend it," says the barber. "Our world changed from color to black and white in just five minutes."

Everything is gray. The cement blocks, torn and crumbled. The insulation, flying free. The soaking mattress caught in a leafless tree. Nothing but white stubs of arms hold up what someone used to sleep on. Everything is dripping and chilly gray.

Shock

1947: Reporting on the victims of the 1947 Woodward, Oklahoma, tornado, Richard Bedard states, "The blankness of expression on so many faces was not from an inability to suffer. Rather, it resulted from an all-too-human nature that suffered too much and slipped into a sort of paralysis as a consequence."

1965: Palm Sunday victims lost awareness. One person didn't notice for two days that a tree in his yard was gone. People made statements such as, "It will probably get back to normal," and "I hope it will wear off." At the time, it seemed far-fetched to think of normal life.[36]

1974: "The totality of destruction was nearly hypnotic," Levine says of the 1974 tornadoes. People refused to come out of their storm shelters.[37] If life had fallen apart so quickly, how could anyone prove the destruction was actually gone?

8
Healthcare

If we could catch someone with an open vehicle, we'd throw a patient in the back with them.
—Jason Smith, paramedic, director of METS ambulance service

Two Oxford HealthCare employees call Cheryl Fitch. They are in town, making their way toward the office to see if everything is okay. Even though the building is usually empty on Sunday, they are worried that a staff member might have gone in to work.

The two staff members are on foot, walking through the rain. They are out of breath. She hears them say they are lost. She can't understand how they could be lost in a town they know so well.

\\\\\\\\\V/////////

The surgery staff in the operating room at St. John's Mercy Hospital find flashlights. They finish the hip surgery, sloshing through water on the operating room floor. Then they discover that they need help to get out of the room.

In the nine-story tower, all communication is lost. No instructions blare over the PA system. Nurses know they should move their patients to a safer area in the hospital, but they soon realize that the entire hospital has been affected. Even without instructions, nurses know that they must get their patients out.

The elevators are not working. The stairwells are dark and filled with debris. Flashlights and cell phones glow as the patients are ushered out. Patients who can walk go first. Patients who cannot walk must be carried. Doors that have been torn off their hinges are used as stretchers. Other patients are carried on their mattresses. Some hospital mattresses are attached to the beds. Nurses cut them loose. However, anything rigid is best, because patients are passed from person to person through the crowded stairwells.

St. John's is also equipped with orange med sleds, rigid backboards that curve around a patient, allowing them to slide gently down a flight of stairs. Unfortunately, these med sleds are on the first floor. Besides, the stairwells are so full of debris that the sleds would not slide well.

The hospital beds can barely move through the hallways, where ceiling tiles are turning to mush in the rising water. The beds will certainly not be going down the stairs.

Many patients are barefoot and dressed only in gowns. Nurses wrap towels around feet to protect them from the debris and glass.

In the ER, Dr. Kitka emerges from under his desk. Water is rising on the floor, and he smells gas from broken gas lines. Everything is dark, but someone brings flashlights.

Ironically, the emergency department is destroyed just at the moment of highest demand. People pour toward the hospital, glass and debris piercing their bodies.

A young man comes to Dr. Kitka, gasping for breath, certain he's about to die. With no anesthetic, Dr. Kitka removes a glass shard and inserts a chest tube. The man is able to breathe again.

Next, Dr. Kitka inserts an airway. For light, he holds his flashlight in his mouth. The staff members continue to treat patients to the best of their ability, working with flashlights as water rains from the ceiling and leaking natural gas threatens to blow up the entire hospital.

Once outside, patients gather in several collection points.

Patients from critical care are given special attention. Special attention in this case means a private pickup bed with a nurse, an Ambu bag to hold over the face and assist with breathing, an oxygen tank, and maybe an extra person to hold the IV bag in the air as the vehicle bounces across the street to Freeman Hospital. With only a name band on their wrists, these patients spill into Freeman with chest tubes and no medical records, their history stored on the computers, which are all out cold.

Vehicles, many driven by strangers, drop off their patients at Freeman, then circle back to St. John's and get in line again. Dr. Kitka instructs a passerby how to help someone breathe by squeezing the Ambu bag as they move across the road to Freeman Hospital.

"You never know that it will be the most important day of your life until the day is over," Dr. Kitka says.[38]

\\\\\\\\\\\\V/////////

Dennis Manley, St. John's safety director who always insisted on proper tornado drills, is on the opposite side of the building, helping evacuate. He makes sure that critical care patients get to Freeman Hospital, accompanied by a nurse.

"They had no idea who or what we were sending them," Dennis says. "I feel like I should apologize."

Although the patients had their name bands on, there were no records to send along explaining their illness or the status of their treatment.

Dennis tries to enter the building to find the hospital's backup supplies for just such a disaster, but he can't reach the right room. The backup disaster trailer, equipped with backup supplies *just in case* the main room would be unusable, has disappeared.

It takes only 90 minutes to evacuate the 183 patients. When the evacuation is finished, Dennis moves command staff to an office outside of town where they will be able to use Internet and phones.

Another storm is coming up, so the emergency department, which has been operating in the parking lot, moves to a safe building in the city. The hospital, not accustomed to emptiness, stands like a ghost against the gray town.

\\\\\\\\\\\\V//////////

Greenbriar Nursing Home residents have two disadvantages in the aftermath. First, the ones with dementia are confused even on a normal day. Second, unlike hospital patients, these people don't even have name bands. This is a positive thing for maintaining a home-like atmosphere, but it adds to the confusion in a time of disaster.

Up on the north end of town, the METS ambulances wait for the tornado to pass. In compliance with METS' tornado policy, ambulance fuel tanks have all been topped off.

When the tornado is gone, the overhead doors open and the ambulances spill into the night, screaming with lights pulsing and dancing on the wet pavement. METS arrives at Greenbriar, where cars have been thrown into the nursing home.

In the first moments after the tornado, ambulances are packed with eight to ten patients.

"If we could catch someone with an open vehicle, we'd throw a patient in the back with them," says a paramedic with METS ambulance.

METS also begins calling St. John's, first on the radio and then by phone. There is no answer.

What in the world, the paramedics think. *Why don't they answer tonight of all nights?* They soon hear the truth. St. John's is no better off than Greenbriar.[39]

9
Documenting the Disaster

You don't need to head that way. There's nothing left.
—man walking out of the disaster zone

Bill Shepherd emerges from his basement and grabs his camera backpack, which is always ready to go. With his home and family safe, he's ready to go out and see what has happened. It's pouring rain, so he waits five minutes.

Bill drives south seven blocks to Parr Hill Park. He drives over a downed power line. Then he bumps over something that gives him a flat tire. He parks and crawls out close to Parr Hill Park.

Gas is shooting out of a broken main line like a torch. The sound is unreal. The smell is so intense that people are vomiting in the street.

"Run for your life!" Bill hollers to the people he sees. "See that broken gas main there? If that blows up, we're all going to die!"

Fires are already glowing across the city. Bill looks back at his vehicle and realizes he's parked just fifteen feet from the broken gas line. He's not sure if he should even start the vehicle, but he does. No explosion. He backs it away, bumping on the flat.

He climbs out again.

"Run for your life!" Bill repeats, taking pictures mechanically as he speaks. His first saved picture says 6:02 p.m. on his camera, but he knows he erased several before that.

The people don't seem to hear him. They wander, dazed. They say they have to help someone out of the rubble, have to look for someone.

Soon Bill realizes that almost every house in the area has a broken gas line. Still, he tries to direct people to a place of safety. The people are so stunned that they just need someone to give them orders. Bill directs them to Parr Hill Park. At least there are no broken gas lines there, and no destroyed buildings. All the while, he's taking pictures.

He still struggles with guilt. Should he put his camera down entirely and just helped people? He makes split-second decisions. He points people in the right direction. He shares first aid tips he remembers, telling people that help will be on the way. At the same time, he takes pictures. If someone complains, he moves on.

For the first forty-five minutes, it rains. People sit in the rain, helpless and stunned. Bill holds a towel over his camera. He records Good Samaritan acts for all to see. A white woman is freed and helped out of the rubble, supported on her right by a Hispanic man and on her left by an African-American teenager.

People go back into their homes, trying to find things. Others praise God out loud, grateful their lives have been spared.

When he first arrived, Bill had an advantage: his brain was steady and clear. His home and family were safe. However, as he circles through the disaster zone, he feels the mask of shock sliding over his face too.

He meets a man who hid in his bathtub. As his house disappeared over his head, the man dropped into the crawl space beneath his house.

"I tried to keep my eyes closed, but the force of the tornado was so strong it pulled my eyes open," the man reports, stunned.

They discuss the sound of the tornado. Even from seven blocks away, Bill found the crunching, destructive sound to be terrifying, unlike anything he ever heard before. From the vantage point of the crawl space, the man agrees.

"Lots of people say a train, but to me, *what train?* The noise was so loud you couldn't hear nothin'."

Bill photographs two women walking down a street, each with a small bundle, their wet hair plastered to their foreheads and shoulders. A young man in a black T-shirt holds a little girl in a pink dress, both pairs of eyes wide with horror. A middle-aged man sits on the muddy road beside a splintered tree limb and a yellow Nike shoe. He seems to be in pain, but it's hard to tell if it's physical or emotional. A man holds both hands of a woman who's just been pulled from a collapsed grocery store. A man stands beside his mangled vehicle, waiting for emergency workers to free his trapped wife. A young woman walks down the street holding a framed photo. People are barefoot or poorly dressed.

Ten men stand in a circle, the ones on the inside digging to free someone. The outer men stand helplessly, arms hanging at their sides.[40] This scene replays itself throughout the city as the closest people free someone while others stand tensely, ready to help, their eyes silent and pained, still chilled from the last thing they saw. Even the sky is the wrong color—a distorted pink.

At the end of three hours, Bill's camera cards are full, and he needs to leave. Emergency personnel have arrived in force. Bill understands why they could not be spread throughout the city right away. The needs were so great.

"Even if there had been five thousand firemen, that wouldn't have been enough," Bill guesses.

\\\\\\\\\\\\V//////////

After checking on the men at the shelter, James and his boys head south into tornado country to see if there's anything they can do to help. As they slowly drive in, they meet a pickup coming out of the city. The man in the vehicle leans out of his window, his expression ghastly, dazed with a kind of wrenching horror.

"You don't need to head that way," says the man, "there's nothing left."

When James can go no farther, he and his boys jump out and start walking. They jog down the railroad track into the city. As they get closer to the devastation and see more and more of what has happened, James feels something inside he's never felt before. His heart is sinking like lead, and at the same time it's racing, a strange effect of horror and desperation to help bursting inside of him.

James and his men near an apartment complex, and they have to leap over power lines and nails. They pass a refrigerator that's been sucked out of somewhere.

They turn in at the three-story apartments and find a dazed man. He and his wife live on the third story, he says. They were up there having a peaceful Sunday afternoon when they heard the sirens.

"Let's go downstairs," the husband said.

"Nah, I'm not coming," the wife said.

"It's pretty bad out there," he said. But she refused to follow.

James is certain the man is not physically capable of clambering up the stack of rubble to search for his wife.

"I'll go look for her," James offers.

His towering frame gives him an advantage as he reaches for footholds and handholds in the mound. He's almost at the top when he finds the body. He can instantly tell she's deceased. He pauses, his head bowed for a few seconds. He glances down at the man, who's still standing there numbly.

James frowns, unsure what to do. The woman is heavyset, and he can't bring her down by himself. Finally, James pulls out his cell phone and snaps a picture of her. The man will know. With a final glance, James descends the ruins.

He silently hands his phone to the man, with the photo on the screen. The man looks at the picture, his forehead wrinkled. "Yes, that's her," is all he says.

James embraces him.

"Is there anything I can do to help?" he asks.

The man shakes his head.

James feels compelled to go on, to meet as many needs as he possibly can on this dreadful day.

A woman panics as she searches for her daughters. But deeper than her hysteria is a deep despair. She spots a picture frame thirty yards away and picks it up as if it were gold. All around him James sees that same "deer in the headlights" look.

"I wish I would have stayed with the man who lost his wife in the apartments," James says later. "At the time, I felt like we had to keep moving. We had to go. There were more people who needed help." He bites his lip and blinks. "But I wish I would have just stayed with him. All day if necessary."

\\\\\\\\\V/////////

A grandmother leaves her Joplin home just before the tornado. She rides out the storm at a friend's house south of the zone.

When the danger passes, she leaves her friend's house and drives back to central Joplin. She comes within about three blocks of her house, and there are no traffic lights.

Wow, there must have been some wind here! she thinks.

She drives another three blocks and realizes that the trouble has just begun. Now she can't drive at all. Desperate to find her children who live close by, she gets out of her vehicle and begins to walk, or rather to climb. She sees with her eyes, but she can't comprehend. She climbs over wood and steps over wires and glass, watching where she places her feet.

Worse, all around her the houses are moving, rubble is being tossed aside, and shouts and cries for help are echoing down what used to be the street. People crawl out of the houses like ants. The looks on their faces can be described only one way: dazed.

The grandmother sees her daughter's neighbor.

"Are you all right?" she asks.

"We're fine," he snaps, and she realizes that he is terrified.

Then he takes off running. There are elderly people living across the street, and he wants to make sure they're okay.

After finding that her children and grandchildren are okay, the woman hauls people in her car, some to the hospital and some to the homes of relatives. The faces of the people who climb into her car are just like all the other faces she's seen: dazed. A woman gets into the car and says to her child, "We're safe; God kept us safe. Our home—it doesn't matter what our house looks like. Daddy's okay and your brothers are safe."

10

Fire Departments and EMS

We've been struck by a tornado. Our trucks are out of service.
—Joplin Fire Stations Two and Four

At the central fire station, Chief Randles comes up from the basement. Calls are beginning to swamp the 9-1-1 dispatchers. Fire Station Two calls the central station.

"We've been struck by a tornado. Our trucks are out of service."

This is not a good start. Randles gets into his personal vehicle. He throws his gear in with him and heads toward Station Two.

He gets a call from Fire Station Four on the way. Station Four is eight blocks north and more than thirty blocks east of Station Two, in the center of the city. He hears them repeat the phrase he just heard moments ago: "We've been struck by a tornado. Our trucks are out of service."

Randles arrives at Station Two. He finds his men freeing someone from a car.

One of their trucks is not crushed, just trapped. He tells them to get this truck out.

Driving down 20th Street into the heart of town, Randles sees the main damage path for the first time, on the street he would have traveled into work had he taken his family home after the graduation.

As the chief turns south on Main Street, the city manager is on the south end of town, trying to come north on Main Street. The two are talking to each other on their radios, but both are having trouble getting through the rubble. The chief hears screaming coming from a Mexican restaurant. He gets out of his vehicle and throws on his gear. It's hailing again, so he quickly dons his helmet.

The people in the restaurant are okay. Randles helps a husband, wife, and young child to a safe place. Then he heads east on 20th Street in the direction of Fire Station Four.

The chief finally meets up with the city manager. They both agree that somehow they have to get a grip on the extent of the damage. The chief leaves and radios what he sees as he goes, creating parameters for the tornado zone.

Because the chief's personal vehicle has a blinking red light, someone sees it and runs out to flag him down. The man says there are people trapped in the basement of a church, and one of them is bleeding.

Chief Randles and the city manager direct the rescue effort at the church. Seven people are trapped in the debris, including several small children. For some of the people, it's too late. The bodies are moved.

The two men move on, past a crushed grocery store and a set of apartment buildings that have been wiped off the surface of the earth. By the time they get to Station Four, the firefighters have dug out a personal vehicle. They've moved their rescue equipment into this vehicle and are back at work.

The chief and city manager make their way back to the central station, where the Emergency Operations Center (EOC) is being set up in the basement. With other department heads, they brainstorm about the most urgent needs. They know there are more rescuers coming to help. The fire stations are beginning to sort things out. The most urgent need is to know the extent of the damage so they can plan rescue efforts more effectively.

It won't work to drive.

"Let's get a helicopter," the two men agree.

They make a phone call, and a medical helicopter comes to take them on a tour. It drops from the sky into the empty parking lot beside the fire station. The city manager and fire chief climb in with the pilot.

By now it's about 9:30 p.m. It's not a good night to fly. Lightning continues to flash. The chopper bumps through the rain. With night vision goggles, the two city leaders stare down at the path of destruction. Chief Randles sketches the path on a map. It's the birth of the "blue fish," as the damage sketch comes to be called. The lines, printed with blue ink, show that the beginning of the path is narrow, like a tail, before widening out like a body.

When the helicopter reaches the east side of town, Chief Randles asks the pilot to hover for a second above his own house. It's hard to assess from the air.

"It doesn't look good," says the chief, but he has more things to worry about than his home.

The helicopter drops the men off at the fire station. Map experts take the chief's sketch and divide it into boxes. They will use these grids to assign search and rescue teams.

\\\\\\\\\\\\V//////////

"Dad, I'm going with you," Keegan says. Because his father is now an administrator of the ambulance company, he no longer does a lot of hands-on paramedic work. But when he does, Keegan is eager to accompany him, putting to practice his EMT training. Keegan races to the basement, tearing off his maroon graduation gown and pulling on boots and a jacket.

Keegan's sister's boyfriend has just graduated from EMT school with Keegan, so he wants to ride along too. Keegan's two sisters, who are ER techs, also jump in the car. Keegan's mother is a nurse practitioner, but she stays home for now. The car is full.

Before leaving, two friends call to say they are trapped. They also hear that St. John's has been hit and will not be accepting patients. Later someone reports that the St. John's operating room is on fire, which proves to be only a rumor.

The carload of uniformed medical personnel drives up Rangeline Road, backtracking the way they just came from the graduation only minutes earlier. The plan is to go to Rangeline and 13th Street and free the first friend, and then go to Joplin High School to free the second friend. After that they plan to drop off Keegan's two sisters at their emergency departments.

Things do not go as planned.

At 20th Street the drive is over. They are stopped by power lines, debris, crushed vehicles, and bodies. They pull into the remains of a car wash and jump out.

Their medical uniforms are magnetic.

"Keegan, Keegan, help me find my mom!" Keegan turns to see a girl in a maroon graduation gown.

Keegan knows he just graduated with this girl. He's gone to school with her for four years. But, beneath the blood and mud, he doesn't know who she is. He runs to help her.

It's also pouring rain. The streets are ankle deep with water in places, and Keegan lifts small children over the deepest spots.

They are the only medical personnel on the scene, so they work out a system. Keegan and his sister's boyfriend provide the muscles to bring people to the car wash lot. In the lot, Keegan's sisters do as much first aid as possible, bandaging wounds and deciding who most desperately needs the hospital.

Keegan's father walks to the collapsed buildings and crumpled cars, looking for more people needing help. He finds bodies in Pizza Hut and Sonic. Home Depot is next door, and its walls have collapsed, killing seventeen. Walmart is close by, its clothing and electronics sections demolished. Thirty people have perished inside. People are trapped all over.

He radios to Newton County Ambulance, asking for help, but the ambulances are all at 20th and Main Street. Someone has declared that intersection to be the worst. Half an hour later, there are still no ambulances at Rangeline and 20th Street.

People walk up to them, most of them barefoot. They're soaking wet. Some are bleeding. Others are covered with mud or insulation.

A woman crawls out of Walgreens. She tells Keegan's father there's someone trapped inside who needs help.

"Ma'am, I got people trapped everywhere," he says in frustration. He's not frustrated at the woman, but at the help he's not getting.

"I was just trying to help," she says and begins to cry.

The administrator feels terrible.

"Unit Four, *are* you doing anything?" he barks over his radio. He doesn't want to yell at people, but right now he's too frustrated to care. People are dying around him, and there are no ambulances.[41]

Overall, emergency radio traffic is calm and matter-of-fact.

"Every house on the other side of Main Street is gone."

"Okay."

Later, "We can't travel safely right now."

"Okay, that's okay."

It's not okay, of course. But this is Joplin, post-tornado.

\\\\\\\\\\\V//////////

As more storms roll in, Keegan's father realizes they have to find a safe building for the patients. He checks Walgreens and the Toyota dealership, but neither building will work. He drives to Lowe's, just outside the tornado path to the south. Lowe's has a backup generator and stands like a lighthouse at the edge of a sea of wreckage.

He meets a Lowe's employee and introduces himself.

"I am about to take over your store," he says.

Lowe's is the next hero. While the medical staff prepares to move the triage center, Lowe's brings them batteries, flashlights, and big tables. There are three wide aisles at the south end of the store where big contractors make their purchases. Lowe's assigns these aisles for medical use.

The EMS personnel decide to bring priority patients to the first aisle and the walking wounded to the second aisle. Supplies are stockpiled in the third aisle.

As more help arrives, Keegan slips away with a man whose regular job is search and rescue diving. They leave on an ATV to do as much searching and rescuing as they can. On this journey, Keegan sees Joplin High School and St. John's Mercy for the first time. He can't believe this is his hometown.

11

Freeman Hospital

Everything is proceeding according to plan. We're making it as we go.
—Freeman Hospital employee

At Freeman Hospital, nurses are circling around the patients in the hallway. They check to make sure that the portable oxygen tanks will last until the patients can be returned to their rooms. After a short power outage, the backup generators have kicked in. There's power, but only on the red outlets. The lighting is dimmed. Water is dripping from a leak in the roof.

At 6:15 an overhead page announces a code: Doctor Astor. This means that the hospital is calling all available staff to help. The announcer's voice is shaking. Soon, another page: Doctor Red. This indicates a fire somewhere. Then there's another page asking all available staff to bring wheelchairs to the emergency department. A charge nurse from downstairs takes three wheelchairs up to the emergency department and sees a trail of blood and bloody handprints on the counters.

Robert Denton and his wife Renee are both registered nurses at Freeman hospital. Both are directors, Bob in the emergency department and Renee on the medical/oncology and pediatric units. Neither is at the hospital at 5:41. When they crest the hill just before they get to the hospital, they see people gathering en masse around the emergency room entrance. Some are walking, some are riding in the backs of pickups, and some are escorted in ambulances. Freeman Hospital, the only light in the dark city, is the place people want to go.

"It's bad," says Bob Denton, driving down the hill with his wife. He stays calm.

Bob's calmness as they approach Freeman Hospital gives Renee a sense of calmness as well. She arrives on her floor just as security personnel are passing out handheld radios to her staff. Patients are lined quietly in the hallways. Things are so calm and quiet that Renee finds it almost frightening. However, she passes on Bob's calmness. She tries to assign any difficult tasks to seasoned nurses. The respiratory department has run out of ventilators and just needs people who can operate the Ambu bags to assist people with their breathing. Renee sends some of her nurses to help.

The day shift workers will stay, and as many people as possible from the night shift are arriving. Sadly, some of the nurses are coming from destroyed homes or are worried about their own family members. Night shift workers are texting to say they cannot get through. Roads are blocked, and staff members without ID cards are turned back.

In the emergency department Bob sees more people than he's ever seen there before. The place is also quieter than the hospital has ever been. Besides the patients with impaling injuries, head trauma, and skin abrasions, Freeman is sorting through patients from St. John's with no medical history available. A dozen patients need surgery *now,* including a young man, one of the first to arrive, holding his intestines in his arms.

An ambulance pulls into the Freeman bay early in the drama. It's a transfer from another hospital.

"You need to take the patient back where they came from," the paramedics are told. They haven't heard about the Joplin nightmare yet.

Other patients need smaller surgeries. Wounds are tricky. They look innocent and easy to close. However, in some cases, debris has entered through a wound and lodged a distance away from the entry point. Leaves and sticks need to be surgically removed.

Technicians prepare IV bags as fast as they can. Chest tubes are placed in patients lying in the hall. Central lines are inserted in fields that aren't exactly sterile. Private rooms are crammed with patients. For some patients, the only thing that can be done is provide a person to stay with them for their last moments.

There has been no time to label patients with disaster tags. The hospital does have 150 numbered bracelets for disasters, but they need 350 more. The challenge is to sort through all the patients and separate those who need immediate surgery from those who are unresponsive.

Although Freeman has fared much better than St. John's Mercy, there has been damage to the building. The backup generators provide only about one third of the normal power. There is one working elevator. Computers are down. Communication inside the hospital is poor, and communication with the outside world is minimal. How widespread is the disaster? No one knows. At least no one needs to answer the phones, because the phone lines aren't working.

\\\\\\\\\\\V/////////

Two people are working in the hospital's central supply room tonight. One is experienced. The other is completely new on the job and probably expected Sunday night to be a great night to start, an easy shift with the normally low patient load. Now supplies are running out in the emergency room, especially chest tubes and central lines. All over the hospital, nurses need keys to get into the electronic med carts.

Although the water is still on, the pressure is pathetic. Across the city, water lines are broken, creating hundreds of small fountains, robbing the water pressure from the lines that are still intact. Toilets cannot be flushed. Instruments cannot be sterilized.

Skip Harper, Freeman's security and emergency director, is relieved that the disaster training of the week before has them somewhat prepared. One big asset from the training is a paper list of phone numbers of all the surrounding hospitals,.

At the same time, things are so crazy that Skip realizes that no one could ever prepare completely. No training exercise has prepared Skip for the smell in the emergency department, which takes him back to his father's butcher shop on slaughter days. He suspects that there should be two levels of disaster planning: one for minor disasters and one for nights like tonight, when a town explodes.

"Everything is proceeding according to plan," someone is heard to say.

"What's the plan?"

"We're making it as we go."

The blood bank begins to run dry, limiting emergency care. In the chaos, one of Freeman's pathologists contacts a pathologist at St. John's. With a little arranging, the St. John's pathologist gives the Freeman pathologist access to the blood in St. John's blood bank.

Security and privacy is also running dry, with patients packed side by side in the same rooms. Skip would like to lock down the hospital to keep unwanted people from wandering in, and he could do this by pressing one button. However, the crowds are just too thick, and people need to come in and out. Locking down will not work. Instead, Skip commissions people to guard the door and help keep order. Janitors and medical secretaries suddenly become security guards.

The security guards are not the only ones working outside of their scope of practice. Psychiatrists at Freeman's mental health facility are treating physical injuries and doing well. Other specialists are doing tasks they would normally never do. Random snatches of dialogue capture the frenzy.

"Are you a plastics doc?"

"No, I'm an OB doc, but I can be a plastics doc."

Skip is also short on runners and scribes. In a world where electronics evaporate, he needs people with feet and pencils. Even when they can get through by radio or text, some things are better relayed face to face. Skip cringes when he hears someone radio, "We need more body bags."

Support begins to arrive. Within an hour, a construction company calls. They are bringing a semi full of generators and telescopic lights.

The electric company arrives. They say they will need to run a new line, which normally takes weeks.

"We'll get it done by morning," they say.

The water company is not responding, because they say the water *is* on. Skip finally calls the EOC, stationed in the basement of the fire department. He asks them to call the governor of Missouri and tell *him* to call the water company.

On an even more practical level, Skip needs an armload of large pizzas. Everyone is hungry. The sandwiches and crackers that are circulating help, but the need for real food grows more intense as the hours wear on.

\\\\\\\\\V/////////

In a downstairs conference room, Renee Denton sets up a forty-bed unit for extra space. In the ER, patients are packed wall to wall, and some are waiting outside. Renee suggests that the walking wounded, the less injured patients, be brought to her new ward.

Renee takes nurses with her, and together they meet the needs of the walking wounded. Things are crazy, but Renee is in control. She and her nurses are using ten-year-old yellow paper charts long replaced by computers. Like the emergency department and the patients upstairs, the forty-cot conference room is quiet.

"Lady, you're doing a good job," one of the patients says quietly.

"Oh no, *you're* doing a good job," Renee replies.

Renee knows exactly what's going on with each of the patients. She knows who needs an X-ray and who needs a CT scan. She doesn't know where her strength is coming from, because she's never done anything like this before.

She looks up. A young nurse is staring straight at her. She looks as if she's about to lose it.

"Do you want to leave?" Renee asks.

"No," the nurse says.

As they begin to see patients, Renee comes to a patient from St. John's. The patient states that she was scheduled for a procedure the next day at St. John's.

Renee steps out of earshot of the patient and vents her frustration. "Are you kidding me? What in the world are they doing, sending us patients that they have scheduled for procedures tomorrow? Don't they know how busy we are?"

Someone tells her. St. John's is destroyed. *All* of St. John's patients have been moved.

Renee stares. In the rush of action, she has not heard. How could the other hospital be gone?

"I just need a minute," she says, and steps out of the room.

\\\\\\\\\\V/////////

Less than twenty-four hours after the patient arrived holding his intestines, Freeman's Emergency Department floor is gleaming again. They have taken 825 X-rays and 396 CT scans. They have seen 1,000 patients and performed 22 emergency surgeries. They have lost 11 lives and transferred 64 patients. Many have been discharged. Missouri Southern State University opens its dorms to house the discharged patients who have no homes.

But in the aftermath of the tornado, an unexpected fright develops—a bizarre fungal infection. It's a sad replay from post-tsunami Japan, a weird side effect of disasters that might be related to spores in the air. The infection takes healthy skin and minor wounds and explodes them into horrifying color. At least thirteen Joplin patients get the fungal infection. Five patients die.

How Do Outsiders View Disasters?

Public attention usually turns entirely away from disasters once the pictures and headlines disappear. Tragedies initially hold the attention of people. Near-death experiences are the most thrilling of all. But disaster stories quickly fade from national consciousness.[42]

At the same time, they fade from the national *conscience*. If you forget something, it can't be your fault for not helping. A month after the disaster, when the city is just barely starting to pick itself back up, visitors are surprised to find things still in disarray. Those who do not see it with their own eyes cannot remember it long.

President Obama recognized this when he visited Joplin a week after the tornado.

"We are going to be here long after the cameras leave," he promised.[43]

At the same memorial service that President Obama attended, Pastor Aaron Brown of Joplin addressed the crowd. "This happened because life on this side of eternity is unpredictable, chaotic, and broken. . . . You may wonder at times, but the fact is . . . God is walking with us through this tragedy, and He will make a way where it seems there is no way."[44]

SHATTERPROOF//JOPLIN, MISSOURI

12
A Search for Life

Everywhere else, people demand food and water. But here, people make sandwiches and serve bottled water from their houses.
—The National Guard

It's Monday night when Keegan hears that Will is missing. He goes home to shower and change, but he can't sleep. He goes back to town and talks to Griffin.

The search begins. Many people the Nortons know, and some people they don't know, are looking for the tall boy with brown hair and a laughing smile.

They look outside in the debris. A logical place to look for Will is in the pond close to the Hummer's wreckage. Using sonar, rescue workers search the pond twice without finding evidence of a body.

They look in other hospitals. Griffin throws himself into the search and rescue, spending many hours himself going from room to room in hospitals, searching for an unidentified male, six foot three, brown hair, straight teeth.

Keegan continues to work with his dad. His mother, a nurse practitioner, joins the effort too, helping to triage injured patients throughout the week. The most critical patients were transported immediately, but now others are streaming in. Some of these people didn't think they were hurt badly enough to need help at first. Still others knew they were hurt but wanted people with worse injuries to receive help first.

\\\\\\\\\\\\V/////////

A report circulates that Will's name has been seen on Freeman's ER log. The Norton family's hopes rise. He must have been transferred. The search intensifies. If Will was at Freeman Sunday night, he has to be somewhere findable.

The CEO of Freeman Hospital is a friend of the family. He visits them in Mr. Norton's room. He explains that the records with Will's name are from January, not May 22.

"It doesn't mean he wasn't here," the CEO says. "It just means we have no record of him being here on Sunday."

\\\\\\\\\\\\V/////////

A Facebook page is started for Will, called "Help Find Will Norton." It quickly gathers thousands of followers. Announcements are posted on this site.

> Tuesday, 7:18 a.m.:
> At this point we are looking for anyone who has actually SEEN Will. Every hospital and possible lead has been called. Please DON'T call hospitals. If you have information, please contact us directly at the number or email below. Everyone, we thank you for your help.

> Tuesday, 10:01 a.m.:
> ****PLEASE DO NOT CALL HOSPITALS**** All of the hospitals in Wichita, Topeka, Tulsa, Oklahoma

City, Springfield, Kansas City, NW Arkansas, and the surrounding areas have been checked. The hospitals are being inundated and overwhelmed with callers. The best thing anyone can do is to pray and keep forwarding this link in the hopes that someone will recognize his face. Thank you again, everyone.

Sara and her mother hear about an unidentified male in a Springfield hospital. They make the trip. "That's not Will," Sara says instantly. She pauses to check his teeth and eyes just to be sure.

It's not Will.

Sara and her parents do DNA swabs. They also collect Will's toothbrush, dental records, and some sweaty socks from his closet and take the items to the morgue. They need to know if he's there.

> Wednesday morning, from Will's aunt:
> I thought I would share with all of you what my brother said yesterday. He said as soon as the tornado grabbed the car, Will started quoting Scriptures, one right after another. As a Christian, this not only makes me cry but makes me smile because I know how strong his faith is.
>
> Wednesday evening, 5 p.m.:
> Everyone, no news yet. Continuing to try to get the word out to search fields, trees, etc. I'd like to have people get on their ATVs or even walk fields, wooded areas, etc. to look for those who are lost. I'd love to find Will and any others who are missing. There is still time to help them. Keep praying! Aunt Tracey

Someone makes fliers with Will's picture on them to distribute to area hospitals.

It's a long week in the hospital. With her mother, Sara stays by her father's side as much as possible. Although only one break was discovered at first, X-rays now show he had fifteen broken bones.

Besides the constant physical pain, there is the emotional pain. He keeps asking about Will.

Sara talks to the ambulance driver who picked up her dad. No, Will was definitely not in the Hummer. Mr. Norton was trapped and had to be freed.

"My son's out here, my son's out here—go find my son," Mr. Norton kept saying.

They couldn't find Will.

The ambulance personnel told Sara that her father was in great pain as they drove over logs and around power lines. Progress was slow. More people wanted to be taken in the ambulance. When the ambulance slowed to crawl over debris, someone handed an injured nine-month-old baby to the driver. By the time the ambulance got to the hospital, it was packed with patients.

> Thursday, 5:20 p.m.:
> We are on foot, going where no one is searching. It's off the beaten path. Not giving up!!!! Aunt Tracey

> Friday, 8:13 a.m.:
> Everyone, I refuse to be a "Debbie Downer" so I'm going to be "Pollyanna" today! No matter what we find or don't find, it's going to be what we're supposed to find. I pray the Lord will guide all of us in the right directions with our many searches today. May He direct not only those who search for my nephew but also the many others who are missing their loved ones. Thanks for your prayers and love! Aunt Tracey

On Friday evening, the pastor arrives and speaks to Sara's mother. Then Sara is called to the hall to hear the news. Will has been found. He is not alive. He was found in the pond on the third sonar search, under debris.

Friday night, Sara stays at the hospital. Her father is on pain medication. He wakes up and falls asleep.

"Do we know about Will?" he asks each time he wakes up.

Each time they tell him again, "Yes, we found him. He's not alive."

\\\\\\\\\\\\V//////////

Keegan's father needs to tell his son about the discovery. He is also the one to tell Griffin. It's the worst moment of the entire week for the administrator of the ambulance service, breaking the news to the two amigos.

Both boys take the news in stride. What else is there to do?

"We didn't sit down and feel sorry for ourselves," says Keegan.

Keegan feels that this attitude is Joplin. When something happens that cannot be changed, there is only one thing to do: be strong and keep going.

\\\\\\\\\\\\V//////////

For four days, Rob is on the missing persons list. This happens to a lot of people, because if anyone knows of someone he hasn't seen since the tornado, he puts that person on the list. As people find each other, the list gets worked down from fifteen hundred to two hundred.

Rob stays at his sister's house for several days. He goes back to see his old house once. He finds a "For Sale" sign randomly in the rubble and picks it up. What an irony, that anyone would want to buy anything in this town of rubble!

He sees a couple of men nearby.

"Hey, you want to buy a house?" he asks.

The men come closer and ask questions. Rob tells them what happened to his house.

"It's not something I can run from," he says. The only thing he can do is move forward.

He steps into the house, overwhelmed by the gray insulation that carpets everything like depressing icing. He sees that spiders have set up their homes in this home that's no longer inhabitable for human beings.

The spiders symbolize ruin to him, and it's time to forever say goodbye to that chapter of his life.

Rob sees a sign, the kind with movable letters: "May 22, When Love Came to Town."

"People are a lot more considerate these days," Rob says. "Before, when an ambulance came through, people ignored it. Now they pull over."

Rob is proud when he hears the National Guard's opinion of Joplin. " 'Everywhere else, people demand food and water,' " he quotes them. " 'But here, people make sandwiches and serve bottled water from their houses.' "

But the choices Rob makes for himself come at a higher price than spreading bread and stacking cheese and lunch meat. Rob does not forget the conviction that settled in his mind when the roof came crashing down. Convinced that his drug addiction is ruining him, Rob checks into Watered Gardens Rescue Mission and begins the journey to stay clean. Can he do it?

\\\\\\\\\\\V/////////

Lee, Tenika, and Jackson move to Lee's mother's house the night of the tornado. They are exhausted and just need lots of rest. It's a big advantage to have a family member to move in with. It's also a big advantage to have a car that works in the immediate aftermath of the storm. Had Lee been at home, their car would probably have been destroyed like so many others.

Here at Grandma's, Jackson gathers an army of chairs and pillows and arranges them in a barricade around the front door.

"What are you doing?" the adults ask him.

"For when the tornado comes," Jackson explains.

Although he's shown maturity already in comforting neighborhood friends right after the tornado, the memories are still too much for such a young person. Jackson does not want to be alone. He remembers the security of his mother's arms in that closet, and he doesn't ever want to think of being out of her reach.

Lee and Tenika discuss the ironies of the tornado and the emotions they feel.

"Yes, it's true, some people not far from us had no damage at all," Lee admits. "I guess it's just like anything in life. There's always someone better off and always someone worse off."

Was it the worst thing that ever happened?

Tenika says no. The emotions of her depression, which have haunted her for years, were worse than the emotions of the tornado.

For Tenika, something big happened inside that closet. "The minute I walked away from that tornado and realized that Jackson was okay, I realized that God had plans for my life," Tenika says.

Because they have the car, Lee and Tenika are able to get around and look for apartments. But just as they are planning a trip out of town, they discover their tire is flat. They stay in town and walk to apartments instead. They find a nice place with one duplex left. As they agree to take it, the landlord replies with regret to four more calls.

\\\\\\\\\V/////////

The Joplin barber recalls the numbness of the first three or four days following the tornado. It was the numbness of going to sleep and forgetting what had happened, only to wake up again and realize, in shock, that the horrible memories were not a nightmare. It was the numbness of remembering that it had all happened in just five minutes, that transformation from color to grayscale.

"This is different from something like a house fire," he says, "where people come together to help the people who've faced a loss. Here, we're *all* in the same boat. The support system is gone. It's each person for himself, in a way."

13

Helping the Needy

I used to get discouraged when things went wrong, but after seeing this, everything we used to call trouble just seemed like absolutely nothing.
—David Wagler, *The Mighty Whirlwind*

With the Oxford HealthCare office destroyed, Cheryl Fitch sends someone to the functioning Walmart at midnight to buy large plastic totes for supplies. With flashlights, they discover that the large black filing cabinets at the office still look usable.

Cheryl sets up a temporary office in a church that graciously opens its doors. The office staff settles in, sitting at round tables, carpeting the floor with stacks of files. The plastic totes line the hall of the church. Tech support personnel in plaid shirts hover around laptops, trying to shake sense out of the chaos. The computers will tell where each employee was at the time of the tornado.

When morning comes, the team begins to drive around searching for patients and staff, guided by GPS and grateful for their ID cards that allow them past police barriers. But the home healthcare office has many troublesome technical details to deal with. They need more oxygen, so they work with Freeman Hospital. The drop boxes have been destroyed, so the hours that were turned in by employees are lost, probably floating in a field somewhere.

Still, when the facts come in, Cheryl is triumphant. All employees stayed with their patients at the time of the tornado. Although 50 staff members lost their houses, and some lost family members, all 500 staff and 750 patients survived the tornado.

Cheryl earns the nickname "Mom" on her visits to the ruined office, because she worries about the employees who try to enter the rubble. One nurse has lost a family member in the tornado, and one of her only pictures of this person was on her desk in the office. A male staff member balances his way through the rubble, determined to find it for her. Although Cheryl does not think he should be in there, she's glad he's so eager to help.

The people of Joplin themselves are not quick to ask for help. Cheryl notices that people are not leaving their ruined houses, but tenting and grilling instead, probably to guard their property from looters by holding claim from their lawn chairs.

Cheryl decides to set up medical tents. The six tents, stocked with 1,100 tetanus shots, serve the community for six weeks.

\\\\\\\\\\\V/////////

The initial chaos at St. John's ebbs away with the Sunday night darkness. When the sun rises, the hospital is standing, four inches off its foundation, its curtains flapping through glassless windows. The light of day reveals piles of crumpled vehicles in the parking lot, including a John Deere tractor that had flown in from the country.

Several huge problems emerge. The building has to be blocked off from looters, such as the "volunteer" seen trying to remove the hospital lobby's ATM. Search teams must go through to find and destroy all medications. Unfortunately, with radiation sources and biohazards, the building isn't safe for anyone, search teams included.

Another problem is that, although the computer records can be recovered, St. John's doesn't know where its patients have gone. There is no way to track them.

In addition, existing patients have desperate questions. Where can I get my medication? Where can I go to take my chemo? Where's my doctor?

An orange fence, eventually replaced with a six-foot-high chain-link fence, is put up around the building. St. John's employees spend two days calling surrounding hospitals, looking for their patients. A special phone line is started to take calls from regular patrons; 2,500 calls are received on the first day.

St. John's is granted the right to use a sixty-bed mobile medical unit recently set up for earthquake disaster practice. Consisting of a combination of trailers and an inflatable, greenhouse-like ward, the unit usually takes four days to set up. It's currently set up in Branson, Missouri, so it will also have to be taken down.

"It's really nice to see this thing set up, but we'll probably never see it used in real life," an observer had said during the earthquake drill.

Working around the clock, crews take the mobile medical unit apart, power wash it, and ship it to Joplin. This takes twelve hours. Other crews prepare the hospital lot to receive the new medical camp. They clear debris, place trailers, and cut through concrete. The electric company arrives, promising to restore power.

"When do you need it?" they ask.

St. John's does have backup generators now, but they tell the company that they would like real power as soon as possible. The electric company will need to bring a large power line from three miles away, a process that usually takes weeks.

"Give us three days," they say.

When the mobile medical unit arrives in Joplin, it takes only eighteen hours to set it up. Workers prepare helipads, ramps, an operating room trailer, an MRI trailer, and showers and laundry rooms. Tech support descends, setting up computers.

St. John's employees are trained to do the special work inside the inflatable hospital. People are skeptical of its sturdiness, although the unit is supposed to be able to withstand 100-mile-per-hour winds.

Exactly one week after the tornado, the mobile medical unit is finished and open for business.

\\\\\\\\\\\/////////

Although Greenbriar Nursing Home is a much smaller facility, tracking its residents down is more difficult. Because nursing homes try to maintain resident dignity, residents are not required to wear bracelets with their names. One elderly lady with Alzheimer's was evacuated from the Joplin facility. Upon arrival at the hospital, she didn't know where she was or who she was.

Besides the nursing assistant who sacrificed his life for his patients, fourteen residents from Greenbriar passed away from tornado-related injuries.

Director Jon Dolan grows frustrated with media crews asking how many people have passed away. He feels that they are just interested in getting a sensational story and then disappearing. It is difficult to explain to them that a death toll could not be reported until news had returned from the morgue.

\\\\\\\\\\\/////////

The healthcare licensing office of the state of Missouri is responsible to review EMS report sheets. Working in a licensing office can hardly be described as an interesting or personal job, and the staff members are used to treating forms and papers with indifference.

In this case, there are no forms. Instead, the ambulances have handed in blank sheets of paper with scrawling notes: "John Doe-trauma, Subaru." "Trauma, Mercury." "Trauma, Camry."

At first the staff is confused. This is a departure from the neatly charted details they are familiar with. Someone remarks that they must have strange names down in Joplin.

Then their internal detective kicks in and they understand. *The paramedics don't know who these victims are. They don't know if they are male or female, only what vehicle they were in.*

Deciphering the scrawls is suddenly an emotional journey. The staff quits making remarks about Joplin names.

\\\\\\\\\\\\\\\\\\\\\V/////////////

Things are bleak at the morgues. Besides running out of space, the coroners have massive identification problems on their hands. Almost no remains are viewable. Some are animal remains accidentally collected. After a first round of confusion, which resulted in a family discovering that a body was in fact *not* their son, Missouri coroners lock down the morgues and turn to dental records, DNA records, and fingerprint records. Because Missouri does not have a lot of staff in this field, they borrow help from the federal government.

\\\\\\\\\\\\\\\\\\\\\V/////////////

In the following days, an outcry arises from people not being allowed to identify the bodies of loved ones. Healthcare workers sympathize but also point out that most people have no idea what the situation is like in the morgue. Tornado victims are not like victims of an H1N1 crisis, or another sudden fatal flu. Most people would not want to know the details. Certainly they would not want to remember their family members that way.

Tornado Deaths

More Americans are killed by lightning than by tornadoes,[45] but this means nothing to those who have had a family member or friend die in a tornado. As one man noted after two deadly tornadoes hit his town, "Who cares how fast the wind was blowing?"[46] Averages and statistics mock the reality of the horrifying extremes, the reality of watching a home explode.[47]

Tornado Alley, part of the Great Plains area from Texas to South Dakota, receives the most tornadoes, but is not where most tornado deaths occur. More deaths happen east of the Mississippi River. Perhaps people living in Tornado Alley are better prepared or build stronger houses. Those living in the middle of a flat prairie can see a tornado coming from farther away, which gives them more chance to escape.[48] Tornadoes in Tornado Alley also tend to be neat, white funnels. Eastern tornadoes are more likely to be supersized, blackish monsters that gobble much wider sections of land.[49]

The blanket invitation from the media for volunteers is a problem. "Anyone who is a doctor or a nurse, please come to Joplin," leaks out on TV. Knowing what will happen, officials try to shut off CNN's announcement, and it stops at 11 p.m. the night of the tornado. But the next morning at 8:00, they open the invitation again to "everyone who can breathe, walk, or carry a stethoscope: come to Joplin."[50]

The problem is, if all volunteers come immediately, there will be way too many. People will be frustrated and return home, vowing to never volunteer again. Then, after the first wave of volunteers tires and retires, no one will be left to take their place. Also, people don't think about the logistics of hosting volunteers. Volunteers will need places to eat, sleep, and go to the bathroom.

Banding Together

1947: In Woodward, Oklahoma, telephone workers had been on strike when the tornado hit. As soon as they saw the damage, they pitched in to do their job. Out-of-town superiors reprimanded them for their weakness at breaking the strike, but they telegraphed back that they would not stop helping.[51]

SHATTERPROOF //JOPLIN, MISSOURI

14
Emergency Workers

I'm trying to recognize the landscape, and there is no landscape.
—quoted in *F5* by Mark Levine

It's 3 o'clock on Monday morning. Chief Randles' family is sleeping in his office.

Down at the EOC under the city administration building, Chief Randles tries to plan where all the volunteers should go. He is told that literally hundreds of fire trucks have arrived.

They decide to separate the various volunteers into four groups, roughly placing one group in each corner of the Joplin tic-tac-toe grid. Volunteer firefighters will group near the fire station. EMS will camp in a car lot not far from their first spot at Lowe's, close to the corner of 32nd and Rangeline. Police volunteers will meet south of town at 34th and Main Street. Public health personnel will be farther north on Rangeline.

At 6 a.m. the chief walks into the engine room to give search and rescue instructions. The huge room is packed with volunteers. The chief doesn't think another person could fit. Although they are not all present now,

5,000 people will help with search and rescue over the next few days. Six full passes will be made through the city. They will not stop until the missing list has dwindled to nothing.

Then the chief steps out and takes a look at 2nd Street. The four-lane street curving over the bridge away from the fire station is stacked with fire trucks all the way across. The street has been shut and is filled with trucks as far as he can see.

In his interview the day after the tornado, Keith Stammer is asked about survivors and if he suspects there will be more victims. With a blank expression he replies, "We don't know yet."[52]

He adds that the most helpful contribution from strangers will be to stay out of town. Not everyone heeds this, though.

Frustrated citizens vent. "This is not a parade," a spray-painted sign announces later in the week.

\\\\\\\\\\V//////////

Somewhere in the beginning of the chaos, a man from Sam's Club arrives, asking Chief Randles if there is anything he needs. The chief says that he thinks they could use some Gatorade, maybe a whole truckload. He's thinking of a pickup truck. Before he knows it, two semi loads of Gatorade arrive, along with a semi load of ice.

The chief begins to be careful about what he asks for. However, as the days pass, another need becomes obvious. Firefighters are working around the clock, sleeping in their wet clothes and then going back to work. Some of them have lost their homes and all their possessions.

The chief tells Sam's Club that he could use T-shirts, underwear, and socks. Again, a semi load arrives.

\\\\\\\\\\V//////////

One of the most intriguing emotions in the wake of a tornado is a sense of being lost. Keith Stammer sums this up well. "Honestly, at the moment it's rather surreal," he says the day after the tornado. "All of our landmarks are gone . . . Places that you always know to turn at, they're all gone."[53]

"I was born and raised in Joplin, and I got lost," Keegan's father says.

By Monday night, many of the roads have been cleared. Because street signs and stoplights are missing, workers paint the road names at intersections.

The weather shows no remorse. There are five thunderstorms in the first forty-eight hours, including two more tornado warnings. A meteorologist is stationed in his own trailer close to the city building. Once, he bolts out of his trailer and races across the street to a sturdier shelter.

"We all followed," says an emergency worker.

On Monday evening, more severe weather heads toward Joplin. Chief Randles pauses in disbelief. Not only is it depressing news to be shared, but the tornado has taken out storm sirens, and the warnings cannot be shared as before. Temporary sirens have been placed, but they cannot be activated from the dispatch office. Someone needs to go out to the high school and press the button near the sirens.

"I'm not sending my people. I'll go do it," says Chief Randles.

"I'll go with you," says the city manager.

Keith Stammer keeps them updated from his desk by the radar screen.

"I think we're going to be okay," he tells them.

Then his tune changes.

"They've issued a tornado warning," he says.

Chief Randles hits the button for the temporary siren.

Nothing happens.

In disbelief, they head back to the fire station. The city manager speaks over the vehicle's PA system.

"Tornado warning, take cover!" the speaker bellows. "Tornado warning, take cover!"

First the bumpy helicopter ride. Now, the city manager and the fire chief are together on another dangerous mission.

Search teams need to be called off because of the new warning, but it's difficult to contact them because cell phones aren't working. Texting does work, however. One leader needs to contact fifty-two team leaders to tell them to abandon search and rescue because of bad weather. It seems like an impossible texting job.

However, the man has five teenagers with him. He turns the task over to them, and in five minutes it is done.

"If you don't know how to text, get your children or your grandchildren to show you," is the word on the street in emergency units now.

This tornado proves not to be a threat after all, but other severe weather is. Monday evening at 5:23 p.m., emergency worker Jeff Taylor, thirty-one, is just finishing up his assignment on the corner of 20th and Connecticut Street when another severe storm comes up. He is struck by lightning and goes into cardiac arrest. EMS manages to bring him back; however, Jeff passes away after being transferred to another hospital. Police escort his body, closing roads all the way to his home town.

\\\\\\\\\V/////////

Search and rescue is done by teams that enter homes, looking for people or animals. If they find nothing, they exit and paint an X on the building. If they find two bodies, they add a 2. At Lee and Tenika's house, Freya is still inside, refusing to budge from the closet. Rescuers paint the X and then add DOG.

When search and rescue ends Monday night, seven more people have been rescued from the rubble.

People who have no place to go head to Missouri Southern State University, where the graduation has just been held. Two weeks before the tornado, the Red Cross signed a contract with the college, which allowed them to use their facilities in the event of a disaster. Of course, many people suspected they would never need to use it. Now the college has become a shelter. In the end, they provide 3,400 overnight stays.

\\\\\\\\\\\V//////////

Chief Randles' family is still camping in his office. They still don't know how their house fared during the tornado. A firefighter who lives near them arrives at the office in the middle of the night. He has recently discovered that his house has been destroyed.

He meets the chief's wife and looks at her with compassion. "I'm sorry about your house," he says.

"What do you mean?" she asks.

He turns away, his eyes sorrowful, and she knows. Their house has also been ruined.

She tells her husband the news.

When morning arrives, a news crew wants to interview Chief Randles. "Were any firefighters' homes destroyed?" they ask.

"Yes, four."

"Was yours one of them?"

"Yes, my house was damaged." The chief is not interested in expounding on the details.

"How bad was it?"

"My home was destroyed."

The chief feels the focus turning on him, and he doesn't like it. "Look, the story's not about me; don't bring it up again. I've got my job to do."

Still, Randles needs a break. He finds the city manager and tells him, "My house is destroyed. I have to check my dogs."

When the chief arrives at his house, he finds their vehicles piled in the front yard. Their RV is in the neighbor's yard. The house is torn open, but for some reason the chief reaches for his key as he steps toward the front door. As he tries to open it, he feels a bumping against his legs. He looks down, and there are his two dachshunds.

The chief collects the two dogs and takes them back to the fire station, where they join the campout in his office.

The calls and emails begin after the interview with the news crew. Chief Randles gets calls from Australia, China, Europe, and New Zealand, and an email from Colombia, South America. Everyone wants to show sympathy and support.

"Where are all these people seeing me?" he asks someone.

"You've been on TV worldwide."

"Oh."

The chief doesn't have time to be dazed long.

\\\\\\\\\V/////////

Two people are recovered alive on Tuesday, but the hope for more live recoveries is very slim. For the first time, Chief Randles takes a four-hour nap, from one to five Wednesday morning.

Along with Cheryl Fitch's home health team, public health also gives tetanus shots. The city is divided into areas called medical pods. A team of four people enters the pod, one registered nurse and three assistants. The assistants go out to the job sites, directing the volunteers back to the nurse who waits by the car, her sharp needles ready.

"We didn't ask, 'Do you want a tetanus shot?' " a nurse explains. "Of course no one wants one. We asked, 'When is the last time you had a tetanus shot?' "[54]

The problem with this pod system is that the volunteers move. If the nurse moves to a different pod the next day, she may meet the same people she injected yesterday.

Finally the tetanus operation is moved to Missouri Southern State University, where many of the volunteers are staying.

No live recoveries are made on Wednesday.

\\\\\\\\\V/////////

By Thursday the fire chief's office is just too small for his family and two dogs. A family member offers to take them in.

Businesses are beginning to re-open in town. There are utility issues, now that the gas is being turned on. Are the leaks all taken care of?

As the chaos subsides, health officials turn to the massive amounts of donated food. In the end, the numbers are staggering: 20 vehicles provide mobile feeding, with 86,000 hot meals and 370,000 snacks being served.

This is wonderful, but basic food handling safety procedures seem nonexistent. With children setting up food stands, officials fear an epidemic similar to the fungus infection down at the hospital. Responders are picking food out of trays with their bare, unwashed hands. There is no place to wash hands. The smell alone in some areas is enough to convince anyone that sickness is lurking.

The food served to the city leaders in the EOC is not monitored for quality or temperature. The last thing Joplin needs is to have the collective brain of the city coming down with food poisoning. Fortunately, with the help of a public health food unit, a disaster is averted.

Today, Thursday, the last body is found.

When the numbers are tallied, 161 people have died from the Joplin tornado. Those who were affected in some way numbered 17,000. There were 7,500 homes damaged. The volunteers numbered 90,000.[55]

15
Joplin's Continuing Story

I trust Him every day.
—Chris Newby, God's Kitchen

Some of Joplin's homeless residents find a temporary home in the tent city at the south end of town. This tent city is fiercely protected by a manager who stands at the entrance demanding identification from all the curious sightseers. Those who have legitimate reasons for desiring entrance are allowed in. The tent-city residents stick up for each other through the summer.

Bayou, the tent-city cook, was leaving Louisiana to get away from storms when he stopped his pickup at a gas station in Joplin. While he and his pit bull took a snooze in the back, strong winds flipped the pickup over, breaking the windshield.

Now Bayou cooks chicken gumbo and other Cajun specialties in the shade of a blue tarp. Tent-city dwellers come over for supper, and visitors are invited to stay. Caramel syrup and strawberry jelly are close at hand at the end of a picnic table.

Bayou's pit bull sleeps close to the woods. Small children dash around the campground, their mothers telling them to stay away from the dog. Bayou insists that he is not dangerous unless irritated.

Big R's is closed for several days. The power is out. Food spoils in freezers and refrigerators.

When the restaurant opens, however, there is a surge of business. Because the restaurant is on the edge of the disaster zone, it's a perfect place to sit down for a barbecue lunch. At lunchtime the lobby is packed with people standing as they wait to be seated. Waiting in line gives people the opportunity to look at the cooler's enormous slices of decorated cream pies.

Close to Big R's, a volunteer tent kitchen starts beside the exposed skeleton of the Joplin High School. When its founders prepare to pull out after several weeks, a young volunteer named Chris Newby offers to stay and keep the kitchen open. All tornado victims or cleanup personnel are welcome to take a free meal.

God's Kitchen, supported by Action Missions, provides three meals a day. Chris serves hot food from 11 a.m. until 9 p.m. Lunch and dinner vary from hamburgers and hot dogs to chicken alfredo and lasagna, with sides of tomato or potato soup. Yellow coolers of Gatorade, labeled by kind, invite the thirsty. Before the main meals are available, breakfast bars, donuts, and cereal can be found. Occasionally the kitchen even serves a hot breakfast.

For the first month, God's Kitchen serves roughly 2,000 people a day. The kitchen stays through July, then August, and then September. The people continue to come, although the numbers drop to about 400 meals a day.

Chris never intended to stay in Joplin serving meals for five months. He recalls the night of the tornado, when a co-worker with Action Missions called him.

"It's bad here. I need you," Chris heard him say.

"I'll come Wednesday," Chris replied.

Later Chris felt God asking him, "Why are you waiting?"

On Monday he called the friend back. "I'll be there tomorrow."

After taking over the kitchen ministry, Chris made a promise to God. "God, I'll do whatever you ask me to do, as long as you provide."

In addition to feeding people, Chris directs a recycling program. Crews clean lumber out of the debris, pulling out bent nails and sawing away broken ends. The lumber is stacked by size, and then the magic begins.

Storage sheds appear beside the lumberyard, crafted from the ruined lumber. Residents who need a place to store their homeless possessions can get a storage shed. Who knows—perhaps their shed contains pieces of their old home.

Chris is twenty-six years old. When asked why he is giving these months of his time, he has a ready answer. "God has opened my eyes to the truth," he says. "It's not about us. And I love people. I've experienced the true joy that comes only from the Lord, and I want everyone else to know how real it is."

He adds that if your faith doesn't change your life, it's not for real. As he talks, Chris's eyes hold secrets of his own past, but he doesn't seem interested in talking about himself.

In the kitchen project, Chris awakes some mornings without knowing if any volunteers will come to help him cook and serve, but people always arrive just in time.

Chris's faith in God is challenged and strengthened. "I trust Him every day," Chris says.

\\\\\\\\\\\\\\\\V/////////

A week after the tornado, a community memorial service is held at Missouri Southern State University, where the high school graduation took place. At exactly 5:41 p.m., the community observes a moment of silence.

Speakers at the memorial include Governor Jay Nixon, President Barack Obama, and local pastor Aaron Brown.

President Obama receives spontaneous cheers when he promises, "Your country will be there with you every single step of the way." The President's words resonate with the conservative community as he quotes Scripture and focuses on brotherhood. He is warmly welcomed.[56]

In his message Pastor Brown says, "We have all spent the last seven days looking for our families and friends. We've all had those moments of unbelievable relief at hearing somebody's voice."

After reminding the audience that death does not get the last word, Pastor Brown ends with an encouragement and a challenge. "We are not a people without hope. We are people from whom hope, life, and light will shine to the ends of the earth."

Later Pastor Brown speaks at the memorial service for Will Norton.

At Joplin High School, the J, L, I, and N have been blown off the school sign. The O and P are still fastened. With duct tape, a creative person adds two more letters, an H at the front, and an E at the back. The sign now reads, "HOPE High School."

C. J. Huff, superintendent of schools, insists that Joplin schools will start on time in the fall.

"I guess you go back to the old [Charles] Dickens quote: 'It was the best of times; it was the worst of times,' " the superintendent said. "In spite of the fact that you were dealing with a terrible tragedy, the 'love thy neighbor' philosophy was very much intact here in Joplin."[57]

Cheryl Fitch is shocked and thrilled by the selfless spirit that appears everywhere, even among her fiercest competitors. She gets calls from home health agencies around Missouri asking how they can help.

Cheryl tries to think of ways that Oxford HealthCare can help its fifty homeless employees. First, the employees are given clothing, but it is evident that it's no use giving people things if they have nowhere to put their belongings. Instead, each homeless employee is given $500 to help create a new life.

Except for two employees who also lost close family members, every employee gives the $500 back. They ask if the money could be given to the patients who lost their houses.

\\\\\\\\\\\\\\\\\\\\\\\\\\\\\\\\\\

St. John's Mercy Hospital plans to open the doors of a new facility in 2014. They will not build on the same site. In the meantime, a temporary hospital has been built, and better buildings will arrive in the spring.

New tornado grab bags will be added to St. John's tornado drills. These will include paper and pencil, gloves, flashlights and batteries, and a small crow bar. Tornado protocol will require that patients' shoes or slippers be brought into the hall during drills. No more wrapping feet in towels to step through glass.

Nurses have come back to Dennis, the safety manager, with gratitude.

"Thank you for making us move the patients in drills," they say.

Learning from Greenbriar, nursing homes now see the need for emergency identification bracelets to give residents in weather disasters so emergency workers can identify who they are. In addition, director Jon Dolan plans to prepare flash drives with important basic information about each person. Even if computers crash, the drive could be loaded onto other computers and read with a basic program like Microsoft Word.

\\\\\\\\\\\\\\\\\\\\\\\\\\\\\\\\\\

On September 1, 2011, Chick-fil-A opens with a shiny arch of red, yellow, and orange balloons. The restaurants that open crawl with people, because there are not enough restaurants to go around yet. Even into late fall, Chick-fil-A patrons are eating outside in the wind because it's too full in the dining area.

Lowe's, once an emergency triage center, becomes a place of comfort and hope, a place where everyone has to go because everyone has something to fix or replace. Customers lean over the paint counter and tell the employees what color they want. The employees mix it and seal it, and then the customers start talking about why they need the paint.

On November 13, 2011, the *Joplin Globe* releases *32 Minutes in May,* a picture book of the May 22 tornado. People bustle to the Joplin Public Library to pick up a book and have it signed by the photographers and editors.

Besides pictures of the rubble, the book lists 161 names. Most of the names have photos above them. Outside the book-signing room, an elderly lady sits in a library chair and turns the pages of the book. As her eyes rest on a photo, tears begin to slide down her wrinkled face.

Chief Randles sits at his desk in his office, leafing through a bulging file. He's tried to answer all the calls and emails, but it's been hard. On top is a check from the fire department in Tuscaloosa, Alabama. The money is for a tornado relief fund. The chief is touched by the show of compassion from firefighters in another state.

"I was on TV a lot as a public face for the search and rescue efforts. It's one of those good and bad things," the chief says.

His eyes dampen as he remembers how people from all over the world just called to say, "Hey, just keep doing what you're doing."

He thinks of the moment he made the decision to turn toward the station instead of down to his house, unknowingly avoiding the path of the storm.

"It was a decision that changed my life. Was it God telling me to turn?"

His wife is sure it was God.

When donations arrive for the chief's house, he splits the money four ways, sharing with the three other firefighters who lost their homes. "There's no way that I as a chief can just keep this for myself," he says. If someone gives him $100, he keeps only $25.

\\\\\\\\\V/////////

Freeman Hospital makes repairs and files away lessons learned. While swelling to hold the patients who can no longer return to St. John's, Freeman adds thirty-two beds and plans to expand even more.

Renee wonders if she made mistakes in taking inexperienced nurses into high-stress areas. She recalls hearing that one of her young nurses, sent to help the respiratory department, was next transferred to the grisly temporary morgue. Still, Renee is pleased with the performance of her staff.

She thinks about the things they did not have enough of. Radios. Food for the staff. Sleep. Red outlets backed by generator power. Keys to access the medicine carts.

She credits her husband Bob for remaining calm that first night at the hospital. Had Bob panicked, she thinks she might have panicked. In turn, her charge nurse could have become unnerved, causing the floor nurses to lose confidence.

She hopes that the rest of the medical community will never have to go through a Joplin-sized tragedy. But if it would happen, her words are these: "Please know that we will be there for you, as you were for us."

\\\\\\\\\V/////////

The injuries to clients of the Ozark Center, Freeman's mental health arm, show up in the months following the tornado. Suicides, drug abuse, gambling, and violence all rise. The Ozark Center is also injured, losing eight of its fourteen buildings, including a well-regarded autism school.

The Ozark Center offers counseling and support to all of Joplin, not just their former clients. They provide tornado debriefings for more than twenty-seven Joplin businesses and seven hundred individuals. Besides those directly impacted by the storm, people at risk for emotional overload include preachers and barbers, who hear story after story.

In the Midwest, people don't typically ask for mental health assistance, the Ozark Center says. The center posts signs around Joplin that say "Healing Joplin after the storm: we listen, we care." Staff dress in blue shirts to go out in the city. They become known as the "blue shirt people" rather than "mental health people."

The Ozark Center receives a plea from prisoners, who have been following the tornado on TV. Locked away in jail, they can't volunteer. They want to do something.

They sew different-colored blocks together to make blankets. Some of the blankets are for elderly people with dementia and are called fidget blankets. These include beads and tags for the elderly people to play with.

The prisoners also make cool ties. The cool ties are gel-filled bandanas. When soaked in water, they stay cool for a long time and can be worn around the head or neck. In the hot summer days of debris-cleaning in Joplin, the cool ties become a big hit.

The Ozark Center does not want to offer a lot of medications. Instead, they remind people to take care of themselves. Basic food and water may be hard for them to get. Many are not sleeping.

To encourage sleep and relaxation in children, the Ozark Center makes early childhood comfort kits. These include lotion, Play-Doh, and bubbles. Parents like the kits a lot.

School starts on time. School children are encouraged to draw pictures to tell their tornado story. High school students create slide shows or videos, choosing pictures significant to their own story. They are then asked to layer messages of hope across the pictures.

One of them says, "Joplin: we built it once—we can do it again."

The Ozark Center receives special grants after the tornado, including one to start a child trauma treatment center. It's going to be called Will's Place, in memory of Will Norton.

16

Preparing to Soar

Like an eagle, I will soar above the clouds.
—Joplin High School graduation song

June 1:

Hi everyone, this is Sara (Will's sister). I just wanted to let you all know that EVERYONE is invited to attend Will's life celebration this Sunday at 4 p.m. at Christ's Church of Oronogo. I hope to see as many of you there as possible. "God is close to the brokenhearted and saves those who are crushed in spirit" (Psalm 34:18).

Griffin speaks briefly at the service for Will. He says he's read that the true definition of success—God's definition of success—is how many lives you impacted, not whether you had a good job or a long résumé.

"Just by the sheer number of people that are here today, it's obvious that Will lived a successful life, and I've found comfort in that," Griffin says to the crowd.

Will's father is at the service in a wheelchair.

Keegan and Griffin are pallbearers. Now they feel the emotion. Besides their grief for Will, they see the faces of many of their fellow classmates for the first time since graduation. It had been impossible to know who had survived and who had not. Mingled with the deepness of grief is the height of joy. *You made it! You're alive!*

Then the memory of why they are gathered returns.

> June 5:
> I had to bury my baby brother today. I never thought I'd have to do that, especially at only twenty-one. Today was by far the hardest. That casket in front of me reminded me that Will's not coming back. Sara

Keegan points out that the support system in Joplin is huge. There's always someone to talk to that will understand. Before, people felt isolated by their troubles. They were afraid to share. Keegan now believes that everyone is more ready to share because they know they can find someone who can relate.

To Sara, it doesn't matter that she didn't get the chance to say one last word to her brother or give him one last hug. She recalls hugging her brother whenever she returned home from college. Every night before they went to bed, they would say, "Love you."

Sara helps to pick out a bench and cross to mark Will's grave. They decide to get a black granite cross. It will be six foot three, like Will.

Keegan has not changed his plans to become an emergency room doctor. Although he will never forget the wild night at Rangeline Road and 20th Street, the experience has not changed his goals. He knows that it will be a long road, but he has always wanted a job that involved helping people. He determines to keep this dream in mind as he writes research papers and goes to class.

\\\\\\\\\\\\\\V/////////

Rob stays at Watered Gardens Rescue Mission for over a month. His old friends offer him a home in a large house outside the city. He knows he can go there at a moment's notice, live with relative ease, and lose the title "homeless."

But something matters more to him. He wants to change, to pull away from his addiction before he collapses under it. Here at the shelter, Rob takes it slow, welcomes visitors, and tells his story. As church volunteers pack up the leftover breakfast, Rob sips coffee and reflects on life. He notes that the reason people find God in jail is that they are left without friends or anybody who will help them through their problems.

By November, Rob is working evenings at Red Lobster, living in a studio apartment, and saving money to buy a scooter. He's become an usher at his church and passes out bulletins as people walk in.

Occasionally, Rob goes back for a visit at Watered Gardens. He's there on a Sunday in November when a visiting preacher speaks to the audience of struggling Joplin citizens.

The preacher talks about "that low, dry place where everything is hard." He tells them, "The devil says your dreams will never come to pass. It's the devil's goal to keep you out of your own personal Promised Land." In the upper meeting room at Watered Gardens, people on folding chairs and benches stare at their fingers and wipe their eyes.

The preacher reads from the Old Testament, the story where they were running out of water and the prophet told the people to dig ditches. Digging ditches was hard, hot work for people who were already parched, but they did it, and the ditches filled with water.

"The devil said, 'I thought I had you; I never imagined you'd dig a ditch. I thought you were shallow. I thought you were weak. I thought you were driven by your emotions.' Just one more shovel," the preacher says, "and that ground might become a little moist."

He encourages the people to have "pit bull faith" that bites down and never gives up. He asks them to prepare a landing strip for God's blessing by having the faith to "dig ditches" in their lives.

Rob knows how hard it is to dig those ditches. In particular, memories of the past haunt him.

"It's really easy to get tied up in that and what should have happened and what could have happened, but I'm forgiven of that," he says.

Memories of the tornado still bring an ache too. Rob visits a memorial display at the Spiva Art Center close to the Joplin library. It's a collection of paintings, prints, and sculptures united by the tornado theme. One piece has the names of all the victims on it.

"I went twice," Rob says. One time he had to leave, overcome with emotion.

A special moment occurs at church one Sunday. Another man who used to frequent Rob's druggie house shows up in church. Not wanting to startle him, Rob doesn't approach him. The next Sunday the man shows up again. This time he sees Rob and comes up to him. He also has a job and is getting clean.

Now there are two of them picking up the pieces and rising from the rubble.

\\\\\\\\\\\\\\V//////////

Tenika cannot believe it, but her depression is gone.

"I walked out of the tornado a different person," she says. "It was life-changing for me. God took my depression away from me."

Some days are still better than others, of course. As the holidays approach, she feels the loss of all her Christmas things. But some of the most painful parts of her story are healing. She can talk to her parents now.

Tenika recalls hearing that for some people, depression leaves through something little, and for others it takes something big.

"It took a big thing for me," Tenika says.

\\\\\\\\\\\\\\V//////////

On a quiet evening in early July, the grandmother who rode out the tornado at her friend's house to the south visits her old house. Her grandchildren join her, and together they dig through the dust and rubble of what was her home, looking for home videos. It's messy work, but if she can discover any of the memories, it will be worth it.

Everything is brown and gray, but she pulls aside pieces of wood and concrete blocks and finds a nest of tapes. She moves something else and uncovers the camera itself.

"I figured these things were such a long way off that I would never find them!" she exclaims. "The cleanup crews already went through, and every time they saw something that looked like it could be valuable, they set it aside."

She turns the video camera over in her hands. "They should be able to make it work," she says. "And the first thing I'm going to do is put all these videos on CD and put them in the safe deposit box!"

One of her grandchildren sidles up to her, carrying a silk lily—once pure white. The child and the lily stand surrounded by the desert of Joplin, an endless stretch of gray and brown with a few stubs of trees, acres and acres of nothingness, and almost no people. An occasional car drives past on the gray streets. Beside the little boy, a bare foundation marks the territory of what used to be his grandmother's house.

Like the city around them, the lily is damaged but not useless—more a symbol of hope in its current state than when it was brand new.

\\\\\\\\\\\\\\\/////////

Winter weather is coming to God's Kitchen. The group will leave Joplin after November 25. On November 23, God's Kitchen begins a three-day Thanksgiving feast. Volunteers feed more than five hundred people on the first day, passing Styrofoam trays heavy with mashed potatoes and gravy and turkey. Fat dinner rolls and banks of colored pasta salad join the hot food under the attack of Thanksgiving forks.

"There is hope, and we're a part of letting them see that hope—that God . . . will continue to restore and bring healing to this city," says Chris.[58]

Chris knows what he's talking about when he speaks of restoration and hope. The story comes out in the dining tent on a chilly November afternoon.

Chris explains that he has been living on his own since he was fifteen. He came from a broken home. He attended church because a friend took him. When he was nine, he confessed Christ and was baptized, but Chris does not feel that he really gave his life to the Lord.

As a young man he began to party. He experimented with drugs. Then he was on drugs. Next he was selling drugs. Finally he was serving jail time.

"I used to be what society would see and say, 'Oh, no, watch out,' " Chris says. "I was locked up in four states."

As his life drained away, Chris continued to feel the tug of a spiritual battle.

The final time in jail, Chris got into the Bible. He read the whole Bible. He didn't plan to quit cussing, but somehow he found his words coming out differently. People discouraged him, assuring him that when he was released, he would go right back to where he had been. They said his jailhouse religion would evaporate when his time was served.

It did not.

Even though he was a felon, Chris got a good job after he left jail. "I never should have gotten that job," he says. But God showered him with grace.

"There is no hope unless you put your trust in the Lord," Chris testifies. "Greater is He that is in you. It's amazing to live and experience it. I'm just so thankful. [We all have] an emptiness or void until we come to know the Lord. We are never fulfilled until we come to Jesus Christ. There's no greater joy than living for the Lord."

Now Chris has left the job for full-time ministry. He doesn't know where God will take him next, but he has learned to listen to God speak. Best of all, he is living proof to Joplin that ruin can be restored. He is proof that fallen people can not only be raised by Christ but can also become part of the miracle of raising others. He is proof that although lives shatter, faith is shatterproof.

Planning a Refuge
Tips for Tornado Safety
—from the Storm Protection Center, Norman, Oklahoma

Houses with basements. The hiding place of choice is a basement. Many people believe they should be in the southwest corner of their basement, but this is a myth. Tornadoes do not always come from the southwest, and their winds are not straight anyway, so debris may fall anywhere. Depending on the construction of a house, if the wind does happen to be straight, the south wall above the ground may be the only one that falls *in,* while the other walls would fall *out*.[59] Far more important is to hide under a table or mattress, even in the basement, since debris may fall from above. Make sure that your basement hiding spot is not directly below a heavy object on the floor above, such as a refrigerator or a piano.[60]

Houses or apartments without basements. If there is no basement, the smallest, lowest, most interior room of the house is the best choice. Countless people have lived through tornadoes by taking refuge in their closets, under stairwells, or in bathtubs.

Outside. Lie in the lowest spot you can find (preferably a ditch or similar low place), as far from vehicles and trees as possible, as either could become airborne. Lie face down, protecting your head with your arms.

Mobile homes and vehicles. If you are in either of these tornado death traps, get out! Mobile homes and vehicles are the two most dangerous places to be in a tornado,[61] and you will almost certainly be safer if you get out, even if there is no shelter to run to.

The only exception for vehicles is if the tornado is clearly far away and not coming straight for you. If it does not seem to be moving to the right or left, it is coming straight for the eyes that are watching it. You should never try to outrun a tornado, but if the tornado is far away, or moving away from you to the right or left, you can escape by turning away from it.

Do not park under an overpass, or hide under a bridge. Besides the fact that they could collapse, the area under the overpass becomes a wind tunnel.

Large buildings, such as churches or shopping malls. Do not panic, for the sake of the people around you. Always move into the middle, away from windows, and into a small room. If this is not possible, hide under a sturdy bench or other piece of furniture, protecting your head with your face to the floor.

Stay away from windows. Always hide in a room without windows. But should you open the windows to equalize the pressure, like the old myth says? Absolutely not. You will waste valuable time, it probably won't help, and you could be hurt by shattering glass.[62]

Conclusion

A tornado story is really two stories. The two plot lines are separate melodies because they concern disparate characters: the tornado and the people.

The tornado starts with some boring but important atmospheric factors miles away from touchdown. Then it becomes a boiling mass of confusion and noise that stretches miles up into the atmosphere. Then it touches down. After wreaking havoc, it shudders weakly before it dies away completely. When it's gone, peace is restored and the tornado part of the story is over.

The people, on the other hand, begin with relative peace in their surroundings. As they near touchdown time, their story has barely started yet, but glances at the sky cause them to shudder with niggling undercurrents of fear. Then the tornado touches down and ushers in mass confusion. The noisy confusion and upheaval sets in and stays for days. It can be seen from miles away, even all the way around the world in these days of Internet reporting.

The tornado's story is front-loaded with all the action. In those brief moments of touchdown, the tornado's story and the people's story come together. Then the tornado's story is over and the people's story begins, as if the tornado has just transferred all those miles of supercell confusion to the surface of the earth.

The tornado has the melody at first. At touchdown time, the song hits a dreadful crescendo, with both characters screaming. Surely this is the reason there is no description for a tornado's sound. Everything is screaming together, the tornado and the people. Then the tornado's sound dies away and the people continue the melody by themselves.

A tornado is a bit like an act of terrorism in which the terrorist kills himself in the end. His story dies out just as the story of his victims starts. Only for those brief moments could their stories be written on the same pages of history, but those are the moments that make all the difference, the desperately unlikely marriage of strangers.

This makes the tornado an unfair character in the story. All good stories keep the hero and the villain until the end of the story. At the end, the hero triumphs and the villain receives justice. No good book ends with, "And then the villain disappeared, never to be seen again."

In tornado stories, though, the writer has no choice, because the villain *does* disappear. There can be no comments about the tornado after it disappears back into the invisible, because it's just gone. There is no neat way to wrap everything up, neither in the pages of a book nor in streets of ruined towns.

Thankfully, there is a third character in a tornado story. Christians recognize this character as God. In the Bible, several things are made clear. First, God is in control of everything, including the weather (Psalm 147:18; Job 37:13). Second, man brought a curse on the whole earth by disobeying God, at which point the earth lost its perfect state, and things have not been right since (Romans 8:20, 21; Genesis 3:17). Third, blessings and tragedies visit the evil and the good, and only God knows the full purpose of what He allows or brings into people's lives (Matthew 5:45; Luke 13:2-5).

Thankfully, God's interest in people stays alive as well, long after the tornado has melted back into the atmosphere. His faithfulness outlives the tornado. His eyesight outlives the cameras. He offers to work with the fragmented sentences of shattered lives. If anything in this world is shatterproof, it is the plot line written by God.

Endnotes

Part One: Hackleburg

[1] Richard Bedard, *In the Shadow of the Tornado,* Gilco Publishing, Norman, Oklahoma, 1996, p. 76.

[2] National Oceanic and Atmospheric Administration (NOAA), "2011 Tornado Information," August 19, 2011, <http://www.noaanews.noaa.gov/2011_tornado_information.html>, accessed on September 22, 2011.

[3] Bedard, *In the Shadow of the Tornado,* pp. 7–57.

[4] Paul Schlemmer, *Columbus Dispatch,* quoted by D. Wagler, *The Mighty Whirlwind,* Pathway Publishing, Aylmer, Ontario, Canada, 1966.

[5] David Wagler, *The Mighty Whirlwind,* Pathway Publishing, Aylmer, Ontario, Canada, 1966.

[6] National Oceanic and Atmospheric Administration (NOAA), "2011 Tornado Information," August 19, 2011, <http://www.noaanews.noaa.gov/2011_tornado_information.html>, accessed on September 22, 2011.

[7] Mark Levine, *F5: Devastation, Survival, and the Most Violent Tornado Outbreak of the Twentieth Century,* Miramax Books, New York, 2007, p. 210.

[8] Ibid.

[9] Stefan Bechtel and Tim Samaras, *Tornado Hunter,* National Geographic Society, Washington D.C., 2009, p. 182.

[10] Ibid., pp. 172–182.

[11] Levine, *F5,* pp. 71–93.

[12] Bechtel and Samaras, *Tornado Hunter,* pp. 159–212.

[13] Levine, *F5,* p. 96.

[14] Bechtel and Samaras, *Tornado Hunter,* p. 181.

[15] Ibid., p. 183.

[16] Ibid., p. 184–185.

[17] Ibid., p. 186.

[18] National Oceanic and Atmospheric Administration (NOAA), "Hackleburg (Marion County) EF-5 Tornado, April 27, 2011," National Weather Service Weather Forecast Office, Birmingham, Alabama, <http://www.srh.noaa.gov/bmx/?n=event_04272011hackleburg>, accessed on December 8, 2011.

[19] Wagler, *The Mighty Whirlwind,* pp. 80, 112, 118.

[20] Levine, *F5,* pp. 51, 156.

[21] P. J. Vesilind, "The Hard Science, Dumb Luck, and Cowboy Nerve of Chasing Tornadoes," *National Geographic,* April 2004, pp. 5–37.

[22] Levine, *F5,* p. 66.

[23] Vesilind, "The Hard Science, Dumb Luck, and Cowboy Nerve of Chasing Tornadoes," p. 16.

[24] Bedard, *In the Shadow of the Tornado,* p. xii.

[25] Bechtel and Samaras, *Tornado Hunter,* p. 161.

[26] Ibid., p. 47.

[27] Levine, *F5,* p. 124.

[28] Bechtel and Samaras, *Tornado Hunter,* p. 23.

[29] National Oceanic and Atmospheric Administration (NOAA), "Hackleburg (Marion County) EF-5 Tornado, April 27, 2011," National Weather Service Weather Forecast Office, Birmingham, Alabama, <http://www.srh.noaa.gov/bmx/?n=event_04272011hackleburg>, accessed on December 8, 2011.

[30] Ibid.

[31] Hannah Mask, "April tornado tragedy hard topic for children," *Times Daily,* October 2, 2011, pp. 1A, 4A.

[32] Theresa Hutcheson (Panther Mart cashier), personal interview, July 8, 2011.

[33] Bechtel and Samaras, *Tornado Hunter,* p. 215.

[34] Ibid., p. 215.

[35] Tom Smith and Bernie Delinski, "Victims deal with memories of tornado," *Times Daily,* August 7, 2011, pp. 1A, 8A.

[36] Levine, *F5,* pp. 224, 232.

[37] P. Gast, "Can America's best hometown survive?" *CNN U.S.,* July 12, 2011, <http://articles.cnn.com/2011-07-12/us/tornado.hackleburg.alabama_1_small-town-town-doctor-tornado/2?_s=PM:US>, accessed on September 3, 2011.

[38] Steve Hood (Hackleburg Fire Chief), personal interview, July 11, 2011.

[39] U.S. Department of Homeland Security, "FEMA History," August 11, 2010, <http://www.fema.gov/about/history.shtm>, accessed on October

11, 2011.

[40]Bedard, *In the Shadow of the Tornado,* pp. 49–55.

[41]Wagler, *The Mighty Whirlwind,* p. 227.

[42]Levine, *F5,* p. 248.

[43]E. M. Varcarolis and M. J. Halter, "Anxiety and Anxiety Disorders," *Essentials of Psychiatric Mental Health Nursing,* Saunders Elsevier, St. Louis, 2009, p. 126.

[44]J. Lavin, "Surviving posttraumatic stress disorder," *Nursing 2011,* Vol. 41, No.9, pp. 41–44.

[45]Varcarolis and Halter, "Anxiety and Anxiety Disorders," p. 140.

[46]Lavin, "Surviving posttraumatic stress disorder," pp. 41–44.

[47]Lisa Singleton-Rickman, "Amid the rubble, Hackleburg, Phil Campbell graduates move on," *Times Daily,* May 27, 2011, <http://www.timesdaily.com/stories/Amid-the-rubble-Hackleburg-Phil-Campbell-graduates-move-on,111412>, accessed on December 8, 2011.

[48]Mask, "April tornado tragedy hard topic for children," pp. 1A, 4A.

[49]Wagler, *The Mighty Whirlwind,* p. 168.

[50]Levine, *F5,* pp. 251–252.

[51]M. McFarland, "Disaster declaration request denied," *Advance News, Nappanee,* Vol. 130, No.47, November 29, 2007.

[52]M. McFarland, "Nappanee Appeals FEMA decision," *Advance News, Nappanee,* Vol. 130, No. 50, December 13, 2007.

[53]Bedard, *In the Shadow of the Tornado,* p. 56.

[54]Levine, *F5,* p. 273.

[55]Corrie Ten Boom, "Invasion," *The Hiding Place,* Chosen Books, Grand Rapids, Michigan, 1984, p. 67.

[56]Vesilind, "The Hard Science, Dumb Luck, and Cowboy Nerve of Chasing Tornadoes," pp. 5–37.

[57]Bechtel and Samaras, *Tornado Hunter,* pp. 161, 181.

[58]Michael Allaby, *Tornadoes,* Facts on File, Inc., New York, 2004, p. 125.

[59]Bedard, *In the Shadow of the Tornado,* p. 63.

[60]Allaby, *Tornadoes,* p. 117.

[61]Levine, *F5,* p. 59.

[62]Bedard, *In the Shadow of the Tornado,* p. 63.

[63]Bechtel and Samaras, *Tornado Hunter,* pp. 200–201.

[64]Levine, *F5,* p. 63.

[65]Bedard, *In the Shadow of the Tornado,* pp. 64–65.

[66]Allaby, *Tornadoes,* p. 84.

[67] Levine, *F5,* p. 64.
[68] Ibid., pp. 94–96.
[69] Wagler, *The Mighty Whirlwind,* p. 184.
[70] Levine, *F5,* p. 171.
[71] Bedard, *In the Shadow of the Tornado,* p. 16.
[72] Levine, *F5,* aluminum foil, p. 115, colors p. 9.
[73] Bedard, *In the Shadow of the Tornado,* p. 6.
[74] Allaby, *Tornadoes,* p. 85.

Part Two: Ringgold

[1] The City of Ringgold, "Ringgold Depot History," <http://www.cityofringgold.com/cms_800.php?page=Ringgolddepothistory>, accessed on December 6, 2011.

[2] National Oceanic and Atmospheric Administration (NOAA), "Summary of North and Central Georgia Tornado Outbreak, April 27th and 28th," May 20, 2011, National Weather Service, <http://www.srh.noaa.gov/ffc/?n=20110427_svrstorms>, accessed on December 6, 2011.

[3] Allaby, *Tornadoes,* p. 98.

[4] James Reid, telephone conversation and personal interview, October 6, 2011.

[5] Phil Cawood, personal interview, October 6, 2011.

[6] Bedard, *In the Shadow of the Tornado,* p. 11.

[7] Ibid., pp. 50–53.

[8] Wagler, *The Mighty Whirlwind,* pp. 115–116, 223.

[9] Levine, *F5,* p. 260.

[10] C. Stephens, "EF-5 tornado deadliest in United States in last 56 years," *The Huntsville Times,* May 8, 2011, <http://blog.al.com/breaking/2011/05/132_miles_of_devastation_ef-5.html>, accessed on September 29, 2011.

[11] James Reid, telephone conversation and personal interview, October 6, 2011.

[12] Danny Jackson, (owner of Walter Jackson Chevrolet), interviewed by *Dealer* magazine, Vol. 18, No. 8, August 2011, pp. 16–19, 70.

[13] W. Katie, "Ringgold Council Agrees to Pick Up Storm Debris Left By FEMA," *Catoosa Weekly,* July 27, 2011, <http://media.timesfreepress.com/epaper/community/ct/07-27-2011/index.html>, accessed on October 10, 2011.

Part Three: Joplin

[1] City of Joplin Fact Sheet, Public Information Office, Joplin, Missouri, read October 24, 2011.

[2] C. F. Boone (publisher), *The Joplin Tornado,* 1971, University of Missouri Digital Library, <http://www.joplinpubliclibrary.org/digitized/joplin_tornado_booklet.php>, accessed on November 16, 2011.

[3] Brown, "Twisters, Cyclones, and Tornadoes of Joplin's Past: Part II," June 29, 2011, <http://www.historicjoplin.org/?p=476>, accessed on November 16, 2011.

[4] Cheryl Fitch, "Home Health Care: An Impacted Agency's Story," Center for Preparedness Education Conference, Omaha, Nebraska, November 15, 2011.

[5] Howard Bluestein, *Tornado Alley: Monster Storms of the Great Plains,* Oxford University Press, New York, 1999.

[6] Bedard, *In the Shadow of the Tornado,* pp. 77–79.

[7] Levine, *F5,* p 57.

[8] National Oceanic and Atmospheric Administration (NOAA), "NOAA's National Weather Service celebrates 140th anniversary," February 9, 2010, <http://www.nws.noaa.gov/pa/history/140anniversary.php>, accessed on October 11, 2011.

[9] Levine, *F5,* pp. 23, 50.

[10] Bedard, *In the Shadow of the Tornado,* p. 79.

[11] Ibid., p. 84–85.

[12] Bechtel and Samaras, *Tornado Hunter,* p. 252.

[13] Bedard, *In the Shadow of the Tornado,* p. 74.

[14] Will Norton, "I nearly died!" *Willdabeast* on Youtube, May 12, 2009, <http://www.youtube.com/Will#p/u/19/DT6_VjoZQh8>, accessed on November 29, 2011.

[15] Sara Norton, "Will Norton's celebration of life memorial service," *TheStyleBlog* on Youtube, June 4, 2011, <http://www.youtube.com/watch?v=Tt_gl0MGDc0&feature=relmfu>, accessed on November 29, 2011.

[16] Scott Meeker (ed.), *32 Minutes in May,* The Joplin Globe, Joplin, Missouri, 2011.

[17] Sara Norton, "The Will Norton Story," *TheStyleBlog* on Youtube, June 18, 2011, <http://www.youtube.com/watch?v=BVSeptS3kec>, accessed on November 29, 2011.

[18] Kevin Kitka, "Joplin Doctor Details Tornado Aftermath," *The City Wire,* Fort Smith region, May 27, 2011, <http://www.thecitywire.com/?q=node/16072>, accessed on November 21, 2011.

[19] Bechtel and Samaras, *Tornado Hunter,* p. 232.

[20] Levine, F5, p. 64.

[21] Bechtel and Samaras, *Tornado Hunter,* p. 224.

[22] Ibid., pp. 43–44.

[23]Vesilind, "The Hard Science, Dumb Luck, and Cowboy Nerve of Chasing Tornadoes," pp. 13–21.

[24]Levine, F5, p. 26.

[25]Vesilind, "The Hard Science, Dumb Luck, and Cowboy Nerve of Chasing Tornadoes," p. 13.

[26]Ibid., p. 17.

[27]National Oceanic and Atmospheric Administration (NOAA), "2011 Tornado Information," August 19, 2011, <http://www.noaanews.noaa.gov/2011_tornado_information.html>, accessed on October 15, 2011.

[28]*The Clinton Herald,* "Daredevil stormchasers survive Joplin tornado," June 8, 2011, <http://clintonherald.com/cnhins/x494184300/Daredevil-storm-chasers-survive-Joplin-tornado/print>, accessed on August 15, 2011. (Go to twisterchasers.com to find out more about Jeff and Kathryn Piotrowski.)

[29]Kevin Kitka, "Joplin Doctor Details Tornado Aftermath," *The City Wire,* Fort Smith region, May 27, 2011, <http://www.thecitywire.com/?q=node/16072>, accessed on November 21, 2011.

[30]Meeker (ed.), *32 Minutes in May,* p.12.

[31]Lee Radcliff (ed.), *The Joplin Tornado, May 22, 2011,* The Ozarks Magazine, Joplin, Missouri, 2011.

[32]City of Joplin Fact Sheet, Public Information Office, Joplin, Missouri, read October 24, 2011.

[33]National Oceanic and Atmospheric Administration (NOAA), "2011 Tornado Information," August 19, 2011, <http://www.noaanews.noaa.gov/2011_tornado_information.html>, accessed on November 30, 2011.

[34](Reuters), November 12, 2011, <http://www.reuters.com/article/2011/11/12/us-tornado-joplin-idUSTRE7AB0J820111112>, accessed on June 2, 2012.

[35]Thomas P. Grazulis, *The Tornado,* University of Oklahoma Press, Norman, Oklahoma, 2001.

[36]Wagler, *The Mighty Whirlwind,* pp. 197, 150, 226–227.

[37]Levine, *F5,* pp. 187, 217; quote from p. 204.

[38]Kevin Kitka, "Joplin Doctor Details Tornado Aftermath," *The City Wire,* Fort Smith region, <http://www.thecitywire.com/?q=node/16072>, accessed on November 21, 2011.

[39]Jason Smith, "Emergency Medical Services Response: Lessons Learned from the Scene," Center for Preparedness Education Conference, Omaha, Nebraska, November 15, 2011.

[40]Scott Meeker (ed.), Bill Shepherd and others (photographer), "The Aftermath: Seven Days That Changed Joplin Forever," *Joplin Metro Magazine,* June 2011.

[41] Rusty Tinney, "Emergency Medical Services Response: Lessons Learned from the Scene," Center for Preparedness Education Conference, Omaha, Nebraska, November 15, 2011.

[42] Levine, *F5,* pp. 195, 247.

[43] Erica Werner, "Obama tours twister-ravaged Joplin," *The Goshen News,* Goshen, Indiana, May 30, 2011, p. A12.

[44] Aaron Brown, "Death does not get the last word," *32 Minutes in May,* The Joplin Globe, Joplin, Missouri, 2011, pp. 90–91.

[45] Levine, *F5,* p. 65.

[46] Ibid., p. 265.

[47] Bedard, *In the Shadow of the Tornado,* p. 67.

[48] Bechtel and Samaras, *Tornado Hunter,* p. 186.

[49] Wagler, *The Mighty Whirlwind,* p. 184.

[50] Dean Linneman, "Public Health: A Story Still Unfolding," Center for Preparedness Education Conference, Omaha, Nebraska, November 16, 2011.

[51] Bedard, *In the Shadow of the Tornado,* p. 44.

[52] ABC News, "Joplin Emergency Management Director on Tornado," ABC News Videos, May 23, 2011, <http://abcnews.go.com/GMA/video/joplin-mo-tornado-jasper-county-emergency-management-director-13663798>, accessed on September 27, 2011.

[53] ABC News interview.

[54] Ryan Nicholls, "Emergency Management Support for Public Health and Medical Response," Center for Preparedness Education Conference, Omaha, Nebraska, November 15, 2011.

[55] City of Joplin Fact Sheet, Public Information Office, Joplin, Missouri, read October 24, 2011.

[56] Werner, "Obama tours twister-ravaged Joplin," p. A12.

[57] Scott Meeker (ed.), "Winds of Change," *32 Minutes in May,* The Joplin Globe, Joplin, Missouri, 2011, p. 122.

[58] Lisa Rose and Cliff Erwin, "Bringing Thanksgiving to tornado victims in Joplin," *KY3 News,* November 23, 2011, <http://www.ky3.com/news/story-bringing-thanksgiving-to-tornado-victims-in-joplin-20111123,0,7798626.story>, accessed on November 28, 2011.

[59] Levine, *F5,* p. 175.

[60] Roger Edwards, "Tornado Safety" and "Tornado Safety Tips," The Online Tornado Frequently Asked Questions, Storm Prediction Center, Norman, Oklahoma, modified May 5, 2011, <http://www.spc.noaa.gov/faq/tornado/index.html#Safety>, accessed on September 27, 2011.

[61] Bechtel and Samaras, *Tornado Hunter,* pp. 254–257.

[62] Edwards, "Tornado Safety."

About the Author

Katrina Hoover is a writer and registered nurse from Goshen, Indiana. She grew up in Stratford, Wisconsin, with two brothers and three sisters, all of whom developed a love of words through the coaching and example of their parents. Katrina moved to Indiana in 2006, where she taught school before enrolling as a nursing student at Ivy Tech Community College and graduating in 2011. Her first book, *On the Winning Side,* was published in 2010 by Christian Light Publications. It is a fictional account, but based on the children's ministries she has been involved in, both in Wisconsin and Indiana. While in nursing school in the winter and spring of 2011, she wrote *Blue Christmas* about her experiences in a Haiti cholera hospital. After graduating, she accepted an assignment from CAM to write about the 2011 tornadoes, traveling to Joplin and the South with her trusty assistant, Sarah Miller.

Along with her writing projects, Katrina thoroughly enjoys her job as a night nurse at Miller's Merry Manor in Wakarusa, where God has spoken to her in unique ways.

Katrina enjoys hearing from her readers and can be contacted at katrina@500-words.com. You may also write to her in care of Christian Aid Ministries, P.O. Box 360, Berlin, Ohio, 44610.

Christian Aid Ministries

Christian Aid Ministries was founded in 1981 as a nonprofit, tax-exempt 501(c)(3) organization. Its primary purpose is to provide a trustworthy and efficient channel for Amish, Mennonite, and other conservative Anabaptist groups and individuals to minister to physical and spiritual needs around the world. This is in response to the command "... do good unto all men, especially unto them who are of the household of faith" (Galatians 6:10).

Each year, CAM supporters provide approximately 15 million pounds of food, clothing, medicines, seeds, Bibles, Bible story books, and other Christian literature for needy people. Most of the aid goes to orphans and Christian families. Supporters' funds also help clean up and rebuild for natural disaster victims, put up Gospel billboards in the U.S., support several church-planting efforts, operate two medical clinics, and provide resources for needy families to make their own living. CAM's main purposes for providing aid are to help and encourage God's people and bring the Gospel to a lost and dying world.

CAM has staff, warehouse, and distribution networks in Romania, Moldova, Ukraine, Haiti, Nicaragua, Liberia, and Israel. Aside from management, supervisory personnel, and bookkeeping operations, volunteers do most of the work at CAM locations. Each year, volunteers at our warehouses, field bases, DRS projects, and other locations donate over 200,000 hours of work.

CAM's ultimate purpose is to glorify God and help enlarge His kingdom. "... whatsoever ye do, do all to the glory of God" (I Cor. 10:31).

Steps to Salvation

The Bible says that we all have "sinned and come short of the glory of God" (Romans 3:23). We sin because we give heed to our sinful nature inherited from Adam's sin in the Garden of Eden, and our sin separates us from God.

God provided the way back to Himself by His only Son, Jesus Christ, who became the spotless Lamb "slain from the foundation of the world" (Revelation 13:8). "For God so loved the world that he gave his only begotten Son, that whosoever believeth in him should not perish, but have everlasting life" (John 3:16).

To be reconciled to God and experience life rather than death, and heaven rather than hell (Deuteronomy 30:19), we must repent and believe in the Son of God, the Lord Jesus Christ (Romans 6:23; 6:16).

When we sincerely repent of our sins (Acts 2:38; 3:19; 17:30) and by faith receive Jesus Christ as our Saviour and Lord, God saves us by His grace and we are born again. "That if thou shalt confess with thy mouth the Lord Jesus, and shalt believe in thine heart that God hath raised him from the dead, thou shalt be saved" (Romans 10:9). "For by grace are ye saved through faith; and that not of yourselves: it is the gift of God" (Ephesians 2:8).

When we become born again in Jesus Christ, we become new creatures (2 Corinthians 5:17). We do not continue in sin (1 John 3:9), but give testimony of our new life in Jesus Christ by baptism and obedience to Him. "He that hath my commandments, and keepeth them, he it is that loveth me: and he that loveth me shall be loved of my Father, and I will love him, and will manifest myself to him" (John 14:21).

To grow spiritually, we need to meditate on God's Word and commune with God in prayer. Fellowship with a faithful group of believers is also important to strengthen and maintain our Christian walk (1 John 1:7).